THE DEFINITIVE GUIDE TO CANADIAN DISTILLERIES

THE **DEFINITIVE GUIDE** TO CANADIAN DISTILLERIES

THE **PORTABLE EXPERT**
TO OVER 200 DISTILLERIES
AND THE SPIRITS THEY MAKE

DAVIN DE KERGOMMEAUX AND BLAIR PHILLIPS

appetite
by RANDOM HOUSE

Appetite by Random House® and colophon are registered trademarks of Penguin Random House LLC.

Library and Archives of Canada Cataloguing in Publication is available upon request.

ISBN: 978-0-525-61058-8

eBook ISBN: 978-0-525-61059-5

Cover and book design by Andrew Roberts

Front cover photograph by Jacob Janco

Back cover photograph by Spinnakers Brewpub

Inside cover map by Tanya Cull

Interior maps by Anthony Tremmaglia

Printed and bound in China

Published in Canada by Appetite by Random House®, a division of Penguin Random House LLC.

www.penguinrandomhouse.ca

10 9 8 7 6 5 4 3 2 1

appetite
by RANDOM HOUSE

Penguin
Random House
Canada

For Janet and Lina

CONTENTS

INTRODUCTION

There is a movement stirring in Canada's spirits world. If you doubt us, just visit the farmers' market in Duncan, BC. There, among the local vegetables, grass-fed meats, cheeses, handcrafted soaps, and wines, you will find the Schacht family, who operate Ampersand Distilling just up the road, selling products they make by hand: gin and vodka. Duncan is typical of the scores of communities across the land where a burgeoning interest in locally produced food and drink has grown to embrace spirits. More than 200 distilleries have sprung up across Canada to meet this surging demand, most of them in the past five years alone. New distilleries are popping up so regularly that it is almost impossible to keep up.

These new enterprises are not small-scale knock-offs of the major distilleries that already provide more than 99% of the spirits that Canadians drink (and yes, that's the real number). Small or large, each of Canada's distilleries has its own distinct, often eccentric, personality. And for the most part, each one turns to local produce to make its fine spirits. While larger distilleries focus on high-volume, mass-market liquors, the smaller distillers specialize in tiny batches of specialty spirits. Often, they sell these products in shops inside their distillery.

What these smaller start-ups may lack in volume, they make up for in cachet. Many of them, for example, are raising terroir to an almost fetish-like obsession. It's not an exaggeration to say that you really can taste Vancouver Island barley in Shelter Point's whiskies, while Cirka's gin telegraphs innovative flavours from Quebec's boreal forest. As well, distillers are creating a new understanding of formerly traditional flavours for spirits. Still Waters Distillery and Dillon's Distillers have each created their own versions of rye whiskies with surprising and appealing new flavours. Pemberton Distillery has been digging peat right on its own property to fuel the kiln that dries and flavours its malt. Distillerie Fils du Roy harvests New Brunswick thuja staves for its barrels, while a collective of Quebec distillers has created an official geographic designation known as *acerum*, for spirits they make from maple sap.

This exciting wave mirrors, in some ways, a bygone era of Canada's distilling past. As they say, history repeats itself. However, there is one difference. These small distillers of yesteryear were not so much commercial enterprises as tiny home stills serving a family or circle of friends. The ubiquity of home stills during this time is one reason the reaction to prohibition was generally not as dramatic in Canada (with notable exceptions) as it was in the US.

For almost as long as Canadians have been making spirits, commercial distilling had been in the exclusive domain of just a handful of giant enterprises, most of them owned and managed by men. However, before the 1890s, hundreds of small distilleries flourished across the country. At that time, most people drank whisky or not at all, and when a law requiring that it be aged for three years came into force, all but the largest distillers were put out of business. Only the larger producers could afford to wait out the ageing period before selling their spirits. And of these many large distilleries, only eight remained in business at the turn of the 21st century due to years of closures, mergers, and acquisitions, not to mention changing consumer demand.

This whisky ageing rule makes eminently good sense from a quality perspective. Canadian whisky is known for its high quality as a result, and has thus been crucial to the longevity of Canada's distilling industry as a whole. Despite its low profile in the whisky press, Canadian whisky is one of the bestselling styles in North America. The wide range of products the major distillers make—and the billions of dollars they inject annually into Canada's economy, despite higher costs (and taxes) than distillers in other countries bear—all happen because, by international agreement, only Canadians can make Canadian whisky. They make many other products as well, but it is whisky that keeps Canada's large distilleries in operation.

While changes in federal and provincial regulations in recent years have led to a microdistillery boom, that important three-year law remains firmly in place, and so it should. For smaller distillers, however, this requirement can be tough to navigate from a business standpoint. To generate much-needed income during the ageing process, smaller distillers sometimes have to get creative. Most make innovative spirits, such as gins and non-traditional vodkas, which do not require ageing, in place of or in addition to whisky. Many operate other businesses too, which often become the gateway into distilling in the first place. Akin to John Mitchell, who began serving microbrewed beer at his Troller Pub near Vancouver in 1982, igniting the craft beer movement, we see a new trend-within-a trend emerging as more and more established brewers install stills. There are also farmers who have so much crop going to waste, they turn it into something saleable in a still. And there are those in the hospitality business who have been riding the wave of the local-food and alco-tourism movements. However, welcoming visitors requires different skills and facilities

than distilling, and this is why larger distillery enterprises tend to stick to their core business and discourage visitors.

All the same, for a new distillery, visitors can provide an important revenue stream. In developing their business plans, small distilling enterprises consider the culture their distilleries create beyond the technical skills. These are not large organizations reporting to boards of directors, but small businesses run by individuals who quickly become a part of their local business communities. And since each is the work of individuals, these small distilleries uniquely reflect the personalities of the people who run them, whether by sharing spirits they know from life in another country, or reflecting the terroir of their Canadian home. This diversity of backgrounds is also represented in how people come to distilling. For some, their distillery is a retirement project. Others have notions of reviving a family tradition of moonshining, but this time legally. There are those looking for a mid-career change, and there are dozens of people from that long-underrepresented group among distillers: women. We invite you to join us in our delight in celebrating the growing cadre of Canadian women who distil, people whom Gail Fanjoy of Sussex Distillery in New Brunswick drolly calls "Mistress Distillers."

Ultimately, there is an entrepreneurial risk in distilling, which has been an underlying theme since distilling began in Canada long ago—with nascent industrialists taking calculated risks. Although the prospects of being legislated out of business are now remote, regulatory challenges created by governments and bureaucracies at all levels remain. They simply cannot keep pace with the change and development within Canada's spirits industry. Yet, despite the often byzantine government regulation that has grown up around distilling—and made small-scale legal distilling unprofitable in the past—in Canada today, people who follow a well-thought-out business plan have a reasonable expectation that their distillery will, in fact, thrive. Each of them is an example of *plus ça change* as today's start-up gig economy mirrors much of the entrepreneurial energy of a bygone era. But this time, they have the support of a reliable power supply, just-in-time delivery, and, it goes without saying, social media.

To talk about distilling these days, you'd almost think the new distillers have taken over the industry. There is no question that they address the needs of spirits aficionados in ways the large distillers often can't. Nevertheless, artisanal distillers serve a niche market, while the general consumer prefers more affordably priced and easily accessible spirits made in large distilleries. As well, smaller distilleries look first to their local markets, and so are much more vulnerable to provincial regulations than large distilleries with national brands. Still, there are synergies between the two groups, as became clear in 2018 when both discovered they had a common enemy. A year earlier, the federal government had introduced a mechanism to raise taxes on alcohol every year and without discussion. The Distillers Guild of British Columbia and other provincial artisanal distillers' associations joined forces to support the largest distilleries in a campaign to oppose this practice. All it took was a common threat and suddenly everyone was friends, regardless of the scale of their production. While there is romance in being a small artisanal producer, ultimately, as in any business, distilleries will come and go. Having seen how the two groups can work together for a common good, though, points to further cooperation and collegiality within a more established industry.

The idea for this book began to take shape while we were travelling across Canada, writing a travel and whisky adventure series. Entering crowded tasting rooms from Eau Claire Distillery in Turner Valley, Alberta, to Forty Creek Distillery in Grimsby, Ontario, showed just how popular "drinking local" is becoming. As we have gotten to know some of these distilleries, we realized each has a unique product and a story that needs to be told, and thus this guide was born.

In all 10 provinces and one territory, you will meet the quirky personalities who create these spirits and who run the distilleries that make them. Some of the distilleries featured have been around for over a century; others are creating their spirits for the first time. Each plays its part in Canada's spirits landscape. There has never been a better selection of rich specialty spirits to tempt the palate and add to your long-time favourites, and the tasting notes we have included will help guide you.

There is a lot to say about the over 200 profiles featured in this book. To make it as comprehensive as possible, you'll find the technical details of each distillery—whether it is their street address, the kinds of stills they use, tour information, or a listing of where you can buy their products—in sidebars on every page. As well, we have included regional maps to plan your next distillery-crawl adventure and to track your progress. We have also mentioned each distillery's nearest neighbours, in each direction, so no matter which way you are heading, you know where to stop next. Once you have taken that first sip, we are confident you will want to visit them all. And when you get home, new discoveries in hand, why not try some of our distillery-specific cocktail recipes—some classic, most unique.

This book is as up-to-date as we could make it. And like every book, it is up-to-date until the moment someone pushes the "Print" button. Given all of the exciting things we have seen in our research, we know there will be new additions by the time it reaches your hands. And this is why, for the latest updates, we invite you to visit us at www.canadiandistilleries.com.

As you work your way through this book, you will—in words, at least, and we hope later in fact—taste all the spirits these distilleries create, and hundreds more. There is a whole new world of flavour in Canada's distilleries, and we hope our book will help you be part of it. ■

FROM FARM TO FLASK
DISTILLING IN A NUTSHELL

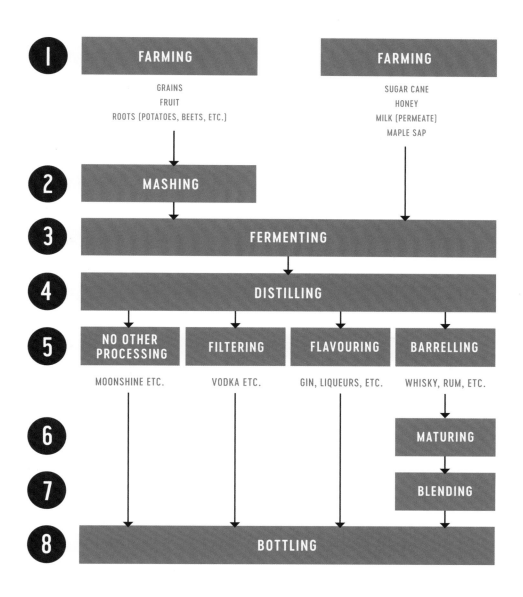

1 FARMING — GRAINS / FRUIT / ROOTS (POTATOES, BEETS, ETC.)

1 FARMING — SUGAR CANE / HONEY / MILK (PERMEATE) / MAPLE SAP

2 MASHING

3 FERMENTING

4 DISTILLING

5 NO OTHER PROCESSING — MOONSHINE ETC.

5 FILTERING — VODKA ETC.

5 FLAVOURING — GIN, LIQUEURS, ETC.

5 BARRELLING — WHISKY, RUM, ETC.

6 MATURING

7 BLENDING

8 BOTTLING

BRITISH COLUMBIA

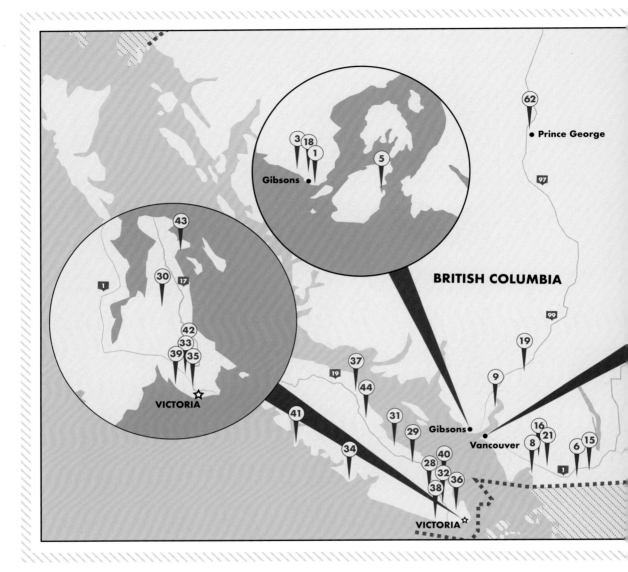

BRITISH COLUMBIA

Prince George

Gibsons

VICTORIA

Gibsons

Vancouver

VICTORIA

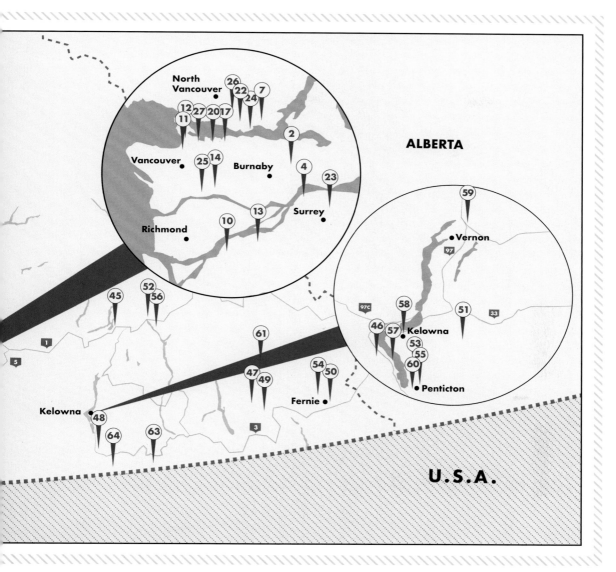

ALBERTA

U.S.A.

BRITISH COLUMBIA

As if out of nowhere, British Columbia has become Canada's ground zero for artisanal distilling. BC's seventy-plus distilleries comprise nearly one third of all the distilleries in all of Canada. Like many overnight success stories, this one took time. Dedicated believers patiently lobbied politicians for more than a decade in order to lay the groundwork for today's flourishing distilling scene. That certainly does not mean distilling is new to BC. What the province is experiencing today is a reprise of another boom that began late in the 19th century. In Victoria, for example, two distilleries and countless breweries kept 24-hour-a-day saloons hopping. Drinkers in BC once knocked back more alcohol per capita than those in any other province or territory.

At the turn of the 20th century, brewer Henrich Reiffel Sr. and his family tapped into that cash cow by purchasing Braid's Distillery in New Westminster, BC. They turned Braid's into the renowned British Columbia Distilling Company. But when BC officially went dry in 1917, Reiffel decided to set sail for Japan, where he opened a brewery.

In Canada, prohibition was a provincial matter rather than a federal one, and for the most part, provincial politicians gave it little more than token attention. British Columbia's brief flirtation with prohibition had very little support and ended in 1921. The public's favourable opinion of wine and beer had survived mostly unscathed, largely because wine and beer are bulky—so less attractive to illicit producers—and therefore largely out of sight. In contrast, bootlegging during that four-year period tarnished the reputation of "hard" liquor, making politicians queasy about supporting its production even after prohibition ended. Then, when America enacted its own Prohibition in 1920, whisky smuggling quickly captured headlines on both sides of the border, leading to the perception that hard liquor was the devil's dram. Smuggling beer or wine just didn't have the same front-page charm as axe-wielding constables smashing barrels of booze.

Shady practices had not been limited to private entrepreneurs during the ban on booze in BC, nor did they end when prohibition was repealed in the province. In 1922, BC's Liquor Control Board Commissioner, JH Falconer, accepted $15,000 from the British Columbia Distillery Company as a "thank you" for the thousands of cases of whisky sold through government stores. This confirmed the growing belief that the liquor business did not always operate above board. For nearly a century after prohibition, this perception of distilling being a crooked business lingered like a bad hangover. While the province supported its small wineries and craft breweries over the years, BC has not welcomed small distillers until very recently.

Large-scale commercial distillers, on the other hand, did thrive when they returned to the province in the mid-1920s. With the sale of alcohol legal again, Reiffel returned to Vancouver and fired up his stills. He wasn't the only one; Reiffel's first competitor locally was Vancouver's United Distillers Ltd. And Samuel Bronfman and his prolific Seagram's Company Ltd. touched down in BC in 1942 when he purchased the British Columbia Distilling

Company, a trendy manoeuvre emulated by other big firms throughout the early 20th century. Similarly, in the early 1970s Schenley Industries acquired the Canadian Park & Tilford Distilleries Ltd. in North Vancouver (which went silent, then closed in the early 1980s). As the century progressed, Hiram Walker expanded its operations to Winfield, BC, in 1971, opening the Okanagan Distillery to keep up with demand for Canadian Club, only to cease operations in 1995. It was the last distillery to operate in BC until 2004, when BC's first small mom-and-pop operation, the Okanagan Spirits Craft Distillery, opened its doors in Vernon. Meanwhile, McGuiness had acquired the Calona firm in the Okanagan Valley in 1990, primarily to bottle Canadian whisky purchased from others, including the former McGuiness Distillery in Weyburn, Saskatchewan, and Hiram Walker & Sons Distillery (page 181) in Windsor, Ontario.

Investing in a small distillery in the political and regulatory climate of 2004 seemed like folly. Provincial officials had only ever dealt with large commercial distilleries; they didn't know what to do with small ones. But the province's wineries opened the doors to artisanal production a decade earlier with an agreement that saw the government support industry-wide restructuring. Nascent microdistilleries had a model to work from—and hope, as the provincial government was keen to be seen as supporting small business in a difficult re-election campaign and encouraged several new distilleries to get up and running. The election was lost and the world's longest poker game began, with the new government constantly shuffling the deck.

Distillers joked that they'd be fine as long as no one bought their products because, by law, the alcohol belonged to the provincial Liquor Distribution Branch (LDB). Whenever a bottle was sold, all the money went to the government, which took a cut, then mailed a cheque to the distillery. At that time, a $40 sale saw a return of about $9—less than the cost of making it.

It took almost 10 years to develop a helpful Craft Production Agreement for distillers. The 2013 agreement required craft distillers to use BC ingredients exclusively, and to ferment and distil them onsite. It significantly increased profitability by exempting small producers from paying the government markup on their first 50,000 litres of finished product. Beyond that, markup was introduced incrementally until annual sales reached 100,000 litres, when full markup was applied. But the hangman's noose awaits: any distillery that goes even one litre over this 100,000-litre cap is reclassified as commercial rather than "craft," even if it continues to distil from 100% BC ingredients. A commercial classification means the provincial liquor board takes over the sales function, the distiller can no longer sell onsite, and thus they endure high markups and low profits.

Still, new distillers eager to get into the game welcomed the changes. The novel concept that the government would support farm-to-bottle production, provided it used 100% BC ingredients, transformed the industry. Craft distilling exploded into a movement across the province. With more than 70 operating distilleries (the most in any province) and dozens of applications waiting in the wings, a groundswell is forming to bring more change and finally soothe any civil servant's pessimistic hangover.

In BC, private liquor stores operate alongside the government-run BC Liquors. These private stores must buy their inventory through the government distribution system, although they do have access to a much broader range of spirits than BC Liquors sells. Unlike the rest of Canada, where distilleries are scattered geographically, BC's distilleries fall naturally into three regional groupings. We begin with those in Vancouver and the Lower Mainland, then tour Vancouver Island, before finishing in the BC Interior.

Alphabetically, then, from The 101 Brewhouse to Yaletown, let's get rolling. ■

THE 101 BREWHOUSE + DISTILLERY
GIBSONS, BC

From 1972 until 1990, the town of Gibsons was the setting for the popular CBC television series *The Beachcombers*. A gritty cast of blue-collar characters invariably became entangled in risky but always heartwarming misadventures while tracking and reclaiming errant logs that had broken away from timber rafts. Today, a new cast of characters has set up in an old Gibsons auto mechanic's shop, giving real-life beachcombers and visitors a place to drink and relax. Rather than chasing logs, head distiller Shawn Milsted makes small-batch gin and vodka. You can enjoy these served in a cocktail, along with a meal in the full-service restaurant, or, as a beachcomber would do, take them straight.

1009 Gibsons Way
Gibsons, BC V0N 1V7
www.the101.ca

NEAREST NEIGHBOURS One Foot Crow Craft Distillery (page 36) — 2 min; Bruinwood Estate Distillery (page 16) — 7 min

ANDERSON DISTILLERIES
BURNABY, BC

3011 Underhill Ave., Unit 106
Burnaby, BC V5A 3C7
(604) 961-0326
www.andersondistilleries.ca

[Instagram] @andersondistilleries

FOUNDED 2014

OWNER Ian Anderson

STILL 400-litre custom-built

PRODUCTS Gin, limoncello, liqueurs, raw flavour spirits for bartenders, soju, tequila

AVAILABLE Onsite, private BC liquor stores, bars

NEAREST NEIGHBOURS Resurrection Spirits (page 38) — 20 min; Mad Laboratory Distilling (page 29) — 30 min

As a recent university grad, Ian Anderson was contemplating postgraduate studies in physics when the BC government introduced its incentives for low-volume craft distilleries. He figured distilling would require about the same amount of work as graduate school, but with greater potential to pay off. Putting his academic pursuits behind him, Anderson purchased an assortment of vessels, pipes, and tubes, rented space in an industrial mall, and set about constructing his own distillery. Before long, he had converted a 400-litre stainless-steel drum into a horizontal cascade pot still. To visualize how a horizontal cascade functions, imagine jumping out of a plane in a hurricane. While gravity has you plummeting downwards to earth, the wind is propelling you violently sideways. Similarly, during distillation, independent forces are moving the spirit in different directions at the same time. "A lot is going on in there," he comments, pointing at the still.

Like so many inventors, Anderson is reluctant to reveal all the mechanical details, though you'd likely need a physics degree to understand them. Put simply, electric coils, like those in a teakettle, heat the wort. After passing through copper packing and gelatinized sapphire for four days, the resulting spirit emerges into a glass column with a copper "cold finger" inside. "The slower you go," he explains, "the bigger your still appears."

Physics aside, the tequila-like flavours you detect in Anderson's products have a biological source. For his first distillations, he let nature provide the yeast, and by grand fortune he produced a spirit that somehow tasted a lot like tequila. Rather than risk losing such uncommon flavours in future batches, he now nurtures that yeast from one distillation to the next.

The term *mad scientist* has become a cliché applied to people tinkering enthusiastically with equipment that we don't understand. As his flavour-rich spirits attest, Ian Anderson's "madness" is in fact technique.

SWEET SERENITATIS LIMONCELLO (20% ABV)

Real lemon rules the scented nose as though you have stepped into a freshly cleaned room, yet without that yellow lollipop flavour. The juicy sweetness of this liqueur is lavish on the tongue without being sticky. A quick, clean finish cleanses the palate. Moreish.

COCKTAIL:
SUNRISE SOUR
MAKES 1 COCKTAIL

1–2 tsp sugar, to taste
1 oz fresh-squeezed lemon juice
Handful of ice cubes
1 oz Anderson Tequila-Process Vodka
1 tsp Anderson Montague Mint
1 orange twist or orange slice, for garnish
½ oz Anderson Montague Sunrise (must be at room temperature)

Dissolve the sugar in the lemon juice. Add the ice, sweetened lemon juice, vodka, and Anderson Montague Mint to a cocktail shaker and mix. Strain into a glass. Garnish with a twist or slice of orange on the rim. Pour the Anderson Montague Sunrise over the top. Do not stir. Billowing and swirling clouds will appear for about a minute after the sunrise is added. Serve immediately.

(Ian Anderson)

2040 Porter Rd.
Roberts Creek, BC V0N 2W5
www.bruinwood.com

NEAREST NEIGHBOURS The 101 Brewhouse
+ Distillery (page 13) — 2 min; One Foot
Crow Distillery (page 36) — 7 min

BRUINWOOD ESTATE DISTILLERY
ROBERTS CREEK, BC

Some people relax or travel to amuse themselves when they retire. Jeff Barringer and Danise Lofstrom approached retirement as an opportunity to do something they had long dreamed of: operate a small distillery on their Sunshine Coast property in Roberts Creek. Their daughter, Sara, joined them and enjoyed the work enough to then train as a distiller.

Inside and out, their attractive shake-sided distillery resembles an art gallery more than a manufacturing business. Samples of Bruinwood's BC craft–compliant vodka, gin, and liqueurs are available to sample before you buy. Producing less than 10,000 litres annually, Bruinwood is a perfect example of the tiny "nanodistilleries" that continue to spring up across British Columbia.

11411 Bridgeview Dr.
Surrey, BC V3R 0C2
(604) 588-2337
www.centralcitybrewing.com

 @centralcitybrew

 @Centralcitybrew

FOUNDED 2013 (as a distillery)

FOUNDER Darryll Frost

STILLS 2,500-litre, 1,250-litre, and 500-litre Holstein pots with reflux columns

PRODUCTS Gin, orange liqueur, rum, whisky

AVAILABLE Onsite, private BC liquor stores

NEAREST NEIGHBOURS Lucid Spirits
Distilling Co. (page 27) — 12 min;
Anderson Distilleries (page 14) — 17 min

CENTRAL CITY BREWERS & DISTILLERS
SURREY, BC

Though he is not a chatty man, Stuart McKinnon smiles easily. As he should. Along with brewmaster Gary Lohin, he created Lohin McKinnon, one of Canada's rising-star whisky brands. Lohin brews the mash and McKinnon distils it, and not just for whisky. They also make the splendid Queensborough London Dry Gin, a four-year-old amber rum, and orange whisky liqueur.

In 2013, after distillery training at Edinburgh's Heriot-Watt University, McKinnon came on board at Central City, which had been brewing beer for a decade. They hired him to launch the brewery's whisky and spirits program. He liked the idea of running a distillery inside an already successful brewery, particularly given the scale of Central City. "We are lucky to have a state-of-the-art 50-hectolitre brewhouse and a very knowledgeable brewing team who can give us the consistent quality we are looking for in our wash."

McKinnon takes advantage of his easy access to the brewery's wide range of specialty beer malts. For a voluptuous chocolate single malt whisky released in 2018, he used highly kilned malt originally intended for beer. Experiments with other grains, such as rye, present more of a challenge in a facility built to process malted barley. For example, compared with barley, rye can be a nuisance to ferment because it creates a lot of sticky foam, which can foul and sometimes overflow the fermenter. However, rye grain contributes desirable whisky flavours not found in barley.

From an operations perspective, seasonal demands for beer and spirits keep Central City busy the whole year round. In summer they brew beer, while distilling keeps the plant bustling in the colder winter months.

From the beginning, Central City planned to focus its spirits program on traditional whisky and gin. Since innovation is the lifeblood of craft beer and spirits, they also make small batches of other spirits such as aged rum, and experimental gins and whiskies. As their bitters and peeled-orange liqueur demonstrate, and as McKinnon confirms, no spirit is off the table. We should continue to expect the unexpected.

COPPER SPIRIT DISTILLERY
BOWEN ISLAND, BC

Every morning, visual effects and video games artist Miguel Kabantsov joined 600 other commuters on the Bowen Island ferry to get to work in Vancouver. With a young family at home, what he really wanted was a way to spend more time on the island. One day he approached his partner, photographer Candice Kabantsov, with the idea of starting a distillery. She was on the same wavelength, but only if they made the healthiest, most sustainable spirits and promoted conscious consumption. Together, they developed a vacant property in Snug Cove near the ferry terminal into a distillery with a lounge and bar, and they began distilling vodka, gin, and unaged rye. Their co-creative natures now lead the Kabantsovs to work with all that the landscape has to offer, and to feature those creations in their distillery's cocktail lounge.

TASTING NOTES: LOHIN MCKINNON SINGLE MALT WHISKY (43% ABV)

Aged in used barrels, this single malt whisky earns the right to decorate its sporran with a Canadian flag. A young, aromatic maltiness joins vanilla and honey on the nose with soft oak, cereals, and fruity citrus on the palate. The delicate, crisp finish reveals a sprightly spiciness.

441 Bowen Island Trunk Rd.
Bowen Island, BC V0N 1G0
www.copperspirit.ca

NEAREST NEIGHBOURS Sons of Vancouver (page 42) — 55 min; The 101 Brewhouse + Distillery (page 13) — 2 hrs; Bruinwood Estate Distillery (page 16) — 2 hrs; One Foot Crow Craft Distillery (page 36) 2 hrs (all include ferry)

CROW'S NEST DISTILLERY
ABBOTSFORD, BC

667 Sumas Way, #117
Abbotsford, BC V2S 7P4
(778) 251-6002
www.crowsnestdistillery.com

 @crows.nest.distillery

FOUNDED 2017

OWNERS Daniel Paolone and Ian Jarvis

PRODUCTS Spiced rum, white rum, vodka

AVAILABLE Private liquor stores in BC

NEAREST NEIGHBOURS Roots and Wings
Distillery (page 40) – 25 min; North West
Distilling Co. (page 31) – 35 min

When money is tight, small distillers need to be creative. Sometimes this includes recycling used equipment initially intended for other purposes. At Crow's Nest Distillery, Dan Paolone converted three 1,000-litre plastic water tanks into fermenters. "They are not jacketed," he explains, so depending on the temperature, it can take from two weeks to two months to ferment a honey mash to about 10% abv.

Paolone believes that you can make vodka neutral two ways: by distillation and by filtration. Traditionally, a vodka column has 20 plates, but Paolone's has only 10, so he runs his spirit through it twice. He achieves his preferred flavours by collecting the spirit within a tight temperature range. That means he saves only half of the alcohol, which he then filters through activated carbon. When he first opened Crow's Nest, an annoying (but tasty) citrus note had a frustrated Paolone working tirelessly to make his spirit more neutral. He had a eureka moment when he discovered the source was not from the process but from his prewashed bottles. They had a slight citrus smell. The solution? Change bottles.

Situated in a rural industrial plaza, Crow's Nest has the simplest of tasting rooms. Paolone and partner Ian Jarvis made a calculated decision to sell their products strictly offsite. A tasting room and bar would generate welcome revenue, but the trade-off would be the need to relocate to more expensive premises. For now, they offer tours just once a month.

"Our products are geared toward the general public. We are not trying to prove we are premium. I can price them at least a dollar less than the lowest competition," says the Schulich MBA. Upcoming innovations include a cold-press coffee cooler co-branded with a local coffee chain, and mead made in beer-making equipment purchased when a local brew-your-own went out of business.

TASTING NOTES: CROW'S NEST VODKA (40% ABV)

A spiced nose is nested in faint dashes of caraway, nutmeg, and cinnamon with bready accents. Then, on the palate, those slight flavours pull a disappearing act. The almost-neutral spirit is clean, with just a touch of vanilla frosting gliding late onto the palate, giving this vodka a tiny peck of sweetness.

DEEP COVE
BREWERS AND DISTILLERS
NORTH VANCOUVER, BC

An aspiring writer, Lucas Westhaver studied English at Simon Fraser University, then sought out jobs that would inspire his writing. He wanted to witness life, so he surrounded himself with people. Meanwhile, a friend (incidentally, also an English major) found work as a distiller and brewer at Deep Cove and invited Westhaver to join him as a bottler. Westhaver liked the environment, stuck around, and eventually took over as distiller. It was a learn-on-the-job situation, though the owners of Deep Cove, who are graduates of Edinburgh's Heriot-Watt, share their knowledge generously. He works alone at Deep Cove now, so yes, even as head distiller he still fills bottles.

With a full-service restaurant and bar that have become a thriving local brewpub, distilling almost seems like a sideline to Deep Cove's operation. A small still in the dining room may look like part of the decor, but this is where Westhaver makes his small-batch spirits. A larger pot still, out of sight in an adjacent room, is for stripping runs. With a BC craft licence, Deep Cove is restricted to distilling solely from BC produce, a restriction that turned into a dilemma when he learned that the pears he made into three barrels of brandy had come from Oregon. As tasty as this pear brandy was, they could not legally sell it. That is, until friends at Vancouver's Long Table Distillery (page 26), which has a commercial distilling licence (rather than craft), came to the rescue. They took the three barrels and released the brandy on their own label, to rave reviews. In addition to gins and vodkas, Westhaver also distils a couple of barrels of whisky each year for a release at Christmas, after about four years of ageing. The first whisky was made from heritage Red Fife wheat (page 166), though he has since switched to malted barley.

TASTING NOTES: OLIVER OLIVE & ROSEMARY GIN (42% ABV)
A Mediterranean essence squeezed into a bottle. Olives and rosemary blend in gracefully without overwhelming the piney juniper's delicate balance. Sweet and savoury with a pleasant brininess accented by lavender. The gin is grounded in a classic juniper profile enhanced by evergreen and citrus notes.

2270 Dollarton Hwy., Unit 170
North Vancouver, BC V7H 1A8
(604) 770-1136
www.deepcovecraft.com

 @deepcovecraft

 @deepcovecraft

FOUNDED 2013

OWNERS Shae DeJaray and Joey Gibbons

STILLS 250-litre and 350-litre Holstein pots with 16-plate column

PRODUCTS Akvavit, gin, vodka, whisky

AVAILABLE Onsite, private liquor stores in BC, bars

TOURS By third parties

NEAREST NEIGHBOURS Sons of Vancouver Distillery (page 42), The Woods Spirit Co. (page 46), and Stealth Distillery (page 44) – all 5 min away

DRAGON MIST DISTILLERY
SURREY, BC

19138 26 Ave., #213
Surrey, BC V3Z 3V7
(604) 803-2226
www.dragonmistdistillery.com

 @dragonmistvodka

@dragonmistdistillery

FOUNDED 2012

OWNER Sherry Jiang

STILL 1,000-litre Dye, 500-litre Dye pots, two 8-plate columns

PRODUCTS Báijǔi, gin, liqueurs, vodka

AVAILABLE Online, private liquor stores in BC, farmers' markets

NEAREST NEIGHBOURS Roots and Wings Distillery (page 40) — 24 min; North West Distilling Co. (page 31) — 30 min

Sherry Jiang studied medicine in her homeland, China, and worked as a physician there until she was 44. Seizing on an opportunity to immigrate, she arrived in a Canada somewhat different from the portrait in glossy magazines back home. She found that learning English was very difficult, particularly the specialized English required for medical certification. With practising medicine off the table, and shocked that China's most popular drink, báijǔi—a traditional, aromatic clear spirit that is high in alcohol—was a rarity in Canada, Jiang decided that she would help abate the báijǔi shortage instead.

As a member of the Distillers Guild of British Columbia, Jiang makes báijǔi, vodka, gin, and liqueurs from wheat grown in BC. For most of her spirits, she ferments the grain mash a week or so, then distils it first in a 1,000-litre Dye brand still imported from China, then a second time in a 500-litre still with a 16-plate split column. The resulting spirit is clean and fresh. Báijǔi, her most popular product, takes longer to make. During a six-week "solid state" (almost dry) fermentation using a special blend of bacteria, yeast, and fungi called *qu* (chew), the mash develops natural aromas that denote authentic báijǔi.

Three sales representatives sell the finished spirits to private liquor stores and Chinese restaurants, while Jiang herself does the bulk of her business personally, selling Dragon Mist spirits through e-commerce, farmers' markets, and craft shows throughout BC's Lower Mainland.

TASTING NOTES: DRAGON MIST BÁIJǓI (56% ABV)

This light-style báijǔi is distilled from wheat, using a traditional Chinese method. Brimming with toasted sweet grains, it launches onto the palate with the heat of a NASA rocket. The finish is long, with pepper, citrus zest, and a countryside earthiness.

COCKTAIL:
WONG CHU PUNCH
MAKES 1 COCKTAIL

1½ oz Dragon Mist Báijǔi
1 oz hibiscus liqueur
¾ oz lemon juice
¼ oz simple syrup
2 handfuls of ice cubes
1 lemon wedge, for garnish

Pour the ingredients into a cocktail
shaker with ice. Shake well. Strain
into a rocks glass filled with ice,
then garnish with a lemon wedge.

(Dragon Mist Distillery)

GILLESPIE'S FINE SPIRITS LTD.
SQUAMISH, BC

38918 Progress Way, #8
Squamish, BC V8B OK7
(604) 390-1122

 @gillespies1

@gillespiesfinespirits

FOUNDED 2014

OWNERS John McLellan and Kelly Woods

STILLS Three homemade stills made onsite using refurbished and recycled factory equipment

PRODUCTS Cocktail ingredients, gin, limoncello, liqueurs, vodka

AVAILABLE Online, onsite, private liquor stores in BC, farmers' markets, bars

NEAREST NEIGHBOURS Sons of Vancouver Distillery (page 42) and The Woods Spirits Co. (page 46) – both 50 min; Pemberton Distillery (page 37) – 1 hr, 15 min

John McLellan and Kelly Woods coined the term "Local Awesome Booze" to describe what goes into every bottle they produce. They use local grains and fruits, which they mash in two repurposed dairy cooling tanks. The liquid then wends its way through a network of homemade retro stills, beginning with "Sputnik." This still is actually reclaimed equipment for processing honey, manufactured in 1957, the year the Soviets launched their Sputnik satellites. Their second still, "Junior," is a repurposed double boiler originally used for Purdy's chocolate. They fashioned a third still, "Anna" (after Woods's late grandmother), by recycling Nature's Path Organic Foods equipment. Working in tandem, the three produce a wide variety of spirits ideal to be shaken or stirred in a cocktail.

Sample the distillery's wares in its sustainably green onsite lounge, dubbed the Squamish G Spot Tasting Lounge. There, enjoy one of Woods's diverse range of cocktails, which are served in vintage glassware rescued from landfill. A perfectly respectable way to engage your taste buds should the name of the lounge make you blush.

TASTING NOTES: GASTOWN SHINE WHEAT VODKA (40% ABV)

Sparkling clean on the nose, this triple-distilled BC-wheat vodka retains sweet suggestions of Frosted Mini-Wheats from the grain. Creaminess on the tongue and delicate vanillas make this vodka a star. Cocktails or straight with a chunk of ice? Your call.

COCKTAIL: GILLESPIE'S ELDERFLOWER SOUR
MAKES 1 COCKTAIL

2 oz Gillespie's Sin Gin
½ oz Boozewitch Elderflower Elixir
Juice of half a lemon
1 egg white

1 barspoon Boozewitch Peach
Lavender Shrub
Handful of ice cubes

Place a coupe in the freezer until chilled, at least one hour. In a shaker, add all of the ingredients except ice. Dry-shake (with no ice) for at least 30 seconds. Add the ice and shake. Strain into the chilled coupe.

(Gillespie's Fine Spirits)

GOODRIDGE & WILLIAMS CRAFT DISTILLERS
DELTA, BC

It occurred to liquor sales representatives Stephen Goodridge and his wife, Judy Williams, that they had invested a lot of time developing brands for other people. Could they not now do this for themselves? So in 2013 the couple successfully launched their distillery in an industrial space in the Vancouver suburb of Delta. That's when fate intervened and Goodridge's former employer lured him back with an offer that was too good to refuse.

Meanwhile, another team of liquor professionals, Paul and Melissa Meehan, were looking for a business opportunity. Serendipity? The Meehans bought the distillery, name and all, then hired Alistair Lindsay as distiller and Adam McDonnell as business manager. They tooled up for increased production and added a 2,500-litre pot still to the 600-litre pot that Goodridge & Williams began with. That and a fancy new 10-head automated bottling machine tell you they do not operate on a shoestring. At 1,500 bottles an hour, this "Ferrari" of a bottling line produces in two hours what used to take 32 hours of manual labour.

Although spirits production continues to abide by BC craft rules, Goodridge & Williams has surpassed the 100,000-litre threshold and, under provincial regulations, has been redesignated as a commercial distillery. Their labels continue to bear the word *craft*, as do their production sensibilities. "We're the bestselling craft distillery in Canada," says Adam McDonnell. The team focuses on gin, vodka, and Italian-style aperitifs, which they sell in every province from Ontario west. Their whisky is also popular. Despite volume production demands, they seem to have a free hand to experiment with new products. Alistair Lindsay's pet project is an overproof rum, while McDonnell wants to venture into Irish-style pure pot whiskies made with malted and unmalted barley. All from BC, of course.

7167 Vantage Way, #8
Delta, BC V4G 1K7
(604) 946-1713
www.gwdistilling.com

FOUNDED 2013

OWNERS Paul and Melissa Meehan

STILLS 2,500-litre and 600-litre Christian Carl pots with 5-plate and 38-plate columns

PRODUCTS Gin, Italian aperitifs, vodka, whisky

AVAILABLE Government and private liquor stores in BC, Alberta, Saskatchewan, Manitoba, and Ontario

NEAREST NEIGHBOURS Lucid Spirits Distilling Co. (page 27) — 10 min; Central City Brewers & Distillers (page 16) — 20 min

TASTING NOTES: NÜTRL VODKA (40% ABV)

It takes two runs through a 38-plate column to strip this rye vodka down to total neutrality. Even an airport K9-unit dog would have a difficult time detecting it. However aroma-free this sippable, crystal-clear drink may be, it feels exceptionally rich on the tongue.

THE LIBERTY DISTILLERY
VANCOUVER, BC

1494 Old Bridge St., Units 1 and 2
Granville Island, Vancouver, BC
V6H 3S6
(604) 558-1998
www.thelibertydistillery.com

 @TLdistillery

 @Tldistillery

FOUNDED 2013

OWNERS Robert and Lisa Simpson

STILLS 140-litre and 220-litre Christian Carl pots with 16-plate split column

PRODUCTS Gin, vodka, whisky, white whisky

AVAILABLE Onsite, online, restaurants, and private liquor stores in BC

TOURS $10; Saturday and Sunday, 11:30 a.m. and 1:30 p.m.

NEAREST NEIGHBOURS Long Table Distillery Ltd. (page 26) — 10 min; Yaletown Distilling Company (page 47) — 10 min

When Granville Island was a manufacturing enclave known as Industrial Island, people went there to work, or not at all. Today, this now-charming neighbourhood is alive with artists, craftspeople, cultural organizations, and lots of tourists. In other words, it is an excellent location for an artisanal distillery.

Veteran wine merchant Robert Simpson reached this conclusion in 2010, when he and his wife, Lisa, secured space at the corner of Old Bridge Street and Railspur Alley. There, they launched a four-year process of establishing The Liberty Distillery. A former banker and business consultant with an MBA, Lisa's involvement began casually. Robert sought her advice to prepare a business plan and deal with the endless bureaucracy through which one must navigate before being granted the right to distil alcohol in Canada. One day, the couple suddenly stopped what they were doing and exclaimed with astonishment, "Look! We're working together." With that surprise realization, Lisa threw herself full time into the project. "This is a woman-owned company," a framed drawing declares. Clearly, The Liberty Distillery is now her baby.

An Old West bar and a mirrored, century-old backbar set the tone for a stylish tasting lounge with tables for 30 people. Loud toots from a steam-powered "donkey whistle" announce the start of happy hour. If you sit for a spell, be sure to taste the oat vodka; you'll not likely find anything like it anywhere else. Like all of its spirits, Liberty's oat vodka is made from BC organic grain and is certified as gluten-free. Afterwards, wander over to the Granville Island Public Market, where you might bump into Lisa purchasing fruit for various vodka infusions.

TASTING NOTES:
ENDEAVOUR GIN
(45% ABV)

A lighter London Dry Gin style, though the juniper is fully liberated. Twenty conventional botanicals, accented with fresh lemon, reach full blossom on the nose. Licorice and savoury spices complement a palate rich in juniper.

COCKTAIL:
BREAKFAST MARTINI
MAKES 1 COCKTAIL

1 oz Endeavour Gin
½ oz triple sec
½ oz fresh lemon juice
1 barspoon marmalade
Handful of ice cubes
1 lemon twist, for garnish
2 Melba toast rounds, for serving

Place a Martini glass in the freezer until chilled, at least one hour. Add all of the ingredients except the lemon and melba toast to a cocktail shaker. Shake and double strain into the chilled Martini glass. Garnish with the lemon twist and serve with Melba toast.

(Dominic O'Driscoll)

LONG TABLE DISTILLERY LTD.
VANCOUVER, BC

1451 Hornby St.
Vancouver, BC V6Z 1W8
(604) 266-0177
www.longtabledistillery.com

 @LT_Distillery

@longtabledistillery

FOUNDED **2010**

OWNERS **Charles and Rita Tremewan**

STILL **300-litre Christian Carl pot with six-plate rectifier**

PRODUCTS **Akvavit, amaro, brandy, gin, limoncello, Marc du Soleil, peppermint liqueur, vodka**

AVAILABLE **Onsite, private and government liquor stores in BC, duty free at Vancouver International Airport, private out-of-province stores**

NEAREST NEIGHBOURS **Yaletown Distilling Company (page 47) – 5 min; The Liberty Distillery (page 24) – 10 min**

"We are a gin house," declares Charles Tremewen. A former park ranger, he is intimately familiar with the BC-harvested wild aromatic plants that imbue his gins. It is, then, a gentle irony that the Long Table gin that critics and customers enjoy most is made using a cultivated species: cucumbers.

Having also worked in the coffee industry, and with a background in organic food, you might expect that Tremewen would have signed on to the BC true craft movement. It certainly would have afforded him significant financial advantages. But he believes that crafting traditional gins requires a truly neutral base spirit. Home distilling would produce small batches of raw spirit that would be almost impossible to make fully neutral in a small still. So, although he ferments his other spirits onsite, unlike many other small distillers who work with the subtle flavours of almost-neutral spirit, Tremewen looked elsewhere for grain neutral spirits (GNS) as the base for his gin. As a result, Long Table is identified as a commercial distillery. For a uniquely BC vodka, Tremewen filters his spirit through limestone mined up the Sunshine Coast on Texada Island.

A full bar, open Thursday through Saturday, complements the distillery in both esthetic and cash flow, and has gained a strong enough following that Tremewen plans to triple his space.

TASTING NOTES: **CUCUMBER GIN** (44% ABV)
This Canadian West Coast–style gin masterfully balances nine botanicals in a complex flavour array. Garden-fresh cucumber yields to citrus zest with a pinch of black pepper. Earthy and citrusy coriander merge into the balance, rounded off with juniper. An incredibly well-composed and refreshing gin.

LUCID SPIRITS DISTILLING CO.
DELTA, BC

For Kashmir Birk, moonshine was just part of growing up in a farming family. "You'd go to someone's house and they would pull out a jar." As a young adult, Birk often talked of opening a real distillery, but the security of a job kept distracting him. Finally, in 2015, Birk quit the corporate world and slowly, and almost entirely on his own, transformed a vacant industrial space into Lucid Spirits Distilling and its tasting bar. "By doing everything myself, I feel like I have a connection," he says. "Everything" includes more than just the jewellery—the shiny 500-litre still and warm, raw-wood tasting lounge. Work began with the physical task of making the towering cement-block walls and a metal ceiling fire- and explosion-proof.

An engaging conversationalist with a philosophical bent, Birk enjoys doing things his own way. "People have a propensity for doing what was always done," he opines. "I prefer to use all the resources in front of me to create something unique." To Birk, Lucid Spirits is a celebration of clarity. He aims to make spirits that are not a soup of many influences, but express the nature of the ingredients he starts with.

His Apple Spirit is an excellent example of this pursuit of clarity. A blend of new wheat spirit and fresh-crushed Okanagan apples, it has a brandy-like appeal. Meanwhile, experiments developing gin recipes moved him toward further clarity, using a smaller, more focused botanical mix. Ultimately, he dropped the floral botanicals altogether for an intentionally uncomplicated gin that focuses on the spicier notes.

Birk initially established Lucid Spirits to make whisky, and that is underway. He is keen for people who visit his distillery to taste the produce of local farms, and they will when they try his rye. The farmer who grows the grain Birk uses is his next-door neighbour.

8257 92 St., #105B
Delta, BC V4G 0A4
(604) 349-3316
www.lucidspirits.ca

@Lucidspirithouse

FOUNDED 2017

OWNER Kashmir Birk

STILLS 500-litre pot with five-plate column

PRODUCTS Apple spirit, gin, vodka, white whisky

AVAILABLE Onsite, private liquor stores in BC, farmers' markets

NEAREST NEIGHBOURS Goodridge & Williams Craft Distillers (page 23) — 10 min; Central City Brewers & Distillers (page 16) — 15 min

(continued)

TASTING NOTES:
APPLE SPIRIT (40% ABV)

A distinct apple cider note on the nose gathers vegetal tones seasoned with a pleasing hint of toasted rice, then takes a delicate step into spring with the sweetness of maple sugar. A touch of bitter apple skins on the finish balances the sweetness of juicy apples and spiced applesauce.

COCKTAIL:
LUCID DREAM

MAKES 1 COCKTAIL

4 oz pineapple juice (not from concentrate)
Tajín seasoning rimmer
1½ oz Lucid Spirits Apple Spirit
2 dashes sugar-free coconut syrup
Pineapple slice, for garnish

Rim a Martini glass with pineapple juice, then with the Tajín seasoning. In a shaker glass, combine the remaining ingredients, except the pineapple, shake, and pour into the rimmed glass. Garnish with the pineapple.

(Brian De Paz)

MAD LABORATORY DISTILLING
VANCOUVER, BC

Whisky was the inspiration. Fifteen years of running bars and liquor stores provided context. Provincial tax incentives gave Scott Thompson the nudge, finally, to turn his distilling hobby into a business. And thus Mad Laboratory Distilling was born. He began by designing and building his own direct-fire pot still and thumper, along with a short column.

Using two-row malted barley fermented in plastic totes, he creates a range of flavoured products, along with gin, vodka, and whisky spirit. It is the continuous fermentation process he uses that offers your first clue to the madness of this laboratory. Thompson begins each fermentation as would any distiller, but before it reaches completion, he transfers the fermenting mash to a stainless-steel tank, where it continues to ferment. Meanwhile, he replenishes the tote fermenter with new mash, which begins to ferment under the action of the yeast residue that was left behind. It's a neat system that keeps the same yeast going, theoretically, forever. "Obviously, the strain will change over time," he concedes, but he remains happy with the results.

This laboratory is not without its limitations. With no temperature controls, fermentation lasts a brief three days in the summer, while in winter it might drag on for a week or more. Thompson's use of natural-gas direct-fire on the still adds another complexity, creating a warm, toasty flavour from sugar that caramelizes on the hot steel surfaces.

Mad scientist Thompson loves to toy with weird and wonderful potions. His tasting room and bespoke gin bar become their own mad lab, offering individually distilled botanicals blended to the customer's taste. They, too, can tinker with solutions, creating their own one-of-a-kind, palate-specific gin. For that, he gets kudos.

618 East Kent Ave. S.
Vancouver, BC V5X 4V6
(604) 727-9521
www.madlabdistilling.com

@madlabspirits

@madlabspirits

FOUNDED 2013

OWNERS Scott Thompson and Ahmet Ulker

STILL 700-litre direct-fire pot and thumper

PRODUCTS Gin, kombucha, raki, vodka, white whisky

AVAILABLE Onsite, private liquor stores in BC, bars

NEAREST NEIGHBOURS Tailored Spirits (page 45) – 2 min; Goodridge & Williams Craft Distillers (page 23) – 20 min; Odd Society Spirits (page 32) and Yaletown Distilling Company (page 47) – both 25 min

TASTING NOTES: MAD LAB VODKA BATCH 11 (40% ABV)

The triple distillation and carbon filtration process makes this vodka so clean, yet deliberately leaves a smidgen of grain flavour behind. Gracefully smooth, refined, and creamy, it flares at just the right moment. Then that heat recedes quickly—a fleeting burst of "madness" in an otherwise decorous drink.

NEW WAVE DISTILLING
ABBOTSFORD, BC

3387 Tolmie Rd.
Abbotsford, BC V3G 2T9
www.newwavedistilling.com

NEAREST NEIGHBOUR Crow's Nest
Distillery (page 18) — 15 min

Paul and Caroline Mostertman and their daughter, Kelsey, have created a destination that resembles a mirage; it's too beautiful to be real. They began with an organic blueberry farm and a lush garden, known as Woodridge Ponds, displaying 150 varieties of pond plants that they grow and sell. Paul and Kelsey then launched Ripples Winery, with a range of blueberry wines fermented from their own crops. The next logical step was a distillery, which has turned this mirage into a spirit lover's oasis. New Wave Distilling brings the blueberry patch full circle, synthesizing the by-products of winemaking into spirits, with the residual spent mash used to fertilize the blueberry plants for next year's crop.

NORTH WEST DISTILLING CO.
MAPLE RIDGE, BC

Kam Price learned the liquor business by importing spirits into Canada. Suddenly, in 2014, one of his key brands, Nemiroff Vodka, dropped out of sight. The distillery in Ukraine had been bombed by dissidents during the Russian annexation of Crimea, disrupting exports. To make things even more difficult, the American dollar was gaining strength, making his American imports more expensive. He needed a new business, and at first, he thought he might open a bar.

Then Price and business partner Kyle Gurniak saw how the BC government was warming up to small distillers, and they made a business decision to start distilling instead. A careful planner with an entrepreneurial spirit, Price calculated what he would need to produce to generate his desired income, then designed a distillery that he could scale up to reach that target. The most challenging piece of equipment to change up later would be the mash tun, he thought, so he installed a 2,000-litre masher. His first 250-litre iStill pot with copper-packed column was soon joined by another 500-litre one. Rather than studying or apprenticing as a distiller, Price learned on his own, watching the Dutch team he purchased the iStills from, and reading distillers' discussion boards voraciously.

The winter wheat he mashes for his vodka comes from Peace River, BC. After 10 distillations, he filters it carefully to ensure that some of the wheat's sweetness remains. He makes use of the residues too. After drying them, Price sends his spent grains to a farm, where he estimates he keeps about 25 cattle fed.

Plans for a lounge on the second floor may mesh with his wife Lainey's dreams of running a library-themed speakeasy. The small industrial enclave that houses North West is surrounded by suburban homes. Wouldn't it be cool if the neighbourhood distillery also turned into the neighbourhood bar?

20120 Stewart Cres., #104
Maple Ridge, BC V2X 0T4
(604) 818-6972
www.northwestdistillingco.ca

🐦 @NW_distilling

📷 @NWdistilling

FOUNDED **2016**

OWNERS **Kameron Price and Kyle Gurniak**

STILL **250-litre and 500-litre iStill**

PRODUCTS **Gin, flavoured vodka, vodka, whisky**

AVAILABLE **Onsite and private liquor stores in BC**

NEAREST NEIGHBOURS **Roots and Wings Distillery (page 40) and Central City Brewers & Distillers (page 16) — both 20 min**

TASTING NOTES: NORTH WEST VODKA (40% ABV)

This traditional winter-wheat vodka is distilled 10 times, then cold filtered through activated charcoal, generating a very clean nose with an understated white-pepper heat. That pepper carries onto the palate, overlaying a minimal sweetness. A spark in the finish vapourizes in the next sip. Ice cream dreams of being this smooth.

ODD SOCIETY SPIRITS
VANCOUVER, BC

1725 Powell St.
Vancouver, BC V5L 1H6
(604) 559-6745
www.oddsocietyspirits.com

 @oddspirits

@Oddsocietyspirits

FOUNDED 2013

OWNERS Gordon Glanz, Joshua Beach,
private investors

STILLS 500-litre and 1,000-litre
Holstein pots with 15-plate column;
3,000-litre mash tun with column
doubles as wash still

PRODUCTS Crème de cassis, gin,
vermouth, vodka, whisky, white whisky

AVAILABLE Onsite and private liquor
stores

TOURS By appointment

NEAREST NEIGHBOURS Resurrection Spirits
(page 38) — 1 min; The Woods Spirit Co.
(page 46) and Sons of Vancouver
Distillery (page 42) — both 10 min

Gordon Glanz graduated from Heriot-Watt University with a master's degree in brewing and distilling. Not long after that, he and some friends were discussing the idea of starting a distillery, a conversation he recalls exactly: "We'll be like a club, a society," somebody declared excitedly. "But what kind of society?" someone else asked. "An odd society!" And so, when the time came, they named their new enterprise Odd Society Spirits.

Glanz and his wife, Miriam Karp, who manages the distillery, are no oddballs when it comes to crafting fine spirits. Though he loves to stretch the bounds of distilling by experimenting with methods and ingredients, his operation is based on sound science. Along with a used 500-litre Holstein still and a 15-plate column still, they have added a column to the top of their mash tun so the tun can do double duty as a wash still. More recently, they installed a new 1,000-litre Holstein still to complement the original. They also collaborate with local brewers, trading barrels back and forth, which is something they wanted to explore from the beginning.

Situated in Vancouver's commercial port area, the Odd Society name has helped shape the ethos of the ex-motorcycle garage turned distillery. Local tattoo artist Shwa Keirstead, recruited to paint a centrepiece over the bar, portrayed the stills as a phantasmagorical mashing of beasts and spirits that define the unworldly character of this odd society. Nonetheless, the spirits themselves, though heavenly, are very much of this world. Enjoy them at the bar, accompanied by appetizers, or at home, served straight or in a cocktail.

TASTING NOTES: SINGLE MALT WHISKY (4-YEAR-OLD UNRELEASED BARREL SAMPLE)

The nose of this lively single malt blends honey, apples, maple, and malty cereals with a touch of oak. Late on the nose, an exotic dry lychee note emerges. Save that bottle of eau de parfum and spritz this on your neck instead. The peppery palate is eyebrow-raisingly crisp. A splash of water quells its youthful vigour and expands the flavour spectrum.

COCKTAIL: **BLACK HEART MANHATTAN**

MAKES 1 COCKTAIL

Handful of ice cubes
1 oz Prospector rye whisky
½ oz Odd Society salal gin
  (or a sloe gin substitute)
½ oz sweet Spanish vermouth
  (such as Miro)
½ oz unsweetened 100% cherry
  juice
1 barspoon Fernet-Branca
Pinch of activated charcoal powder
1 lemon peel
1 brandied cherry, for garnish

In a mixing glass, combine ice and all of the ingredients except the lemon and cherry and stir. Strain into a coupe glass without ice. Express the lemon peel by twisting it over the cocktail to release some zest and then rubbing the peel on the rim of the glass. Toss the peel. Garnish with a brandied cherry.

(Mia Glanz)

A MAN ON A MISSION
MEET ALEX HAMER

Not everyone has the good fortune to discover their true calling in life and then pursue it. Alex Hamer wasn't certain what his mission might be, but he knew that his IT career was not it. He had lived in Scotland for a couple of years and considered himself a Scotch guy. His curiosity led him to a one-week distilling course, where he debated whether his interest in distilling would lead him to a more fulfilling career. The course revealed a stumbling block that many distillers were facing: they could make great spirits, no problem, but how would people find them? The real issue, he realized, was promotion and distribution. He was inspired to do something to raise the profile of artisanal distilling in Canada. But what?

In 2014 he launched BC Distilled, not as an industry association, but as a forum to promote artisanal spirits and to foster a sense of community. Hamer had in mind a Canadian version of the American Distilling Institute, which had so successfully nurtured microdistilling throughout the US. If exposure was what the industry needed, that was where he would begin. Hamer was aware of all kinds of consumer drink events where distillers introduced their products to the public and consumers came to taste new spirits. But it seemed to him that such events were geared more toward the big distilleries and brands. The small distilleries that did take part seemed peripheral. Hamer decided that BC Distilled would host an artisanal distillery festival reserved exclusively for small distilleries in Vancouver, the beating heart of Canada's microdistilling scene. His first event filled the hall. By year two, he had to turn people away.

Hamer's reputation for fair and honest dealing is unparalleled. Mention his name to almost any small distiller and you will be met with yet another glowing report. His support for aspiring distillers includes an introductory course he organizes with the Sons of Vancouver Distillery (page 42). In 2017 he launched the prestigious Canadian Artisan Spirit Competition (CASC), in which a cross-country team of drinks professionals assesses spirits blind, returning scores and comments, which Hamer then shares with the competitors. No chocolate medals here—a CASC medal tells customers that experts endorse this spirit.

With his credibility well established, Hamer is expanding his activities beyond British Columbia with a new organization, Artisan Distillers Canada. National events, including a conference and expo for Canada's growing wealth of artisanal distillers, are just around the corner. ■

ONE FOOT CROW
CRAFT DISTILLERY
GIBSONS, BC

1050 Venture Way
Gibsons, BC V0N 1V7
www.onefootcrow.com

NEAREST NEIGHBOURS The 101 Brewhouse
+ Distillery (page 13) — 2 min; Bruinwood
Estate Distillery (page 16) — 7 min

One Foot Crow is not a dance fad, nor is it rural slang for a sobriety test. It is a distillery named for a one-footed fledging that dropped by one day. The bird, which eventually matured into a healthy adult crow, returns regularly to catch the peanuts people throw to it. One Foot Crow Craft Distillery infuses its organic vodka with humic and fulvic acids, which turn the spirit black, like the glimmering feathers of their one-footed friend. A mineral-infused black Gunpowder Gin is also available.

PEMBERTON DISTILLERY INC.
PEMBERTON, BC

Signs declaring "Seed Potato Control Area" indicate you've arrived in the Pemberton Valley. This is spud-growing country. Protected Pemberton potatoes are so prolific that farmers all over western North America buy them for seed. Still, supply exceeds demand, and in 2002 Tyler Schramm and his younger brother, Jake, were looking for new ways to use their farm-grown organic leftovers. Distilling seemed to be the best possibility. Thus, by 2008 Schramm had returned from Edinburgh with a degree in distilling from Heriot-Watt. Together with his wife, Lorien, he launched Pemberton Distillery and started turning potatoes into vodka in the fifth microdistillery in the province.

But you can't study distilling in Scotland and not get the whisky bug. Before long, he was mashing BC-grown organic grains—some grown by the Schramms themselves, some from neighbouring farms. In 2014 Schramm installed a drum malter, becoming the first Canadian distiller to make his own peated malt. He had learned about peat and its influence on Scotch whisky during his studies. But unlike the distillers of yesteryear, who imported peated malt from Scotland to emulate it, he drew on his coursework to harvest local peat, which sat untapped on his property. He also grows herbs for his liqueurs and absinthe.

A decade after launching the distillery, the Schramms have expanded production to include BC apple brandy, and rye and bourbon-style whiskies. They are also increasing production beyond the 100,000 pounds of potatoes they distil each year to make about a dozen liqueurs, absinthe, gin, schnapps, and, of course, vodka—adding prolific to their designation as the world's first certified organic potato distillery.

TASTING NOTES: PEMBERTON VALLEY SINGLE MALT WHISKY 8-YEAR-OLD SINGLE BARREL [44% ABV]

Pemberton's pale-yellow single malt begins with a captivating grainy goodness. The malt's nose displays a folksy earthiness with understated style. Grassy malt cereals, biscuits, and a distant caramel shift to the palate, bringing lightly roasted almond nuttiness to an already enjoyable dram.

1954 Venture Place
Pemberton, BC V0N 2L0
(604) 894-0222
www.pembertondistillery.ca

🐦 @pembydistillery

📷 @Pembydistillery

FOUNDED 2008

OWNERS Tyler and Lorien Schramm

STILLS 1,000-litre Holstein pot and 500-litre Holstein hybrid pot stills with column

PRODUCTS Absinthe, brandy, gin, liqueurs, potato vodka, schnapps, whisky

AVAILABLE Onsite, online, private liquor stores, restaurants, and bars

TOURS $15; Saturday, 4 p.m.

NEAREST NEIGHBOURS Gillespie's Fine Spirits Ltd. (page 22) — 1 hr, 15 min

RESURRECTION SPIRITS INC.
VANCOUVER, BC

1672 Franklin St.
Vancouver, BC V5L 1P4
www.resurrectionspirits.ca

⊙ @resurrectionspirits

FOUNDED 2016

OWNERS Brian Grant, David Wolowidnyk,
Adrian Picard

STILL 1,000-litre Still Dragon with six-
plate column and 250-litre Still Dragon

PRODUCTS Gin, vodka, whisky, white rye

AVAILABLE Onsite tasting lounge and
private liquor stores

NEAREST NEIGHBOURS Odd Society Spirits
(page 32) — 1 min; The Woods Spirit Co.
(page 46) and Sons of Vancouver
Distillery (page 42) — both 15 min

After two decades tending bar in Vancouver, it was not so much a career change as a logical next step for David Wolowidnyk to put his stamp on a product by opening a distillery. In 2018 he and his partners, Brian Grant and Adrian Picard, did just that, and of course their Resurrection Spirits includes an ample lounge. "It is interesting for a bartender to make cocktails using just spirits from your own distillery," says Wolowidnyk.

As a top-gun bartender, cocktail stylist, and leader in Vancouver's—and Canada's—cocktail culture, Wolowidnyk relishes the challenge. Above the distillery, a heavily reinforced floor supports an expanding collection of barrels filled with whisky or gin. A smaller upstairs tasting room hosts special guests, some of whom have small barrels of Resurrection spirits maturing onsite.

Beginning with rye grain, the spirit for each product follows its own distillation path. For whisky, two passes through the pot still yield a flavourful spirit that goes into barrels at 68% abv. For white rye, the second pass includes a column, resulting in the alcohol content rising to 90% abv. "It would be a shame to take it to neutrality," Wolowidnyk comments, calling the end product a grain eau-de-vie. Finally, the spirit for making gin is distilled to 92% abv. "We want the botanicals to sing," he explains.

Inspired by Jim McEwan's Botanist Gin, from Scotland's Isle of Islay, the distillery uses both cold and vapour infusion to optimize particular flavours. Resurrection gin is classically rich in both citrus and juniper notes. Being bartenders, the team could not settle on just any old botanicals. When they found that BC juniper was too aggressive for their palates, they tried Hungarian before settling on Tuscan juniper. It had the flavours they were seeking. A tasting panel of 75 bartenders agreed. You will too.

TASTING NOTES: WHITE RYE (45% ABV)

Don't let the light nose fool you; this 100% organic rye spirit is a heavyweight—a spirit with a classic rye grain profile on the nose and an earthy floral attitude lightly accented by spices. On the palate, toasted rye grain with sweet puffy marshmallow transitions to chest-warming rye spice. This white spirit resuscitates any rye cocktail in need of CPR.

COCKTAIL: **GOOD THYME**
MAKES 1 COCKTAIL

SPICED APPLE CORDIAL:
½ cinnamon stick
1 tbsp allspice (whole berries, then cracked)
2 cups plus 2 tbsp apple juice (not from concentrate)
1 cup sugar

COCKTAIL:
2 oz white rye
¾ oz spiced apple cordial
4 dashes Angostura Bitters
Handful of ice cubes
Fresh thyme sprig, for garnish

For the Spiced Apple Cordial, break the cinnamon sticks into a few pieces and combine with the cracked allspice. In a saucepan over medium heat, add the spices and dry toast them for five minutes, constantly moving the pan. Add the apple juice and simmer over high heat for 5 to 10 minutes, until the apple juice is reduced by half. Once cooled, strain through a fine strainer, and again through a coffee filter. Return the apple juice to the saucepan and add the sugar. Over medium heat, simmer the juice until the sugar dissolves, roughly 10 minutes. Cool and store in a sealed container. The juice can be refrigerated for up to three weeks.

For the cocktail, in a mixing glass, stir in all of the ingredients except the ice. Strain into a rocks glass over ice, and garnish with a sprig of thyme.

(David Wolowidnyk)

ROOTS AND WINGS DISTILLERY
LANGLEY, BC

7897 240th St.
Langley, BC V1M 3P9
(604) 371-2268
www.rootsandwingsdistillery.ca

 @rawstillhouse

@rawstillhouse

FOUNDED **2017**

OWNERS **Rebekah Crowley and Rob Rindt**

When business travel took Rebekah Crowley to distant places, she often returned with a bottle of the only drink her partner, Rob Rindt, enjoyed: potato vodka. "We could make this ourselves," Rindt, a third-generation farmer, told her one day. That was all it took for Crowley to quit her job and take a one-week distilling course. The couple soon bought an old potato harvester and a 30-gallon HBS still from Kentucky. HBS stands for "Hillbilly Stills," and they truly look the hand-hewn part. Next, they dedicated six acres of their farm to Kennebunk potatoes, a french-fry variety. They have since added a 100-gallon HBS still.

"Working with potatoes, you really have to squeeze hard to get the alcohol out," Crowley discovered. Rindt's solution was simple: plant three acres of Jubilee sweet corn to fortify the potato mash. This not only increases the yield, it also makes the spirit a little bit sweeter.

By June, when fall-harvested potatoes are past their prime, Crowley turns to making whisky. All-corn whisky matures on one rack of barrels, with a 75% rye/25% corn blend on another. Their forays into infused vodkas yielded a particularly tasty horseradish vodka that has you asking, "Where's the beef?" Bitters and non-alcoholic beverages are coming next.

Roots and Wings Distillery is housed in a spacious, rustic wooden barn. From its cedar walls, deck, and Old West facade, you'd never guess that the adjacent store and tasting room were converted from a humble trailer. If you drop by to pick up your favourite gin, vodka, or infused spirit and find the shop closed, look closely. Crowley and Rindt live right across the street and have left their phone number on the "Closed" sign for you. And that name? When Rindt asked Crowley what they should call their new distillery, she recalled the sentiment of a poem that celebrated the importance of "Roots and Wings." In conversation, though, Crowley is just as likely to refer to her distillery as RAW Stillhouse.

TASTING NOTES:
JACKKNIFE GIN
(40% ABV)

Like a Swiss Army knife, this gin is ready and armed for any occasion. Fourteen botanicals, many grown in the distiller's own garden, fold into a base spirit made from homegrown potatoes and corn. An herbal, vegetal, floral nose foretells a palate underscored with rose blossoms, juniper, lavender, and a sweet, spicy glow.

COCKTAIL:
SIDEKICK SIMPLETON
MAKES 1 COCKTAIL

2 oz Roots and Wings Sidekick
2 oz unsweetened coconut milk
1 oz cold-brew coffee simple syrup
Handful of ice cubes
1 cinnamon stick, for garnish

Pour all of the ingredients except ice into a cocktail shaker. Add the ice and shake to incorporate. Serve in a toddy glass with a cinnamon stick.

(Rebekah Crowley)

SONS OF VANCOUVER DISTILLERY

NORTH VANCOUVER, BC

1431 Crown St.
North Vancouver, BC V7J 1G4
(778) 340-5388
www.sonsofvancouver.ca

 @SonsofVancouver

 @Sonsofvancouver

FOUNDED 2015

OWNERS James Lester and Richard Klaus

STILLS Self-designed and built 20-plate column; two modified Hillbilly Stills

PRODUCTS Amaretto, chili vodka, specialty liqueurs, vodka

AVAILABLE Onsite

NEAREST NEIGHBOURS The Woods Spirit Co. (page 46) — 1 min; Stealth Distillery (page 44) — 5 min; Deep Cove Brewers and Distillers (page 19) — 5 min

Richard Klaus and James Lester are cooler than crystal-clear ice cubes. The two friends met while working in Alberta's oil patch. Klaus then tried bartending before heading off to Latin America in search of more adventure. Meanwhile, Lester set sail for Australia, where he, too, tended bar. When it became clear that the American craft distilling movement was coming north, Lester spent a year working in a small bourbon distillery in Seattle. Returning to Canada, the pair joined forces to build Sons of Vancouver Distillery. Licensed journeymen in instrumentation and process control, the two were well prepared to design and build their own distilling equipment.

A copper shell-and-tube heat exchanger that zigzags up the black cement-block wall looks like the end of the day in plumbing school. A tiny 17-plate continuous column resembles a submarine's periscope. Both were designed and built in-house to complement two equally inelegant, yet eminently functional Hillbilly Stills pots and columns. Beauties, all of them. Beauty, of course, being on the tongue of the imbiber.

Along with their flavoured spirits, the Sons have 100% rye whisky maturing in full-sized barrels. They didn't like the woody trade-off that comes with more rapid ageing in smaller barrels. They also chose to use rum yeast for their whisky fermentations, hoping it would generate grassy rhum agricole flavours.

The tiny bar at the front of their shop has become a weekend destination for those in the know. Like the distillery itself, it exudes the earnest yet unrestrained vibe of skate park meets climbing gym. They also offer a week-long distilling school several times a year, to show students firsthand how to run a distillery. It is structured learning, yes; but, true to their ethos, it is mercifully PowerPoint free.

TASTING NOTES:
CHILI VODKA
(40% ABV)

Local aquaponic chilis, infused
into Sons vodka, generate
tongue-searing heat. As close as
your palate will come to a near-
death experience and survive.
Grandma, is that you? But does
this vodka's stunning orange glow
betray that it was secretly made
by juicing a volcano?

COCKTAIL:
AMARETTO SOUR
MAKES 1 COCKTAIL

1½ oz Amaretto
½ oz lime
1 egg white
Handful of ice cubes
2 dashes Angostura Bitters,
    for garnish

Pour all of the ingredients except
ice and the bitters in a cocktail
shaker. Dry-shake until the egg
whites meringue in the shaker.
Add ice and shake for eight more
seconds. Double-strain into a coupe
glass. Garnish with bitters drops.

(James Lester)

10316 152a St.
Surrey, BC V3R 4G8

NEAREST NEIGHBOUR Central City Brewers
& Distillers (page 16) – 15 min

SR WINERY & DISTILLERY
SURREY, BC

Soju is an incredibly popular drink that, by volume, outsells every other spirit on the planet. Korea's thirst for soju is especially voracious. So when small-scale distilling became feasible in BC, master distiller Yoo set out to help the locals quench their thirst with his handcrafted Korean soju. Yoo had already earned a solid reputation in Metro Vancouver for the unpasteurized makgeolli, a cloudy Korean rice wine, that he sold to restaurants. He makes his soju, branded under the maQ name, in traditional fashion, using local ingredients, then he bottles it at various strengths, ranging from 18% to 41% abv.

20 Orwell St., #3
North Vancouver, BC V7J 2G1
www.stealthvodka.com

@stealthdistilleries

FOUNDED 2015

OWNERS John Pocekovic and Randy
Poulin

STILLS 500-gallon (US) Vendome wash
still with two-plate column; 250-gallon
Vendome spirit still with three-plate
column

PRODUCTS Vodka

AVAILABLE Private liquor stores

NEAREST NEIGHBOURS Sons of Vancouver
Distillery (page 42), The Woods Spirit Co.
(page 46), Deep Cove Brewers and
Distillers (page 19) – all 5 min

STEALTH DISTILLERY
NORTH VANCOUVER, BC

John Pocekovic pours two glasses of vodka for you to taste. His flourish and twinkling eye are those of a magician. You nose the first glass and smell . . . nothing. Maybe a hint of alcohol wafts up. Glass 1 is about as neutral as distilled water. Not sure what Pocekovic was expecting, you set it down and pick up glass 2. It smells even more neutral than the other. Wait a sec! More neutral than nothing? Grabbing glass 1 in your other hand, you draw a deep breath and this time detect marshmallows and butterscotch. Back to glass 2. Still nothing. A smiling Pocekovic has just performed his magic trick: he illustrated a difference between two "neutral" vodkas. The first, made from wheat, is soft as silk on the palate, with a slight lingering bitterness as its sweetness fades. The second, a corn vodka, feels almost creamy in your mouth, with an earthy sweetness and bristling hot pepper. The name Stealth is well deserved for a vodka that sneaks up on your palate.

With 30 years as a banker, Pocekovik thought his experience in a heavily regulated industry would help him negotiate Canada's tangled liquor bureaucracy. Nevertheless, his forays into the cooler business using sourced vodka were especially challenging. After the taxes and government levies were paid, merely 15 cents of each dollar's sales remained to cover production costs. Distilling, particularly in BC's encouraging environment, looked more attractive. His family agreed, and son-in-law Randy Poulin, a mechanical engineer, set off for Kentucky's Moonshine University (yes, that really is its name.) They abandoned the cooler business altogether and Poulin set to distilling Stealth vodka. "No one touches the equipment unless they are trained," says Pocekovic. "Science and art merge in the vodka still. If it's not right, it's waste." And neutral? Well, it seems that is a matter of tasting.

TASTING NOTES: **STEALTH CORN VODKA** [40% ABV]

A texture-perfect, juicy vodka with hints of sweet candy corn and corncobs. This elegant potion is creamy to the nth degree, with Celsius degrees of heat sneaking into a quick finish. Go ahead, sip it, while vodka-forward cocktails wait patiently with open arms to welcome it.

TAILORED SPIRITS
VANCOUVER, BC

418 East Kent Ave. S., #101
Vancouver, BC V5X 2X7
www.tailoredspirits.com

NEAREST NEIGHBOUR **Mad Laboratory**
Distilling (page 29) — 2 min

Christopher Konarski, Max Smith, and Taylor Dewar drew on their diverse experience in the food and beverage industry to found a distillery that makes vodka and gin from cider apples. Homebuilt stills provide a unique distilling environment, while careful filtering ensures some apple sweetness remains in the spirit.

THE WOODS SPIRIT CO.
NORTH VANCOUVER, BC

1450 Rupert St.
North Vancouver, BC V7J 1E9
www.thewoodsspiritco.com

 @woodsspiritco

 @Woodsspiritco

FOUNDED 2018

OWNER Fabio Martini

STILLS 800-litre Wenzhou Yayi pot with 15-plate column; self-designed vacuum still

PRODUCTS Amaro, gin, limoncello

AVAILABLE Online, private liquor stores, restaurants

NEAREST NEIGHBOURS Sons of Vancouver Distillery (page 42) — 1 min; Stealth Distillery (page 44) and Deep Cove Brewers and Distillers (page 19) — both 5 min

"When you break open a chanterelle, you can almost smell apricots," says Fabio Martini. This former gasfitter and amateur mycologist (someone who studies fungi) is somewhat of a forager who harvests wild food in BC's lush rainforest. After studying organic agriculture at the University of British Columbia, Martini worked as a brewer, which led to his fascination with yeasts. He then worked at the Sons of Vancouver Distillery (page 42). His own distillery would be born out of these experiences and his work in the woods, hence The Woods Spirit Co.

Martini takes an unusual approach to crafting infused spirits. After macerating each botanical, he cold-distils it, under vacuum. It's a lot of work, but it enables him to bring the ingredients together in harmony and balance. His Pacific Northwest Amaro incorporates vacuum-distilled rhubarb, gentian, wormwood, grand fir needles, and imported citrus peels. The sweet-bitter flavour is dead on and, most importantly, so is its colour. It seems the creativity and innovation of Canada's small distillers are limited only by their imaginations.

TASTING NOTES: BARREL AGED AMARO (28% ABV)

Warm orange hues convey a twilight character to the nose. A touch of wood shavings rounds out bright orange peel, striking fruits, and spice. As the palate transitions from sweet to a traditional bitter five-spice mix, grapefruit zest emerges in an endless finish.

COCKTAIL: DRAWING LOTS
MAKES 1 COCKTAIL

1 oz rye
1 oz Woods Pacific Northwest Amaro
1 oz egg white
½ oz lemon
½ oz grapefruit

½ oz lavender honey
Handful of ice cubes
1 large ice cube
1 grapefruit peel, for garnish
Fresh lavender sprig, for garnish

Pour all of the ingredients into a shaker except the ice and garnishes, and dry-shake for 30 seconds. Add ice cubes, then shake for 15 seconds. Strain into a rocks glass over one large ice cube. Garnish with a grapefruit peel and lavender sprig.

[Benedict Simon Lloyd]

YALETOWN DISTILLING COMPANY
VANCOUVER, BC

Google Maps will direct you to Yaletown Distillery Bar + Kitchen, a spacious restaurant on Mainland Street in Vancouver's Yaletown. Windows at the back of the restaurant peer into the distillery, but there is no public access. Worry not. Leave your car on Mainland and walk around the block to Hamilton Street. There, Craig Harris, the manager, offers a warm welcome. A peek around the corner into the distillery finds distiller Tariq Khan monitoring a spirit run, tasting products, or formulating new ones.

Khan began his distilling career in France as a boy, helping his grandmother make pear eau-de-vie. Moving to England, Khan studied brewing, then spent five years as a brewer until the Mark James Group brought him to Vancouver. While brewmaster at Yaletown, Khan went to Washington for a week to study distillation. By 2013 he was ready to bring Yaletown Distilling online. It had been a brewery for almost two decades.

London Dry Gin and Blacktop Vodka, both made from malted two-row barley, are Yaletown's flagship products. Khan scratches his distiller's creative itch with new formulations of vodka, hopped gin, fruit-infused vodkas, and a respectable single malt whisky matured in full-sized French oak barrels. He has also secured a few tequila barrels to broaden the palate of some of his spirits. Production is still well below the threshold for craft designation in BC, and since there is no room to expand, it will remain that way for the near future.

You may want to enjoy an Italian meal at the restaurant on Mainland Street (or breakfast, if you're early) before you head around the corner to see Khan. Do yourself a favour, though: before you leave the distillery, stop at the bar for a taste of what's new, and chat with Harris, the bartender, turned liquor salesperson, turned distillery manager. He's certainly got some fascinating tales to tell.

1132 Hamilton St.
Vancouver, BC V6B 2S2
(604) 669-2266
www.yaletowndistillingco.com

@YTdistilling

@YTdistilling

FOUNDED **2013**

OWNER **Mark James Group**

STILLS **500-litre Holstein pot with 13-plate column**

PRODUCTS **Gin, vodka, whisky**

AVAILABLE **Onsite, private liquor stores in BC, bars**

NEAREST NEIGHBOURS **Long Table Distillery Ltd. (page 26) – 5 min; The Liberty Distillery (page 24) – 10 min**

TASTING NOTES:
YALETOWN SMALL BATCH BC GIN (42% ABV)

The nose of this London Dry–style gin has depth and range. Under the juniper foundation lies a fresh, forest mushroom-like tone with a zesty orange scent akin to fresh mandarin orange peel. An invigorating pepper complexity balances juniper notes on the palate, while the citrus bitterness offsets a gentle sweetness. Beautiful and intricate.

(continued)

COCKTAIL: A COOPER'S PARADISE

MAKES 1 COCKTAIL

1½ oz Yaletown Whisky (Canadian or rye whisky)
1 oz fresh-squeezed lemon juice
¾ oz pasteurized liquid egg white
½ oz Yaletown Honey Spirit (honey liqueur)
2 dashes aromatic bitters
Handful of ice cubes
1 tsp cinnamon sugar, for garnish

Pour all of the ingredients except the ice and cinnamon sugar into a cocktail shaker. Dry-shake vigorously for 15 seconds to develop a rich foam. Add ice and shake again for 15 seconds. Fine strain into a cocktail glass and garnish with cinnamon sugar, sprinkled over the foam.

(Craig Harris)

AMPERSAND DISTILLING COMPANY
DUNCAN, BC

Each spirit's subtle nuance expresses the delight the Schacht family takes in the distillery they designed and built. For 30 years, Ramona Schacht ran a juried craft show in Victoria, until she and Stephen bought two hectares outside of Duncan. They intended to establish an organic farm on the land, some 50 kilometres north of Victoria. The work, though rewarding, was backbreaking. Stephen, an electrical engineer and occasional jeweller, thought that distilling would be a logical offshoot of farming. Their son, Jeremy, a chemical engineer, and his wife, Jessica, a dramaturge, were keen but inexperienced.

Combining their various individual skills and collective enthusiasm, they converted sheets of stainless steel and copper into a distillery. Stephen and Jeremy designed the equipment, including two unusual cedar-clad stills, and then fabricated it on site. Then came the challenging part: making lush, flavourful spirits. Jessica and Jeremy set to work developing gin recipes. The gin, as Jessica puts it, had to make as good a Negroni as it does a Martini. Nonetheless, a rich, sweet, bitter, digestif called Ampersand Nocino, if it is not sold out, could kick sweet vermouth to the curb in a Negroni.

Each year, the Schachts transform 60 tonnes of organic Okanagan wheat into Ampersand spirit. Enzymes, added slowly to prevent boil-up, convert the wheat starch to sugar in the mash tun; then the wort is filtered and transferred to a fermenter. A week later, distiller's beer at about 10 to 12% alcohol goes into the 1,000-litre wash still for a first distillation. Then things get interesting. From the wash still, the low wines pass to a 500-litre spirit still—a stainless-steel pot topped with what looks like a column. Packed with copper and stainless-steel pellets, the column works as a lyne arm would, returning distillate back for redistillation, thus creating a cleaner spirit. Cleaner, richer, more flavourful, organic: Ampersand Distilling illustrates the synergies of four people using their diverse talents for a common purpose.

4077 Lanchaster Rd.
Duncan, BC V9L 6G2
(250) 737-1880
www.ampersanddistilling.com

🐦 @ampdistillingco
📷 @ampdistillingco

FOUNDED 2014

OWNERS The Schacht family: Stephen, Ramona, Jessica, and Jeremy

STILLS 1,000-litre self-built pot and 500-litre self-built packed column

PRODUCTS Gin, seasonal liqueurs, vodka

AVAILABLE Onsite, private liquor stores in BC, farmers' markets

TOURS By appointment

NEAREST NEIGHBOURS Stillhead Distilling Inc. (page 66) — 15 min; Arbutus Distillery (page 51) — 55 min; Salt Spring Shine Craft Distllery Ltd. (page 61) — 1 hr, 20 min

(continued)

TASTING NOTES: **NOCINO** (27.1% ABV)

The skins of unripe black walnuts deliver a deep shade of brown and aromatics that tussle playfully from the moment the bottle is opened. An exotic fruity sweetness pushes, then pulls a leathery bitterness into elegant harmony, then terse opposition. The walnut's tannins are both bracing and refreshing. Gloriously sippable.

COCKTAIL: **SWEET DREAM**
MAKES 1 COCKTAIL

LAVENDER SIMPLE SYRUP:
¼ cup lavender blossoms
2½ cups sugar

SWEET DREAM COCKTAIL:
1½ oz Ampersand Gin
¾ oz Lavender Simple Syrup (see here)
½ oz fresh-squeezed lemon juice
2 handfuls of ice cubes

To make the Lavender Simple Syrup, place the lavender blossoms in a 1 cup measure, then fill with boiling water. Steep, covered, for 10 to 12 minutes. Strain into a medium-sized bowl. Top up the lavender tea with water to yield a total of 2½ cups. Pour the lavender tea into a small saucepan, and add the sugar. Dissolve the sugar over low heat. Set aside to cool. Store, covered, in the fridge for up to a month.

To make the cocktail, place a rocks glass in the freezer until chilled, at least one hour. Pour all of the ingredients into a shaker over ice. Shake until combined, and strain into the chilled rocks glass over ice.

(Ampersand Distilling Company)

ARBUTUS DISTILLERY
NANAIMO, BC

Distiller Mike Pizzitelli earned two master's degrees, the first in cell biology, the second in brewing and distilling. Despite such academic credentials, a trace of wizardry wends through his creations—a mystical throwback to a time when distillation *was* alchemy. Blue gin that magically turns pink with tonic could be a sorcerer's trickery—or a chemist's litmus.

Walking into Arbutus Distillery, you might think you've entered the wrong door. A bartender behind a long bar polishes glasses as a handful of people sit at tables, eating pizza. "This is a testing ground," says Pizzitelli. "The lounge has synergies with the distillery and helps the cash flow." In the distillery itself, a large chrome cube on legs looks like a space-age still of tomorrow, until he explains, "It's a pizza oven." Owner, distiller, and pizza chef (and alchemist)—that's Mike Pizzitelli. He flicks the lights on in the distillery so you can have a look around, but just briefly. A window throws light into the tasting lounge and might spoil the ambiance for his dining patrons.

If his alchemical spirits foretell anything, it is that racks of former bourbon barrels filled with whisky (and one with amaro) hold great promise. Pizzitelli tries to make all of his spirits a little more flavourful than is usual, so he tweaks them in contemporary ways—conifer gin with pine and spruce buds, vodka infused with yam, cashew, and Scotch bonnets (read: searing-hot peppers), and floral gin with local hops and lemon verbena. Each begins with locally grown barley, malted in Victoria by Phillips Fermentorium (page 60). Next up: 100% rye. Pizzitelli, who was once a brewer himself, lends barrels to local breweries for seasoning. At three years, his whisky is a great sipper. What will it be at seven? The wizard's crystal ball is in the shop; you'll just have to wait.

TASTING NOTES: EMPIRIC GIN (40% ABV)

This gin is inspired by the "Empiric Death Doctors," whose beak-like masks were stuffed with botanicals to ward off illness and plague. Juniper and coriander rule heavy citrus notes of lemon verbena. Balancing the gin's strong earthy and spicy forest tones, hints of lavender keep it fragrant and flavourful.

1890 Boxwood Rd.
Nanaimo, BC V9S 5Y2
(250) 714-0027
www.arbutusdistillery.com

@ArbutusDistill

@arbutusdistillery

FOUNDED **2013**

OWNER **Michael Pizzitelli**

STILLS **1,000-litre Koethe with two 9-plate columns**

PRODUCTS **Absinthe, amaro, brandy, gin, liqueurs, vodka, whisky**

AVAILABLE **Onsite, private liquor stores in BC**

TOURS **Restaurant and bar**

NEAREST NEIGHBOURS **Wayward Distillation House (page 71) — 1 hr, 5 min; Stillhead Distilling Inc. (page 66) and Ampersand Distilling Company (page 49) — both 50 min**

DE VINE WINES & SPIRITS
SAANICHTON, BC

6181B Old West Saanich Rd.
Saanichton, BC V8M 1W8
(250) 665-6983
www.devinevineyards.ca

FOUNDED 2007 (winery), 2015 (distillery)

OWNERS John and Catherine Windsor

STILLS 650-litre Kothe Pot still with four-plate column

PRODUCTS Genever, gin, rum, grain spirits, seasonal spirits, vermouth, vodka, whisky

AVAILABLE Onsite, BC restaurants, and private liquor stores

NEAREST NEIGHBOURS Victoria Caledonian Distillery (page 68) – 15 min; Victoria Distillers (page 69) – 20 min

When John and Catherine Windsor converted 10 hectares of overgrown Saanich farmland into a vineyard in 2007, Ken Winchester helped them get the vines into the ground. Winchester is a microdistilling legend. From across the street, he operated Winchester Cellars, a winery that became the first microdistillery on Vancouver Island.

By 2015 Winchester was de Vine's full-time winemaker. He returned to distilling when he learned of a vintage 25-year-old Kothe still sitting unused in a barn. His first spirit was Vin Gin, a London-Dry-meets-Pacific-Northwest gin made from a base distillate of the winery's Grüner Veltliner Pinot Gris and other island grapes.

Winchester is also a historian of spirits and has a passion for traditional distilling methods, on which he enthusiastically puts his own contemporary spin—a modern-day Willy Wonka without the hat and bow tie. In Ancient Grains, Winchester does something no one else is doing in Canada. He distils the ancestors of modern grains—spelt, emmer, khorasan, and einkorn—with malted barley. He then ages the heritage-grain spirit in new oak quarter casks—a golden ticket to flavour. A Dutch-style genever is made with 100% malted barley and 20 botanicals—grown on a farm nearby in a greenhouse and a large outdoor garden. Then there is an Old Tom gin he calls New Tom, plus two vermouths, rum-like spirit, and Glen Saanich—a single malt whisky.

Winchester has also revived sloe gin thanks to a local farmer who showed up one day with a branch of berries, asking if he had any use for them. Winchester recognized them as sloe berries. Not interested in making a traditional sloe gin liqueur, he soaked the berries in Vin Gin, transforming both the colour and the flavour.

TASTING NOTES: GLEN SAANICH (45% ABV)

Its fragrance hits the palate as delicate fruits careen into rich grain flavours. Dry spices complement the clean, malty, and vaguely nutty charm, as cloves and cinnamon spice leap into a searing, cohesive, peppery finish. A gentle spirit on the cusp of becoming a giant.

COCKTAIL: THE DE VINE INTERVENTION
MAKES 1 COCKTAIL

1½ oz de Vine Genever
½ oz de Vine Moderna Vermouth
2 handfuls of ice cubes

Tonic, to taste
1 lemon twist, for garnish

Pour the Genever and Moderna in a cocktail shaker. Add ice and shake until combined. Strain into a cocktail glass with fresh ice. Add tonic to taste. Finish with a lemon twist.

(de Vine Wines & Spirits)

ISLAND SPIRITS DISTILLERY
HORNBY ISLAND, BC

4605 Roburn Rd.
Hornby Island, BC V0R 1Z0
(250) 335-0630
www.islandspirits.ca

OWNER Pete Kimmerly

STILLS A constantly evolving collection of handmade stills, including a 120-litre Holstein pot still with 6-plate column and a 350-litre Holstein pot still with 10-plate column

PRODUCTS Eau-de-vie, gin, spirit infusions, vodka

AVAILABLE Onsite, private BC and Alberta liquor stores

NEAREST NEIGHBOURS Wayward Distillation House (page 71) — 1 hr, 35 min; Arbutus Distillery (page 51) — 2 hr, 10 min (both include ferries)

The water at the "Little Hawaii" beach in Hornby Island's Tribune Bay Provincial Park is warm and crystal-clear. Almost as clear as the spirits this former sea captain makes nearby. Pete Kimmerly, a professional mariner, spent 41 years at sea and towed giant oil rigs across the top of North America for a time. Kimmerly also ran a still while on board. "It was a dry company, so the still was skunk works. It had to be on gimbals to deal with the sometimes extreme motion," says Kimmerly. A post-retirement job as master of the Hornby Island Ferry led him to settle on the island. Kimmerly's interest in distilling goes back to when he was 16, when he built a still out of an old barbecue and his grandmother's pressure cooker. "We have come a long way since then," he says.

MERRIDALE CIDERY & DISTILLERY
COBBLE HILL AND VICTORIA, BC

In 1999 lawyer Rick Pipes and his wife, Janet Docherty, bought a struggling cidery with the goal of rejuvenating the business. Today, visitors linger over lunch in Merridale's spacious restaurant, wander groomed orchard grounds, and learn firsthand how craft cider differs from that made by larger producers.

In 2007 Pipes installed a still and began putting spirit away in barrels. At the time, the provincial liquor model encouraged high-volume products, which made it difficult to achieve the quality Pipes wanted. Nevertheless, he continued to distil apple and pear spirits but did not sell them. When microdistilling became more viable in BC, Pipes had plenty of long-aged spirit in store, just ready to bottle. Barrels from every year since 2007 ensure Merridale's 10-year-old apple and pear brandies will remain core products. That is good news, as their flavours are nothing short of sensational.

Merridale has adopted an Old World practice for reducing spirits from barrel to bottle strength. Adding water to alcohol generates heat. Pipes and his distiller, Laurent Lafuente, agree this changes the aromas of the spirit, so they add water gently over several days to avoid these sudden fluctuations. Bottling at 47% abv allows gentler filtering, and this in turn leaves flavours, such as oils from the pear skins, well and truly intact. Pipes ferments apple juice to make fruit spirits. His vodka, though, is a little bit different. Here, he uses the lees left behind from the cider-making process. His fruit spirits mature in French oak barrels. Whisky, though, spends five years in new American oak.

Merridale Cidery & Distillery is a family-friendly destination just 40 minutes north of Victoria. Success in Cobble Hill has led to a second distillery, Merridale at Dockside, across the new bridge near Songhees Point in Victoria. There, you can dine on a rooftop patio or watch from a catwalk as distillers craft spirits below.

1230 Merridale Rd.
Cobble Hill, BC V0R 1L0
(250) 743-4293 / 1-800-998-9908
www.merridale.ca

@merridalecider

@merridalecider

FOUNDED **2007**

OWNERS **Rick Pipes and Janet Docherty**

STILLS **Small Mueller pot**

PRODUCTS **Apple brandy, pear brandy, gin, vodka, whisky**

AVAILABLE **Onsite**

TOURS **Guided for groups of 10 or more, $10; walking tour of property, free**

NEAREST NEIGHBOURS **The Moon Distilling Co. (page 56) and Phillips Fermentorium Distilling Co. (page 60) — both 45 min; Stillhead Distilling Inc. (page 66) — 15 min**

TASTING NOTES: COWICHAN PEAR BRANDY (47% ABV)

You'd almost think someone swung a Louisville slugger to pick the fruit for this striking combination of fresh-picked pears and wood. Juicy, ripe pears dominate the nose and the palate, but a sip elevates it, thanks to the tropical fruits, slight pear-skin tannins, and nutty, peppery oak.

THE MOON DISTILLING CO.
VICTORIA, BC

350 Bay St.
Victoria, BC V8T 1P7
(250) 380-0706
www.moonunderwater.ca

 @moonbrewery

@moonbrewery

FOUNDED 2017

OWNERS Clay Potter, Anne Farmer,
Steve Ash

STILLS 500-litre Genio still

PRODUCTS Flavoured vodka, gin, grain
spirit moonshine, liqueurs, Shaft coffee
liqueur

AVAILABLE Onsite, private BC liquor
stores, restaurants

NEAREST NEIGHBOURS Phillips
Fermentorium Distilling Co. (page 60) —
2 min; Victoria Caledonian Distillery
(page 68) — 15 min

In his 1946 essay *The Moon Under Water*, George Orwell described the qualities of his favourite pub, before lamenting that such a pub was a wishful figment of his imagination. "There is no such place as the *Moon Under Water*," he confesses. "That is to say, there may well be a pub of that name, but I don't know of it, nor do I know any pub with just that combination of qualities."

Well, Mr. Orwell, you should have visited Victoria.

Clay Potter graduated from Heriot-Watt University's brewing and distilling program in 2011. The next year, with his parents, Anne Farmer and Steve Ash, he bought the Moon Under Water Brewery and got straight to work getting the business *above* the water. He expanded the brewpub's operations to include a distillery, which he designed to resemble the facade of a prohibition-era general store. In the store's back office, Potter distils a wide range of spirits, including vodka, gin, and whisky, in a 500-litre Genio still. That still is the one feature that Orwell neglected to mention in his description of his ideal pub.

COCKTAIL: THE SHAFT

MAKES 1 COCKTAIL

2 oz Shaft liqueur
2 oz half-and-half cream
Handful of ice cubes

Pour the Shaft liqueur and cream into a mixing glass and stir until combined. Serve over ice in a rocks glass.

(The Moon Distilling Co.)

PACIFIC RIM DISTILLING
UCLUELET, BC

Vancouver Island's Pacific Rim is peppered with natural wonders. In 2018 Luke Erridge added a distillery to the list of its seaside treasures. Erridge's great-uncle Alfie introduced distilling skills to the family in pre-prohibition days. "Alfie's spirits could power a tractor, my grandfather's could run a lawnmower, my mother's was getting there, and I've refined it," reflects Erridge, the first to make the family passion a business.

Inspired by what the generations before him might have used for ingredients had they landed here 250 years ago, Erridge got to work. He filled a jar with sugar water, topped it with cheesecloth, and left it in the woods to ferment. From that, he developed the distillery's yeast culture.

Oceanfront botanicals, such as salal and shore pine for Lighthouse Gin, are equally of this place. First, Erridge adds four botanicals directly into the still with barley malt spirit, while another four rest in the rising vapours above, in a gin basket. He then steeps salal berries in the resulting distillate, giving the gin its distinctive red hue. His flagship Humpback Vodka has also been a smash hit, with complete batches known to sell out in a single weekend.

317 Forbes Rd., #2
Ucluelet, BC V0R 3A0
(250) 726-2075

[] @pacificrimdistilling

FOUNDED **2018**

OWNER **Luke Erridge**

PRODUCTS **Gin, vodka**

AVAILABLE **Onsite, bars and restaurants**

NEAREST NEIGHBOURS **Tofino Craft Distillery (page 67) – 35 min; Arbutus Distillery (page 51) – 2 hrs, 35 min**

SIX BREEDS OF DISTILLER

Two hundred distilleries and counting in Canada, and no two are alike. Seriously. Each one has a still, of course, but other than that, just as the Hiram Walker & Sons Distillery (page 181) in Windsor, Ontario, bears almost no resemblance to the Gimli Distillery (page 154) in Manitoba, the Sons of Vancouver (page 42) differs in every way imaginable from The Woods Spirit Co. (page 46), just a five-minute walk away.

Regional differences? Surely that's naive even to imagine, but then you start talking about all those local gin botanicals. These distilleries are so different because they are reflections of the individuals who run, and in many cases created, them. Who, then, are these people?

Some are chefs who have exchanged their knives for copper pots. Others are university-trained distillers who look at spirits through a microscope. Some began as brewers and now take beer in another direction. Sometimes, farmers with excess grain, potatoes, or fruit added a still to process it. There are mid-career dropouts now chasing a dream, and financial wizards intent on chasing a dollar. Often, people choose to do their own thing, while other times they come together, bringing their complementary backgrounds to the single purpose of making flavourful spirits. Each of them (with some shoe-horning, perhaps) fits into one of six broad categories:

THE FLAVOURIST

These bartenders, chefs, artists, and artisans, who have turned their hand to making spirits, combine flavours to make the most exciting spirits possible. Regional or inventive, they are inspired to create new flavours just to flex their artistic muscles.

THE SCIENTIST

Some are educated in whisky schools such as the internationally acclaimed Heriot-Watt University. Others—chemists, physicists, and engineers—may bring to mind the mad scientist cliché, using hard-science degrees to solve spiritual problems. They tinker, they tweak, they adjust the process, perhaps to maximize output, and most certainly to make it consistent.

THE BREWER

Mashing, cooking, and fermenting grain, the basic processes in making beer, are also key steps to make whisky. Some of Canada's great distillers started out brewing beer, then they took the extra step of distilling it.

THE FARMER

Fallen fruit, ugly potatoes, and excess grain cost money to produce, and though perfectly edible, they're unsaleable. This is lost income to the farmers who grow them. Farmers who distil them into spirits end this needless waste while creating another revenue stream.

THE INVESTOR

In much of Canada, you almost need a trust fund or a second income to operate a successful small distillery. In British Columbia, though, recent laws have created business opportunities that attract hard-core entrepreneurs and investors. By restricting these opportunities to distillers who use BC produce, some of those profits find their way to farmers in that province. Now, other provinces are toying with similar models. Silent investors themselves don't distil. They hire talented professionals to make spirits the most profitable way they can.

MID-LIFE RETIREE

Then there are early retirees who are too young to slow down and too old—or successful—to work for someone else. Perhaps they made a bundle as IT executives, bankers, or the like, then cashed out early and turned to distilling in Canada, instead of shuffleboard or golf under the Florida sun. Most often, when they left the boardroom, they began an involuntary physical fitness program that involves wrestling barrels and lugging around heavy bags of grain. ■

Distiller, Simon Buttet, pours a sample in his tasting room at Alchemist Distiller (page 74). Today's distillers are often the face of the distillery, not only making the spirits, but also serving samples to curious imbibers.

PHILLIPS FERMENTORIUM DISTILLING CO.
VICTORIA, BC

2010 Government St.
Victoria, BC V8T 4P1
(250) 380-1912
www.fermentorium.ca

 @phillipsbeer

 @phillipsbeer

FOUNDER Matt Phillips

FOUNDED 2001 (brewery) and 2014 (distillery)

STILLS 1920s 2,600-litre pot still and 500-litre Mueller pot with eight-plate column

PRODUCTS Gin (whisky coming soon)

AVAILABLE Onsite, private BC liquor stores

NEAREST NEIGHBOURS Spinnakers Brewpub (page 65) and The Moon Distilling Co. (page 56) — both 5 min

On the seventh day, Matt Phillips rested his beer-exhausted palate with a gin and tonic. And saw that it was good. This was the genesis of the Fermentorium—a distillery that would explore the interaction between gin and tonic from the comforts of Phillips's brewery. But the project wouldn't come to fruition until Phillips moved to new digs that gave him the additional room he needed.

In 2012 Phillips applied his brewing aesthetic to making old-fashioned sodas. This opened the doors to creating tonics using traditional extraction methods and real ingredients. The Fermentorium was reborn.

When the Hiram Walker & Sons Distillery quit the Okanagan in 1995, a 1920s British copper pot still was left behind. A winery acquired the still, but then left it to collect dust and dents. When the winery went out of business, Phillips rescued the still and baptized it as Old George.

By late 2013 Old George was making Phillips's debut run, stripping barley mash into low wines to be rectified into gin in a modern Mueller still. The brewery has since added a malting plant to control the quality of the grain used for making beer and whisky for Phillips as well as several other distilleries. And for that palate-cleansing gin and tonic at the end of the week.

TASTING NOTES: STUMP COASTAL FOREST GIN (45% ABV)

The stump is all that's left after juicing a fragrant grand fir to make this gin. Herbs and flowers balance appealing woodsy tones, coriander, and lavender, but beneath its assertive nature lies delicate grapefruit zest, disclosing a hint of Cascade hops.

MAKES 1 COCKTAIL

1½ oz of Stump Coastal Forest Gin
¾ oz lime juice
½ oz Hop Drop (available at the distillery)

½ oz simple syrup
Handful of ice cubes
1 lime wheel, for garnish

Pour all of the ingredients into a cocktail shaker with ice and shake until combined.
Double-strain into a large cocktail glass. Garnish with a lime wheel.

[Phillips Fermentorium Distilling Co.]

SALT SPRING SHINE CRAFT DISTILLERY LTD.
SALT SPRING ISLAND, BC

Bears from Vancouver Island rarely swim across to Salt Spring Island, but when they do, they head straight to the honey pots at Michael and Rie Papp's distillery. The Papps use 100% BC honey to make their small-batch vodka, gin, and moonshine. With their Cordon Bleu–trained palates, the couple has developed a fruity, floral gin, balanced by the sting of juniper without any grizzly notes. They invite you to try it at the live-edge maple wood counter in their distillery tasting room.

194 Kitchen Rd.
Salt Spring Island, BC V8K 2B3
(250) 221-0728

FOUNDED **2016**

OWNERS **Michael and Rie Papp**

PRODUCTS **Gin, moonshine**

AVAILABILITY **Onsite**

NEAREST NEIGHBOURS **Stillhead Distilling Inc. (page 66) — 1 hr, 10 min (includes ferry)**

SHELTER POINT DISTILLERY
CAMPBELL RIVER, BC

4650 Regent Rd.
Campbell River, BC V9H 1E3
(778) 420-2200
www.shelterpoint.ca

 @shelterpoint

@shelterpoint

FOUNDED **2011**

OWNER **Patrick Evans**

STILLS **5,000-litre and 4,000-litre Forsyths pot stills; 1,000-litre Specific Mechanical pot with 20-plate column**

PRODUCTS **Gin, liqueur, vodka, whisky**

AVAILABLE **Onsite, online, private stores**

TOURS **Free; 12–5 p.m. daily (includes tasting)**

NEAREST NEIGHBOUR **Wayward Distillation House (page 71) – 30 min**

Shelter Point Distillery, with its 155 hectares of farmland and two kilometres of Salish Sea beach, couldn't be more beautiful. There, third-generation dairy farmer and distillery owner Patrick Evans grows barley. If barley grows well here, he thought, why not make whisky? The first few batches were not encouraging. Today, though, the team—including head distiller Leon Webb, operations manager James Marinus, and distillery manager Jacob Weibe—successfully make vodka, gin, and single malt whisky that is a genuine Canadian sensation.

The gin uses juniper and other botanicals that Evans cultivates right on the farm. From a tonne of grain, the team distils Shelter Point gin, 1,200 bottles at a time, in their new Specific Mechanical pot still. Another wonderfully briny gin, which they flavour with sea asparagus from their own seashore, makes a vaguely dirty Martini without the nuisance of olive juice!

Although Shelter Point is best known for its single malt whisky, Evans has not forgotten his Irish ancestry. He fills a few barrels with Irish pure pot-style spirit made with 50-50 malted and unmalted barley. Late in 2018 a new triumph emerged from the warehouse behind the distillery: 100% rye whisky that Webb believes is the best he has ever tasted.

And if you ever get tired of gazing across the Salish Sea, turn around to see some of the highest mountains on the island, including Mount Washington, a famous training ground for Olympic snow sports.

TASTING NOTES:
SHELTER POINT SINGLE MALT (46% ABV)

Clean grain, breakfast cereal, and grassy pastures drift from the glass as sweet undertones shift onto a palate that bursts into fiery cinnamon spices. A maltiness weaves through the whisky, providing structure leading into a sweet and gentle finish. Made from double-distilled two-row barley aged in once-used American oak.

SHERINGHAM DISTILLERY
SOOKE, BC

6731 West Coast Rd., #252
Sooke, BC V9Z 0S9
(778) 425-2019
www.sheringhamdistillery.com

 @SheringhamBC

@sheringhamdistillery

FOUNDED 2015

OWNERS Alayne and Jason MacIsaac

STILLS 2,000-litre, 650-litre, and 350-litre pots with 12-plate column, all imported from China

PRODUCTS Akvavit, gin, vodka, whisky

AVAILABLE Onsite, online, private liquor stores

TOURS Tasting room and shop (contact the distillery for seasonal hours)

NEAREST NEIGHBOURS The Moon Distilling Co. (page 56) – 40 min; Phillips Fermentorium Distilling Co. (page 60) – 45 min

After riding from Goldstream to Sooke on the wriggling serpent that maps call Highway 14, you may find yourself in need of a break. Head straight to Sheringham Distillery, where distiller Jason MacIsaac crafts locally sourced grains and botanicals into whisky, akvavit, and vodka. They are all wonderful, but when you walk up to the bar in Sheringham's tasting room, ask for Seaside Gin. Winged kelp, which grows in the Pacific waters nearby, gives this gin oomph. The first sip is restorative, the next as refreshing as a Juan de Fuca breeze. And the next . . .

MacIsaac and his wife, Alayne, founded Sheringham 20 minutes farther down Highway 14, in the rural community of Shirley. They moved to Sooke in 2018 after maxing out the capacity of their original location. It's a different experience here, from new distilling equipment to a more reliable source of water.

For 23 years, before he took up distilling, Jason was a chef. Working at a resort in Jordan River, even farther down Highway 14, he lived in what was reputed to have been a moonshiner's shack. What else was he to do but build his own still? Later, as the chef of a private club in Victoria, he met a group of distillers who were there to discuss legislation that could help make distilling more viable. Whether it was eavesdropping or post-prandial chit-chat, Jason got the gist of what they were up to and went home and got going full bore.

Today, Sheringham's spirits are as much an adventure as the ride from Victoria is. Delicate flavours, balanced carefully, become one. So don't look for the yuzu, cherry blossoms, green tea flowers, the tea itself, or juniper, coriander, and angelica individually in Jason's Kazuki Japanese gin. Enjoy it for the blissful synthesis it is. "I think having a chef's palate helped me with the flavour," Jason explains modestly.

TASTING NOTES:
SHERINGHAM DISTILLERY AKVAVIT (42% ABV)

This Scandinavian-style spirit offers a citrus brightness on the nose without overpowering a fresh, herbal tang of caraway and dill. Full-bodied and bready, the spirit's anise sweetness balances a peppery bite and delicate brine that drift into a lingering finish.

SPINNAKERS BREWPUB
VICTORIA, BC

When Paul Hadfield launched Spinnakers Brewpub in 1984, he set the wheels in motion for a whole new industry. A former architect, Hadfield's interest was piqued by what John Mitchell was doing at Troller Pub in Horseshoe Bay, near Vancouver: becoming the first pub in Canada to serve microbrewed beer. Hadfield built Spinnakers from the ground up to produce the interesting beer flavours he and Mitchell could only taste when travelling abroad. Canada's craft beer boom quickly followed. Spinnakers soon embraced the blossoming local-food movement. Given such momentum and great timing, it makes sense that Hadfield's latest venture is distilling. In 2018 he installed a 500-litre iStill. Brewmasters Matt Stanley and Kala Hadfield (Paul's daughter) have begun with gin and vodka for the brewpub's backbar. Canned coolers and vodka soda are next, with whisky somewhere further down the line. Once they find their feet as distillers, they will also begin selling through private liquor stores.

308 Catherine St.
Victoria, BC V9A 3S8
www.spinnakers.com

NEAREST NEIGHBOURS Phillips Fermentorium Distilling Co. (page 60) – 5 min; The Moon Distilling Co. (page 56) – 10 min

STILLHEAD DISTILLING INC.
DUNCAN, BC

5301 Chaster Rd.
Duncan, BC V9L 0G4
(250) 748-6874
www.stillhead.ca

🐦 @StillheadDstlry

📷 @stillheaddistillery

FOUNDED 2017

OWNERS Ron & Christal and Brennan &
Erika Colebank

STILLS 500-litre Holstein pot with
12-plate and 6-plate columns

PRODUCTS Apple brandy, blackberry
vodka, gin, kirsch, vodka, whisky

AVAILABLE Onsite, online, private liquor
stores (and at 37 Grill near Kitwanga)

TOURS Tasting room and shop

NEAREST NEIGHBOURS Ampersand
Distilling Company (page 49) — 15 min;
Merridale Cidery & Distillery (page 55) —
15 min

The twinned bridges that span the Cowichan River, two minutes from Stillhead Distilling, are short, and the water below, though fast, is shallow. This is ideal spawning territory for ocean-going steelhead trout. The head of a still, on the other hand, is where the vapours gather until pressure pushes them into the condenser. The name Stillhead is Brennan Colebank's wistful, punning nod to the once-abundant fish. A steelhead logo on labels and signs is complemented by wrought-iron fish welded into the security bars on the doors and windows.

Generating income is always difficult for start-up whisky distilleries since, by law, the spirit must spend at least three years in oak barrels. Stillhead makes several different spirits, but whisky is a special focus. To keep its balance sheet positive, Colebank sells barrels of spirit to individuals and whisky clubs. Five-litre barrels go home with the customer; 30-litre ones mature at the distillery. And those six square barrels on the maturing racks? They are an American innovation that allows distillers to customize small numbers of barrels to their own specifications.

The Cowichan Valley, where Duncan is located, is home to nearly 5,000 Hul'q'umi'num', the People of the Warm Land. Come blackberry season, band members descend on the distillery with pails of wild blackberries. Whether they arrive in pickups with pails of berries in the back or on a 10-speed with a single small pail hanging off a handlebar, the pickers know they will be paid top dollar for good-quality berries. Stillhead's most popular product—blackberry-infused vodka—sells 4,000 bottles each year.

Brennan's father, Ron, lives in Prince George and distributes Stillhead products in northern BC. When travellers on the Yellowhead Highway near Kitwanga get the munchies, 37 Grill makes a decent meal. Thanks to Ron, it also serves Stillhead spirits exclusively.

TASTING NOTES:
WILD BLACKBERRY INFUSED VODKA (35% ABV)
Ripe wild blackberries are much more flavourful than those you buy at the grocer's, as this bestseller amply demonstrates. The berries imbue the creamy vodka with a fetching all-natural wine tone as a subtle tartness underlines its blackberry sweetness.

TOFINO CRAFT DISTILLERY
TOFINO, BC

Beaches interrupt the temperate rainforests that hug the rugged western shoreline of Vancouver Island leading to the town of Tofino. Here, local paramedic Adam Warry and firefighters John Gilmour and Neil Campbell made their own waves by setting up a distillery. The trio produces two gins, both with regional flavours. Their West Coast Gin is a traditional non-chill-filtered dry gin made with 10 botanicals. For Old Growth Cedar Gin they use the same botanical mix, then pack their gin basket with western red cedar tips. The distillery also makes vodka and a tripped-out absinthe called Psychedelic Jellyfish. You can sample all of these spirits and more in mini-cocktails at their snug tasting room.

681 Industrial Way, Units G and H
Tofino, BC V0R 2Z0
(250) 725-2182
www.tofinocraftdistillery.com

FOUNDED 2017

OWNERS Adam Warry, John Gilmour, Neil Campbell

STILLS 500-litre and 250-litre Genio stills

PRODUCTS Absinthe, gin, vodka

NEAREST NEIGHBOURS Pacific Rim Distilling (page 57) — 35 min

VICTORIA CALEDONIAN DISTILLERY

SAANICH, BC

761 Enterprise Cres.
Saanich, BC V8Z 6P7
(778) 401-0410
www.victoriacaledonian.com

 @VCaledonian

 @victoriacaledonian

FOUNDED 2016

OWNERS Graeme Macaloney and several
hundred investors

STILLS Forsyths pots

PRODUCTS Whisky

AVAILABLE Onsite, private liquor stores

TOURS $22–$46

NEAREST NEIGHBOURS de Vine Wines &
Spirits (page 52) – 15 min; The Moon
Distilling Co. (page 56) and Phillips
Fermentorium Distilling Co. (page 60) –
both 15 min

Victoria Caledonian Distillery certainly has what Scottish distillers call "the kit." Against an emerald wall, sparkling copper pot stills from Forsyths of Rothes stand sentry on either side of an equally sparkling brass spirit safe. A few barrels in feng shui–perfect position complete the photo-ready backdrop.

Scottish-born and raised founder and president Graeme Macaloney is trying to replicate Scotch whisky in a Canadian locale, and is making all the right moves. He began by hiring the late Dr. Jim Swan, a renowned Scottish distilling consultant, to advise him. Together they developed a rapid-ageing regimen that they claim reduces the time needed to make mature whisky.

While the whisky matures, their in-house brewery generates income. Macaloney also hired Scotch whisky heavyweight distiller Mike Nicolson to get the distillery running, before turning it over to an experienced brewer, Nicole MacLean. In 2018 Macaloney installed a smoker so that the distillery could make its own peated malt, just as Pemberton Distillery (page 37) had done four years earlier and Distillerie Fils du Roy (page 261) in 2016.

It is difficult to tell whether this picture-perfect distillery is in regular production yet because visitors are not permitted inside the warehouse. Selling investment opportunities is a key element of Victoria Caledonian's business model, and Macaloney's ultimate intention, stated in one of many fundraising campaigns, is either to list on a public stock exchange or be acquired by a global spirits firm. So far, his project has raised about $10 million and has annual sales of about $1 million, primarily from the in-house brewery. For some of its whiskies, Victoria Caledonian Distillery blends spirits imported from Scotland.

TASTING NOTES: MAC NA BRAICHE MALT SPIRIT (50% ABV)

The way it wears its kilt and tosses its caber *au naturel*, you'd swear this full-bodied spirit was made from malted barley soaked in steroids. Stone fruits, charred oak, and malt transition easily from nose to palate. Assertive spice betrays the spirit's untamed youth, while anticipating a splendid single malt whisky.

VICTORIA DISTILLERS
SIDNEY, BC

In 2007 winemaker Ken Winchester and his business partner, Bryan Murray, bought a small wood-fired pot still to make eau-de-vie. All they needed now was a distiller. A degree in molecular biology and 10 years tending bar had given Peter Hunt an understanding of spirits, and so Murray and Winchester brought him on board shortly after they first fired up their still. Grape spirits didn't sell well, so they pushed forward and found their true niche in juniper's romance. It was 2008, and Canadian small-batch gin was born—and named Victoria.

Murray retired in 2015, when an investment firm acquired the distillery. Hunt stayed on as president and master distiller. A year later the business moved into a new seaside distillery that was more than meets the eye with its shiny Canadian Specific Mechanical still. Like a Transformer, this still quickly changes from a six-plate rectification head to a spirit head or a stripping head for whisky. They've since added a second still.

Victoria's Empress Hotel hosted the 2008 launch of Victoria Gin, laying the groundwork to create another gin to celebrate the storied hotel's past. Empress 1908 is now a worldwide sensation. Six organic botanicals, including ginger root and cinnamon bark as a spicy bow to Queen Victoria's title as Empress of India, marinate in corn spirit and water for 24 hours, before mixing with corn distillate in the still. After the gin is reduced to 42.5% abv, a second magical infusion of butterfly pea blossoms and the Empress Hotel's secret tea blend are added. Within hours, the gin develops its signature cobalt blue hue.

This blue butterfly pea blossom, incidentally, is coveted in traditional Chinese medicine to boost brainpower and promote hair growth, among many other health benefits. Judging by the staff's healthy glow, after testing 50-plus trial recipes, the blossom is certainly doing its job.

(continued)

9891 Seaport Place
Sidney, BC V8L 4X3
(250) 544-8217
www.victoriadistillers.com

Founded 2007

OWNER The Marker Group

STILLS 200-litre Mueller copper pot still with three-plate column and two Specific Mechanical stills with six-plate rectification heads

PRODUCTS Gin, liqueurs, rum, vodka, whisky

TOURS $7; call for reservations

AVAILABLE Onsite, private liquor stores, and internationally

NEAREST NEIGHBOURS de Vine Wines & Spirits (page 52) — 20 min

TASTING NOTES:
EMPRESS 1908 GIN
(42.5% ABV)

Its cobalt blue light show is dazzling. Equally radiant flavours of Bulgarian black juniper, citrus pith, candied ginger, and spring flowers balance a gorgeous, full-bodied, oily texture. Fairmont Empress-blend tea enhances the floral and citrus notes while synthesizing seamlessly with the butterfly pea blossom's earthiness.

COCKTAIL:
THE AVIATION
MAKES 1 COCKTAIL

2 oz Victoria Gin
½ oz fresh lemon juice
½ oz maraschino liqueur
1 dash crème de violette (optional)
Handful of ice cubes
1 lemon twist, for garnish

Place a cocktail glass in the freezer until chilled, at least one hour. Pour all of the ingredients except the lemon twist into a cocktail shaker with ice. Shake and strain into the chilled cocktail glass. Garnish with a lemon twist.

(Victoria Distillers)

WAYWARD DISTILLATION HOUSE
COURTENAY, BC

Math quiz: Wayward Distillation House makes all of its spirits from honey. It takes about a kilogram of honey to produce one 750-millilitre bottle of spirit. When it reaches maximum production, Wayward will make 50,000 litres of spirit each year. Golden Clover Apiary maintains 1,400 hives of bees, which it leases out to pollinate pesticide-free farms in northern BC. Bees collect nectar from 4.5 million flowers to make one kilogram of honey. While they gather the nectar, the bees also pollinate the flowers, causing them to produce seeds. Wayward buys all of its honey from Golden Clover.

Question: How many flowers must the bees in Golden Clover's 1,400 hives visit in order make enough honey to keep the stills working at Wayward Distillation House?

Answer: About 300 billion flowers.

Savour that thought the next time you sip on a Wayward beverage, and marvel at what a wonderful person you are to help grow another generation of flowers in the farm fields of northern BC, to say nothing of sustaining the bee population.

"Honey makes a fabulous spirit—there are no off-flavours," says distillery co-owner Andrea Brimacombe. "We looked at all kinds of fermentables." Andrea, along with her former husband, Dave Brimacombe, and Curt and Laura Carbonell, had already experimented with making mead. It seemed logical to take things a step further. This is why Wayward's gins, vodkas, rums, and liqueurs all begin as honey. In the hands of Wayward's distillers, this honey retains a little sweetness even after it has been distilled. The team uses six local botanicals for their gin, toning down the juniper so that they can push other floral notes forward. Like Wayward's honey-based rum, some of this gin then ages in oak barrels.

TASTING NOTES:
WAYWARD ORDER DEPTH CHARGE (33% ABV)

Coffee notes, so sweet on the nose, dissolve into untempered coffee flavours on the palate. Infused raw organic cacao nibs accent the natural bitterness of espresso from the nearby Royston Roasting Company, bringing an earthy quality to this good-to-the-last-drop honey-vodka-based liqueur.

2931 Moray Ave.
Courtenay, BC V9N 7S7
(250) 871-0424
www.waywarddistillery.com

@drinkwayward

@waywarddistillery

FOUNDED 2014

OWNERS Andrea Brimacombe, Dave Brimacombe, Curt and Laura Carbonell

STILLS 1,200-litre Cage & Sons with 20-plate column

PRODUCTS Gin, honey spirit, liqueur, rum, infused vodka, vodka

AVAILABLE Onsite, online, private liquor stores, bars and restaurants

TOURS Tasting room and shop

NEAREST NEIGHBOURS Shelter Point Distillery (page 62) — 25 min; Arbutus Distillery (page 51) — 1 hr, 5 min

AFTER DARK DISTILLERY
SICAMOUS, BC

1201 Shuswap Ave.
Sicamous, BC V0E 2V0
(250) 836-5187
www.afterdarkdistillery.com

@After_Dark_Dist

@after_dark_distillery

FOUNDED 2017

OWNERS Dean and Louise Perry

STILLS 1,000-litre Still Dragon with double column; 160-litre Mueller stripping still (purchased from Okanagan Spirits)

PRODUCTS Gin, moonshine, vodka, whisky spirit

AVAILABLE Onsite, private liquor stores

NEAREST NEIGHBOURS Jones Distilling (page 80) and Monashee Spirits Craft Distillery (page 86) – 50 min; Okanagan Spirits Craft Distillery-Vernon (page 88) – 1 hr

When Dean and Louise Perry were looking for a place to set up a distillery, Sicamous town councillors suggested a location right up their alley: the three-lane bowling alley, no longer in service, on the main street. As an incentive, the town promised a new sidewalk and parking spaces to accommodate visitors. "They welcomed us with open arms," says the barrel-chested trucker with an easy smile. After 20 years working in Alberta's oil patch, Dean and Louise decided that if they were going to pursue their dreams, now was the time.

"After Dark" echoes the storied past of moonshine and bootlegging. But why moonshine? "We needed a product that could go out the door while we waited for our whisky. That means vodka and flavoured moonshine." Then, with a grin, Dean adds, "We do our best work after dark!" Handmade, one-of-a-kind moonshine jugs from a pottery in nearby Enderby add to the moonshine's aura. This distillery is no moonshiner's hovel though.

Grain stored in outside silos is dropped 1,000 kilograms at a time into one of four bright yellow, custom-built hoppers inside the distillery. Below these, a fifth hopper, this one on wheels, collects the grain and carries it to a grinding mill. After five days of fermentation in large plastic totes, Dean distils it to 83% abv.

While most of their whisky matures, the Perrys have released an 11-month-old grain spirit, playfully named Loud Mouth Soup. Although they have no plans for a restaurant, in summer, visitors can opt for the food stand in the parking lot, and sit and listen to live music on the patio. That's probably a better idea. Word is that you shouldn't eat in a restaurant with a bowling trophy on the cash register anyway.

TASTING NOTES:
MONASHEE MOUNTAIN MOONSHINE ESPRESSO COFFEE
(24% ABV)

Scientists should study just how a Mason jar lid can withstand the pressure of this moonshine's rise-and-shine coffee flavour. Colossal dark-roasted espresso notes bolster touches of raw coffee bean and sugary coffee candies.

COCKTAIL:
CREAMSICLE
MAKES 1 COCKTAIL

1 cup of ice cubes, plus an extra handful
2 oz vanilla almond milk
1 oz of Copper Island Gin
1 oz orange juice concentrate
¼ large mandarin orange
1 orange wedge, for garnish

Combine all of the ingredients except the orange wedge in a blender, and blend until smooth and frothy. Pour into a soda glass containing additional ice, and garnish with an orange wedge.

(After Dark Distillery)

ALCHEMIST DISTILLER
SUMMERLAND, BC

18006 Bentley Rd., #101
Summerland, BC V0H 1Z3
(250) 317-6454

FOUNDED 2017

OWNERS Simon Buttet and Sandrine
Jacques (Buttet by now)

STILL 1,000-litre self-designed with
2 metre glass column and spiral heat
exchanger

PRODUCTS Absynthe, apple liqueur, gin

AVAILABLE Onsite, private liquor stores

NEAREST NEIGHBOURS Okanagan Crush Pad
Winery and Distillery (page 87) — 5 min

In October 2014 Simon Buttet and Sandrine Jacques immigrated to Canada from France. Simon is a chemical engineer who had home-distilled absinthe in France and dreamed of being his own boss in a venture that provided large toys to play with, while making something that would bring joy to his customers. Voilà! A distillery would do just that.

Looking for work to get them through the winter, Buttet knocked on the door of every distillery in the Okanagan Valley. Eventually, Legend Distilling (page 82) hired him. A year and a half later, he was ready to venture out with Sandrine to launch a business of their own: Alchemist Distiller. Today, they are known for distilling spirits from apples.

BOHEMIAN SPIRITS
KIMBERLEY, BC

Of all the birds Wade Jarvis and Erryn Turcon enjoyed watching from their Marysville distillery, the Bohemian waxwing is their favourite. Why? Because the pigments of their wing tips, over time, become a waxy red thanks to the fruit they gorge on. Come winter, the fruit has fermented on the vine, sending flocks of drunken vagabonds sloshing and dropping all over town.

After adopting their feathered friends' name, the distillery followed their roving lifestyle. Having outgrown the former craft brewery it had taken over, Bohemian Spirits moved to a larger space with a tasting room, store, and cocktail lounge in nearby Kimberley. Although the brewery had failed, turning distiller's beer into spirits has been a great success.

And remember those red wing tips? It seems the birds sometimes have to share the berry bounty with the distillers. Bohemian Spirits' Colossal Gin derives its pink hue from pigments in locally harvested huckleberries and is their biggest seller. With barrel-aged gin and whisky maturing, Jarvis and Turcon keep the cash flow positive by making vodka. "Vagabond Vodka represents the wanderer in all of us," says Jarvis. "We proofed it at 42% in homage to the answer to the ultimate question of life from Douglas Adams's book *The Hitchhiker's Guide to the Galaxy.*" It is this kind of deep thought that keeps Bohemian Spirits moving forward "with infinite majesty and calm."

215 Mark St.
Kimberley, BC V1A 2B2
(250) 427-5430
www.bohemianspirits.com

 @goodcheerhere

 @goodcheerhere

FOUNDED **2014**

OWNERS **Wade Jarvis and Erryn Turcon**

STILLS **750-litre Red Boot pot with 20-plate reflux column**

PRODUCTS **Gin, liqueurs, vodka, whisky**

AVAILABLE **Onsite, private BC liquor stores**

NEAREST NEIGHBOURS **Elder Bros. Farms Distillery (page 77) – 15 min; Taynton Bay Spirits (page 92) – 1 hr, 30 min**

TASTING NOTES:
COLOSSAL GIN
(40% ABV)

Tart huckleberry on the nose blends with a pleasing cucumber tone, giving this pink gin a refreshing quality. The palate soars into the trees to find the gin's framework of subdued pine and dry, peppery wood. And above this, juniper berries cap a simply splendid drink.

THE DUBH GLAS DISTILLERY LTD.
OLIVER, BC

8486 Gallagher Lake Frontage Rd.
Oliver, BC V0H 1T2
(778) 439-3580
www.thedubhglasdistillery.com

 @dubhglasd

@thedubhglasd

FOUNDED 2015

OWNER Grant Stevely

STILLS 300-litre Holstein pot still with nine-plate rectifying column

PRODUCTS Gin, single malt whisky, white whisky

AVAILABLE Onsite, online

TOURS Friday—Sunday, 11 a.m.–6 p.m.

NEAREST NEIGHBOURS Tumbleweed Spirits (page 96) — 30 min; Old Order Distilling Co. (page 90) — 30 min

About 10 minutes north of Oliver on Highway 97, keep an eye peeled for the Gallagher Lake Campground. It is an easy way to spot the Dubh Glas Distillery, which is on a service road just across the highway. Dubh Glas (pronounced *dugh-luhs*) is Gaelic for "from the dark water," an apt image for this operation. An aquifer deep beneath the distillery feeds the dark depths of a cavernous well with pure water from the Cascade and Columbia Mountains. The property was once slated for more camping, but you won't find any toasted marshmallows here, just barrels. Grant Stevely bought the land in 2010, then built his whisky distillery from the ground up, to resemble a deep-woods cabin. He did much of the construction work himself.

Stevely's passion for distilling, especially single malt whiskies, began long before he put a shovel in the ground here. As head of security at Banff's Sunshine Village ski resort, he secretly fermented and distilled barley syrup in a 20-litre Portuguese copper alembic still in one of the staff bathrooms. He soon added a mill and switched from buying syrup to grinding barley.

Camped front and centre in the 140-square-metre distillery, a sparkling 300-litre Holstein pot still turns 100% BC-malted barley mash into whisky spirit. Sixty-plus barrels of maturing whisky are about all the space can hold, making expansion a next step, even as evaporation claims 10% annually from Stevely's 200-litre recoopered bourbon barrels. Although Stevely refers to this evaporation as "the angel's share," talk about whisky thieves!

While his whisky is nestled in oaken sleeping bags, Stevely produces his acclaimed Noteworthy Gin, again using 100% BC-grown barley. Ceres, the Roman goddess of agriculture, grain, and fertility, adorns a label most noteworthy for its colour. It matches Stevely's bright orange attire. We never said distillers were boring.

TASTING NOTES: SINGLE MALT WHISKY LAUNCH CASK STRENGTH (79.7% ABV)

Lively and brisk with freshly ground black pepper, spices, and promises of oak. A drop of water reveals a pleasant grassy character and a fruity, sweet softness. Suggestions of grain and cereals tantalize the palate through a very long finish that grows somewhat floral. Over time, exotic sandalwood spices and char still buzz around the empty glass.

ELDER BROS. FARMS DISTILLERY
WYCLIFFE, BC

In Hungary, where elderberries are popular, distillers Attila and Naomi Lepsis acquired a taste of elderflower syrup as children. Later, in Canada, when Attila closed The Hun, his Hungarian eatery in Barrie, Ontario, and moved to the Okanagan, he decided to work with those same flavours. Antioxidant-rich elderberry bushes grow well here. Their sons, Cyrus and Damian, mix elderflowers with honey from the farm's hives and make a syrup, which they ferment and then distil in a Canadian-made four-plate North still. Atilla then dilutes the resulting spirit down to 30% abv with fruit juice to make schnapps.

3121 Mission Wycliffe Rd.
Wycliffe, BC V1C 7C8
www.elderbrosfarms.com

NEAREST NEIGHBOUR **Bohemian Spirits** (page 75) — 15 min

FERNIE DISTILLERS
FERNIE, BC

531 1st Ave.
Fernie, BC V0B 1M0
www.ferniedistillers.com

@fernie_distillers

FOUNDED 2018

OWNERS Jillian Rutherford and Andrew
Hayden

STILLS 600-litre Wenzhou Yayi Column
still with copper helmet and 12-plate
split column; 200-litre Wenzhou Yayi
with copper helmet exclusively for gin

PRODUCTS Gin, liqueurs, vodka, seasonal
products

AVAILABLE Onsite and private liquor
stores in BC

TOURS By appointment

NEAREST NEIGHBOURS Lost Boys Distilling
(page 84) — 5 min; Elder Bros. Farms
Distillery (page 77) — 1 hr, 10 min

In their downtown distillery, in a former Royal Canadian Legion hall, Jillian Rutherford and Andrew Haydon distil Fernie's colourful history and bottle its essence. They invite customers to immerse themselves in Fernie's past by drinking the answers to a history quiz. There are no prizes beyond bragging rights, but here are a few clues to save any embarrassment.

In 1887, a little better than a decade before the Canadian Pacific Railway connected Fernie to the rest of Canada, prospector William Fernie found coal. Rutherford's Prospector Gin celebrates his discovery and the prospectors who followed his path. No. 9 Mine Vodka evokes the mine in Coal Creek where, in 1950, British Columbia's first underground diesel locomotive functioned. Okay, there's a quick history lesson to start you off. The rest is up to you.

TASTING NOTES: FERNIE FOG (40% ABV)

The Canadian Pacific Railway that connected Fernie with the country in 1898 allowed miners and prospectors to arrive by steam engine. This Earl Grey tea infusion shines subtly through the foggy steam, with sweet vanilla balancing the tea's trademark citrusy bergamot nose.

FORBIDDEN SPIRITS DISTILLING CO.
KELOWNA, BC

Adam and Eve never set foot in the Okanagan, but the Tomiye and Casorso families did. There, they farmed a vast area that included a large apple orchard that is now owned and cultivated by Blair and Kelly Wilson.

The Okanagan, with its orchards and rich farmland, is its own Garden of Eden, except this time, *the Wilsons* banished the serpent. That's because they ferment those apples and distil them into vodka. A tasting room in the distillery features century-old wood reclaimed from the Casorso property. Search out a label with a bat-winged angel tumbling to earth while grasping for a golden apple. That is Rebel Vodka—distilled 25 times. The angel took the risk, now you reap the reward.

4400 Wallace Hill Rd.
Kelowna, BC V1W 4C3
(250) 764-6011
www.forbiddenspirits.ca

🐦 @FSD_Co

📷 @forbiddenspiritsdistillingco

FOUNDED 2018

OWNERS Blair and Kelly Wilson

STILLS 1,000-litre Kothe pot still and twin 24-plate rectifying column

PRODUCTS Gin, rum, vodka

AVAILABLE Onsite, private liquor stores, restaurants, and bars

TOURS By appointment

NEAREST NEIGHBOURS Okanagan Spirits Craft Distillery-Kelowna (page 88) — 15 min

JONES DISTILLING
REVELSTOKE, BC

616 Third St. W.
Revelstoke, BC V0E 2S0
www.jonesdistilling.com

@jonesdistilling

Founded 2018

OWNER Gareth "Jonah" Jones

STILLS Two 500-litre iStills; 200-litre Genio stripping still

PRODUCTS Gin, cinnamon liqueur, cream liqueur, vodka, whisky (forthcoming)

AVAILABLE Onsite, online, private liquor stores

TOURS Tasting room open daily in summer

NEAREST NEIGHBOURS Monashee Spirits Craft Distillery (page 86) — 5 min; After Dark Distillery (page 72) — 1 hr

The solid two-storey red-brick cube on Revelstoke's Third Street so recalls the elementary school it once was that you can hardly believe it's now a distillery. Climb the grand staircase that has felt a million tiny footsteps since Mountain View School opened in 1914, though, and you will not find any classrooms. In 2016 British expat Gareth "Jonah" Jones bought the landmark, which had been vacant since 2012, to house Jones Distilling.

While still a child, Jones caught the distilling bug from his father. Family lore says Jonah's father once pilfered a still from a police lockup where it was being held as evidence. Jonah was 19 when his dad passed away, and the memory of those home distillations lived on until he revived them, legally, in a vodka he named for his father. Jones has hired ex-brewer Megan Moore to run the stills.

Moore looks like she knows her way around a mogul. "Sometimes I come in, check the stills, then head straight to the mountains," she says. Nonetheless, she enjoys distilling. "I love the smell of mash when I walk in the door." Moore turned from brewing beer to distilling to be on the leading edge of something new. Although her official title is "master distiller," earned by succeeding on a distilling course, she dismisses it with a shrug. "I've barely scratched the surface," she says, grinning. Employing technical elements of molecular mixology/gastronomy, Moore controls her fermentation temperatures to within a tenth of a degree. She also uses an auger to ensure there are no unfermented spots in the mash. And what does Moore drink après-ski? "IPAs—the hoppier, the better."

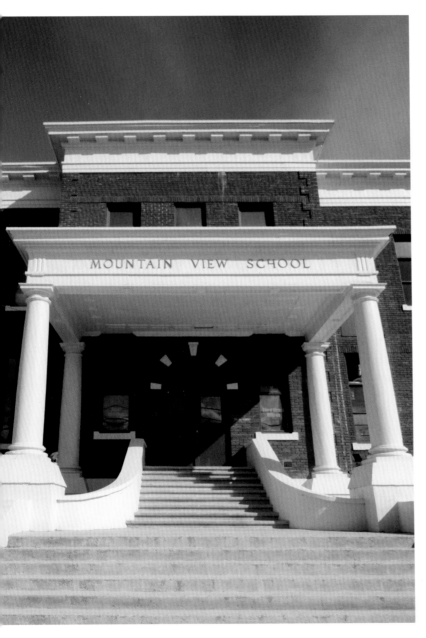

TASTING NOTES:
MR. JONES VODKA
(40% ABV)

School's out with this lightly sweet vodka. Local grains distilled, then filtered through activated charcoal give it a mark of A+ in pure and smooth. Perfect for a cocktail in the teachers' lounge, chilled in a shot glass, or last-day-of-classes streaking down the hallway in a tumbler full of ice.

COCKTAIL: HOLIDAY SPICED APPLE FIZZ
MAKES 1 COCKTAIL

Handful of ice cubes (optional)
2 oz real apple cider
1½ oz Mr. Jones Premium Vodka
Splash of ginger beer
1 cinnamon stick, for garnish

For the cold version, fill a rocks glass with ice. Add the vodka and cold apple cider and stir. Add a splash of ginger beer to fill the glass. Garnish with a cinnamon stick.

For the warm version, simmer the apple cider on low heat for five minutes. In a camp mug, add vodka and the warmed apple cider and stir. Add a splash of ginger beer to fill the glass. Garnish with a cinnamon stick.

(Megan Moore)

LEGEND DISTILLING
NARAMATA, BC

3005 Naramata Rd.
Naramata, BC V0H 1N1
(778) 514-1010
www.legenddistilling.com

 @LegendNaramata

 @LegendNaramata

FOUNDED **2014**

OWNERS **Doug and Dawn Lennie**

STILLS **600-litre Artisan Still Dragon**

PRODUCTS **Amaro, flavoured vodka, gin, liqueurs, vodka, whisky**

AVAILABLE **Onsite, online**

TOURS **Tasting room**

NEAREST NEIGHBOURS **Maple Leaf Spirits (page 85) — 10 min; Old Order Distilling Co. (page 90) —15 min**

Brew beer or distil spirits? Dawn and Doug Lennie couldn't decide until BC's distilling laws changed. Having run an artisanal food market, artisanal spirits were a natural for Dawn. The couple enrolled in distilling courses, and in 2014, after six months of trial runs, they opened Legend Distilling. For Doug, distilling was a welcome mid-career change from running a construction company. Watching him heave barrels around the metal shipping containers that serve as maturing warehouses, you realize that, like construction, distilling takes a lot of muscle.

Legend is a pretty hillside distillery with all the production fixings, a well-appointed tasting room, and a visitor centre. In summer, the patio restaurant serves exotic local foods (stinging nettle soup?) for the adventurous palate, and burgers for the kids. Naramata is a small Okanagan town in winter, but come summer, wine tours turn it into a bit of a traffic-jamming madhouse.

Every successful spirit needs a story, and the couple looked to local legends for theirs. Their Ogopogo Vodka recalls the mysterious Okanagan Lake monster. Sometimes, though, the story influences the spirit. The recipe for Black Moon Gin, named for the shadowless moonlight under which local bootleggers worked, taps into a local moonshining legend, and it is a flavour sensation. This juniper-heavy gin integrates indigenous wild sage and flame-torched local rosemary. Local legend has it these were first included by accident in some dimly lit moonshiner's shack.

Similarly, Manitou orange and sumac liqueur observes the millennia-old lead of Indigenous inhabitants, who used sumac berries for their citrus flavours. Nature shapes Legend's whisky too. A haze found in some early bottlings disappeared when newer batches were filtered after a chilly night outdoors—chill filtering, yes, and authentically so.

TASTING NOTES:
DOCTOR'S ORDERS
GIN (40% ABV)

Wildly aromatic with orchard apple, lavender, and lemon citrus, enhanced by coriander. Then waves of licorice and juniper waft into the fold. The palate builds on floral aromatics and crisp apple-a-day to keep you-know-who away. A restrained bitter berry accent punctuates the finish.

COCKTAIL: NARAMATA
HANKY PANKY
MAKES 1 COCKTAIL

1½ oz Doctor's Orders Gin
⅓ oz Blackmoon Gin
1½ oz sweet vermouth
1 large handful of ice cubes
1 orange peel twist, for zesting and
    garnish
1 Campari ice cube (optional)

Place a coupe glass in the freezer until chilled, at least one hour. In a separate glass, pour the gins and vermouth, and add lots of ice. Stir for 30 seconds until nice and cold. Strain into the chilled coupe glass. Twist the orange peel over the drink to express the zest, then drop the twist into the drink. Add a Campari ice cube to make it into a Negroni.

(Harry Dosanj)

LOST BOYS DISTILLING
FERNIE, BC

1441 7th Ave.
Fernie, BC V0B 1M0
www.lostboysdistilling.com

@lostboysdistilling

FOUNDED 2019

OWNERS Trevor Semchuck, Spencer
Schey, Pat Coughlin

AVAILABLE Onsite, private liquor stores,
farmers' markets, craft fairs

NEAREST NEIGHBOURS Fernie Distillers
(page 78) — 5 min; Elder Bros. Farms
Distillery (page 77) — 1 hr, 10 min

"Fernie is a drinking town with a skiing problem," explains distillery cofounder Trevor Semchuck. Like the lost boys in Peter Pan, Semchuck and cofounders Spencer Schey and Pat Coughlin share the bonds of lifelong friendship and adventurous spirits. Lost Boys is also a local metaphor for the distilling process. In Lost Boys Pass in the nearby Kootenay Mountains, warm, moist air rises and collides with cold air, causing condensation. That is also how distilling works— except the precipitate in Lost Boys Pass becomes Fernie's famous powder snow, rivalled only in local popularity by the "sippage" falling from the stills at Lost Boys Distilling.

MAPLE LEAF SPIRITS
PENTICTON, BC

Vineyards that overlook Okanagan Lake and the mountains beyond dot the Naramata Bench. But don't let the inspiring view distract you from Maple Leaf Spirits. In a small red-clad building, up a picturesque winding lane, Jorg and Anette Engel distil equally inspiring Okanagan spirits.

When they came from Germany in 2001, the Engels wondered why, with such expansive fruit farms, there were no distilleries here. Jorg soon found the answer. The political tax machine and laws at the time made it virtually impossible for small distilleries to make any money. Nevertheless, he applied, and by 2004 he had obtained his distilling licence.

At that time, distilling was restricted to industrial areas. A cabinetmaker by trade and a distiller by passion, Engel installed a still in the back of his cabinet shop. Distilling quickly proved a costly hobby; sales were low and profits nonexistent until 2013, when the province introduced tax incentives for craft distilleries. Maple Leaf Spirits quickly evolved into a serious business.

The Engels distil a diverse range of local fruits in their German Kothe still, including plums, apricots, pears, and grapes from their own vineyard. From these, Jorg makes a range of liqueurs, fruit brandies, and grape spirits. Sticking to tradition, Engel doesn't distil grain spirits. He had ordered a mash tun in the early days, but woke up one morning thinking, "Why would I do grain? I should stick to my original plan to do fruit." That mash tun soon became a blending tank.

A decade after the Engels pioneered sustainable production methods for Canada, they were recognized with a Green Tourism Canada Award. Today, the couple is content to convert tourists along the busy Naramata wine trail into spirits lovers.

948 Naramata Rd.
Penticton, BC V2A 8V1
www.mapleleafspirits.ca

🐦 @mapleleafspirit

📷 @Maple_leaf_spirits_inc

FOUNDED 2005

OWNERS Jorg and Anette Engel

STILLS 150-litre Kothe still with three-plate column

PRODUCTS Eau-de-vie, fruit brandy, liqueurs, marc

AVAILABLE Onsite, online, private liquor stores

TOURS Daily in summer, by appointment in winter

NEAREST NEIGHBOURS Legend Distilling (page 82) – 10 min; Old Order Distilling Co. (page 90) – 10 min

TASTING NOTES: **PEAR WILLIAMS** (40% ABV)

A rich and aromatic eau-de-vie that never strays from its core: freshly picked ripe Bartlett pears. The traditional clear spirit is slightly sweet on the palate, but slowly dries off on the finish, introducing hints of pear peel and seeds. The fruit maintains its charm from first pour to empty glass.

MONASHEE SPIRITS CRAFT DISTILLERY
REVELSTOKE, BC

307 Mackenzie Ave.
Revelstoke, BC V0E 2S0
(250) 463-5678
www.monasheespirits.com

 @Monashee_Spirit

 @monasheespirits

FOUNDED 2017

OWNERS Josh and Jen McLafferty

PRODUCTS Cinnamon liqueur, cream liqueur, gin, vodka, whisky (forthcoming)

AVAILABLE Onsite, online, private liquor stores

TOURS Free; Wednesday–Saturday

NEAREST NEIGHBOURS Jones Distilling (page 80) – 5 min; After Dark Distillery (page 72) – 1 hr

Until an accident left him unable to walk, Josh McLafferty lived to ride motocross. A six-month struggle to regain his feet, though successful, convinced McLafferty and his wife, Jen, that they had to change their lifestyle. For a Moose Jaw native living in Vancouver, the Monashee Mountains seemed an odd place to start over, but in 2017 the couple opened the doors of their distillery in downtown Revelstoke.

Each winter, an influx of skiers and snowboarders more than triples the town's size and can lead to a crowd control problem. The McLaffertys had to hire a doorman to manage the avalanche of tourists descending on the distillery's small, 20-seat tasting bar. Renovations have since made the original storefront distillery/bar more accommodating for visitors. However, as the 250 bottles of certified organic gin they make weekly still don't meet demand, their distilling is expanding to a dedicated location nearby.

McLafferty's interest in his community and commitment to using local ingredients have led to some interesting and imaginative spirits. For example, a garlic-infused vodka marks the Revelstoke Garlic Festival in October. Meanwhile, he vies with local bears for fruit ripening in people's yards. For the bears, it is food; for McLafferty, it is the base for a brandy called Bear Aware, and a way to reduce residents' surprise encounters of the ursine kind. Monashee's annual target of 20,000 bottles includes whisky made with a Japanese yeast known to impart stone-fruit flavours.

TASTING NOTES:
MONASHEE SPIRITS BIG MOUNTAIN CREAMER (23% ABV)

This succulent cream liqueur oozes silky indulgent flavours. Chocolate-covered almonds, fresh cream, vanilla biscuits, honey, maple syrup, and a splash of coffee—an avalanche of flavour that justifies the lineup during ski season.

OKANAGAN CRUSH PAD WINERY AND DISTILLERY

SUMMERLAND, BC

The towering, broad-shouldered Kiwi Matt Dumayne stands in front of his shiny 200-litre Still Dragon pot still and crosses his tattooed forearms. Make no mistake, Okanagan Crush Pad is a winery first. What they distil, though, reveals Dumayne's New Zealand winemaker's sensibility: complexity with balance. His gin, for example, forgoes trendy "granny's perfume" botanicals in favour of a dry, heavy, juniper style.

In 2014 Dumayne purchased 1,000 litres of spirit from Maple Leaf Spirits (page 85) just across Okanagan Lake. He wanted to make a fortified wine. He liked the results, and the next year applied for and received his distillery licence. "Once you have a still, why not make other spirits too?" he thought. So, he added a vodka-like white brandy called Spirit of the Vineyard, as well as the gin. He still makes his fortified wine, and to keep it interesting, he changes the grape varietals with each production.

16576 Fosbery Rd.
Summerland, BC V0H 1Z6
(250) 494-4445
Okanagancrushpad.com

 @OKcrushpad

 @OKcrushpad

FOUNDED 2015

OWNERS Christine Coletta and Steve Lornie

STILLS 200-litre Still Dragon

PRODUCTS Barrel-aged brandy, fortified wine, gin, white brandy

AVAILABLE Onsite, online, private stores, provincial liquor stores

TOURS Tasting room; summer during business hours, by appointment in winter

NEAREST NEIGHBOURS Old Order Distilling Co. (page 90) — 20 min; Alchemist Distiller (page 74) — 35 min

OKANAGAN SPIRITS CRAFT DISTILLERY
VERNON AND KELOWNA, BC

5204 24th St.
Vernon, BC V1T 8X2
(250) 549-3120
and
267 Bernard Ave
Kelowna, BC V1Y 6N2
(778) 484-5174—Kelowna
www.okanaganspirits.com

 @OkanaganSpirits

 @okanaganspirits

FOUNDED 2004

OWNERS The Dyck family

STILLS In Vernon 700-litre Adolf Adrian pot called Egg; 1,000-litre, 50-plate Adolf Adrian pot with 27-foot column called Stilla; 2,000-litre Arnold Holstein pot called Godstilla; in Kelowna 250-litre Mueller still

PRODUCTS Absinthe, aquavit, eau-de-vie, fruit brandy, gin, marc, vodka, whisky

AVAILABLE Onsite, online

TOURS Drop in; groups of six or more, call 1-888-292-5270

NEAREST NEIGHBOURS TO VERNON LOCATION Okanagan Spirits Craft Distillery—Kelowna (see here) — 50 min; After Dark Distillery (page 72) — 55 min

NEAREST NEIGHBOURS TO KELOWNA LOCATION Okanagan Crush Pad Winery and Distillery (page 87) — 35 min; Okanagan Spirits Craft Distillery—Vernon (see here) — 50 min

Okanagan Spirits in Vernon is where BC's distilling renaissance began. As Tyler Dyck tells his team at BC's original microdistillery, "You are not selling booze, you are selling an experience." Tyler designed a new spacious distillery to resemble "moonshiner's shack meets prohibition era," complete with an authentic "whisky-six" rum-runner's car in the showroom. However, it was only after a decade-and-a-half-long slog in more humble digs, and only after distilling became more profitable in BC, that these trappings of success appeared. They also opened a small demonstration distillery in the tourism capital of Kelowna.

Changes the BC government had made, beginning in 1989, to support the province's wine industry inspired three Okanagan Valley families. Together, in 2004 they launched Okanagan Spirits, putting award-winning European distiller Frank Dieter at the helm. The Dyck family then waited until 2013, nearly a decade, for a craft distillery production agreement with the government. It was tough. As their partners dropped out, they brought in their son, Tyler, to run the distillery. He began attending meetings of the BC distiller's guild, ultimately becoming its president. Eventually, the government came onside, and a version of gold rush fever hit microdistilling in BC.

"We benefit from being five generations of family in the Okanagan; we know where to find certain varieties of heritage fruit," says Dyck. The original small distillery, now referred to as "the garage," made fruit spirits. Once a year, they bought enough beer from a local brewery to make a single barrel of whisky. Consumer demand has shifted, resulting in four different whiskies in today's lineup. To keep the distilling team fresh, Dyck encourages them to experiment regularly with different beer mashes. A gorgeous hopped whisky with the nose of an IPA is one result; a chocolate BRBN (pronunciation hint: sounds like *bourbon*) is another. "Craft distillation stopped with prohibition," Dyck opines, and at Okanagan Spirits, he is doing his best never to repeat that history.

TASTING NOTES: BC RYE WHISKY (40% ABV)

This seductive dram is made from 51% Coldstream Valley rye, blended with 49% locally malted BC barley, and aged in heavily toasted and charred American white oak barrels. Delicate cooked grains become more pronounced on the palate and evolve through the finish. And it's these grains that set the tone for a pleasing fruity and floral rye spice that flashes late onto the palate, setting up for fresh dry oak.

COCKTAIL: THE MANHATTAN ORCHARDIST (CHERRY MANHATTAN)

MAKES 1 COCKTAIL

Handful of ice cubes
2 oz Okanagan Spirits BRBN Bourbon-Style Corn Whisky
½ oz Okanagan Spirits Cherry Liqueur
1 dash Bittered Sling French Quarter Bitters
Okanagan Spirits Drunken Cherry, for garnish

Place a coupe glass in the freezer until chilled, at least one hour. In an ice-filled mixing glass, add ingredients and stir for 45 seconds. Strain into the chilled coupe glass. Garnish with the Drunken Cherry.

(Tyler Dyck)

OLD ORDER DISTILLING CO.
PENTICTON, BC

270 Martin St.
Penticton, BC V2A 5K3
(778) 476-2210

www.oldorderdistilling.ca

 @oldorder_spirit

 @Oldorderdistilling

FOUNDED 2015

OWNERS Graham Martens and Naomi
Gabriel

STILLS 226-litre Mueller pot with
five-plate column

PRODUCTS Gin, liqueurs, vodka,
black vodka, whisky

AVAILABLE Onsite, online, private liquor
stores

TOURS Book online

NEAREST NEIGHBOURS Maple Leaf Spirits
(page 85) — 10 min

Naomi Gabriel and Graham Martens saw opportunity in the orchard on the farm that Martens's parents owned in Summerland's rolling hills. Unfortunately, when the BC government first made distilling BC fruits profitable, the legislation did not yet go as far as to allow distilling on farms—this was changed soon afterwards. All the same, the couple liked the idea of blending farming with distilling. By 2015 they had filed the paperwork requesting to rezone a 280-square-metre space in downtown Penticton. Objections from the fire department were quelled in part by putting the still behind explosion-proof glass.

A peek through that glass reveals enough barrels to make you wonder if the distillery has extended its reach beyond fruit spirits, and sure enough, Martens is now distilling grain. As well as laying down whisky spirit, Old Order makes single malt vodka using BC-grown barley from North America's smallest malting house in nearby Armstrong. For each batch, Martens typically ferments eight to ten 25-kilogram bags of grain for five to seven days, using a Champagne-style yeast. He then triple-distils it, taking care not to strip out any of the key grain flavours. After collecting the spirit in milk cans, he uses it as the base for Old Order's other spirits, including Black Goat Vodka. A rarity in Canada, black vodka has been infused with plant minerals that darken the spirit without affecting the vodka's flavour.

The Old Order cocktail lounge offers a dynamic menu of seasonal and "tipple" cocktails. This tipple list includes both classic and innovative cocktails that feature local ingredients where possible. Ingredients such as citrus fruits are freshly squeezed. Malted barley is also the base for Legacy, a Dutch genever-style gin made with traditional botanicals. The recipe for Legacy also includes dried apples from the Summerland family orchard, which brings them back to that family-owned farm where the idea first bore fruit.

TASTING NOTES:
BLACK GOAT VODKA
(43% ABV)

Glowing malt notes on the palate reveal the malt base of this dazzling black vodka with its vibrant inky tones. A soft, glossy mouthfeel bursts into searing white pepper, followed by a sweet, fruity denouement.

COCKTAIL:
OLD ORDER BLACK
GOAT VODKA MARTINI
MAKES 1 COCKTAIL

Splash of vermouth
Handful of ice cubes
2 oz Old Order Black Goat Vodka
1 long lemon twist, for garnish

Splash some vermouth in a Martini glass, tip and revolve the vermouth around the rim to coat the glass. Add ice to a shaker and pour the Old Order Black Goat Vodka over top. Shake until combined, and pour into the martini glass. Finish with a long lemon twist, ensuring one-quarter of it is draped and folded over the rim of the glass.

(Rocco Pollonio)

TAYNTON BAY SPIRITS
INVERMERE, BC

1701B 6th Ave.
Invermere, BC V0A 1K4
(778) 526-5205
www.tayntonbayspirits.com

◎ @tayntonbay

FOUNDED 2017

OWNERS Justin Atterbury, Ricky Eubenga, Jason Powers

STILLS 30-gallon (US) HBS with 12-plate column; 50-gallon HBS with 14-plate column; 250-gallon with 6-plate column

PRODUCTS Flavoured vodka, gin, Gringo's Revenge, matcha teas, vodka

AVAILABLE Onsite, private liquor stores

NEAREST NEIGHBOURS Elder Bros. Farms Distillery (page 77) – 1 hr, 30 min; Park Distillery (page 126) – 2 hrs

The town of Invermere sits atop bluffs along the headwaters of the Columbia River, where, sometimes, a group of young boys will toss small stones at the trains that chug along the shoreline below. It sounds dangerous but is harmless target practice. When you live in a town of 3,500, you learn to make your own fun. And when you grow up, you can learn to make your own spirits.

However, Port Alberni, BC, native Justin Atterbury credits his wife, a local, with piquing his interest in distilling. It all began when she set about making her own Baileys-like cream liqueur, to great acclaim. Atterbury owns The Station Neighbourhood Pub, about a 20-minute walk from the railway station where those stone-pinged trains once stopped for passengers. The pub, by chance, has a basement where he has set up three small Hillbilly Stills (HBS) from Kentucky. An assistant darts between stirring mash in a plastic tote in the tasting room and stirring fermented mash in one of the stills downstairs. True to his hillbilly-bootlegging persona, Atterbury's assistant smiles vacantly when you ask where he learned to run a still, and he isn't too keen to have his picture taken either.

When he named a spirit that tasted like tequila "Tekila-eh," Atterbury landed in hot sauce with the government of Mexico, which sent him a cease-and-desist letter. By international agreement, tequila must be made in Mexico. Atterbury still makes the spirit, which sells well under its new tongue-in-cheek moniker, Gringo's Revenge. He also makes a range of flavoured vodkas and a gin, but his bestsellers are his matcha teas. They come in an assortment of flavours and, with alcohol levels comparable to wine, are quite sippable. You are welcome to taste the full lineup at the tasting bar, but if you want a cocktail (or a genuine Baileys), you'll have to head upstairs to the pub.

TASTING NOTES:
TAYNTON TEA GINGER MATCHA BATCH 6 (14% ABV)
Taynton Bay has teamed up with the Naked Leaf tea company to create this vodka/loose-leaf cocktail infusion. A citrus nose floods the senses with holistic refreshment. Sweet honey balances a bounty of fresh citrus, black pepper, coriander, cardamom, floral tones, and exotic spices. Honey sweetness softens the tartness of quince and lime in a refreshing spa retreat for your palate.

COCKTAIL:
HIBISCUS SUNRISE

MAKES 1 COCKTAIL

Handful of ice cubes
4 oz Sprite
2 oz orange juice
1½ oz Taynton Bay Spirits
   Raspberry Vodka
Hibiscus bitters, for garnish

In a glass full of ice, add all of the
ingredients except the bitters. Float
Hibiscus bitters overtop by holding
the bitters bottle close to the
surface of the cocktail and gently
drizzling a few drops so it floats
atop the drink.

(Theresa Wood)

TRENCH BREWING & DISTILLING INC.
PRINCE GEORGE, BC

399 2nd Ave.
Prince George, BC V2L 2Z4
(236) 423-0065
www.trenchbrew.ca

🐦 @trenchbrewing

📷 @trenchbrewing

FOUNDED **2018**

OWNERS **Craig & Esther Schwenning
and Bailey & Jesse Hoefels**

STILL **1,000-litre Still Dragon kettle
with 12-plate copper column**

AVAILABLE **Onsite**

NEAREST NEIGHBOURS **After Dark Distillery
(page 72) – 7 hrs, 15 min; Park Distillery
(page 126) – 7 hrs, 20 min; Hansen
Distillery (page 120) – 7 hrs, 30 min**

An eight-metre-tall roadside attraction waves a Canadian flag, has a Pinocchio-like nose, and flashes a giant grin. Spotting Mr. PG means travellers on the Yellowhead Highway have finally reached Prince George. Locals swear that his wooden smile got broader when a still arrived and Trench Brewing became the city's first distillery. Visitors can sample vodka and gin distilled onsite, while listening to live music and enjoying nibblies in the distillery lounge. Six Mile Stout and other beers on pour are each named for various landmarks along the Rocky Mountain Trench.

TRUE NORTH DISTILLERY
GRAND FORKS, BC

Stoplights on the Crowsnest Highway bring traffic to a halt in front of a low cement-block building in Grand Forks. As you wait for the light to turn, it's hard not to glance over at the bright red home of True North Distillery. Those curious enough to investigate may find Scot Stewart in a back corner, tending to what looks like two gleaming copper hot-water tanks. These are pot stills that he made from scratch back in 2011, when he established True North. Stewart was scouting locations when a friend suggested he visit Grand Forks and look at a property for sale there. "Build your distillery here," he said, "and I can visit and stock up on whisky whenever I want."

Stewart named his first whisky Black Dog After Dark in honour of a very large black dog that helped make the first batch by selflessly keeping the distillery free of rodents. Another, 54-40 Whisky, refers to an old slogan—"54-40 or fight"—popular among Americans during the Oregon boundary dispute of the 1840s. Stewart's great-grandfather often recounted the story of Britain's resistance to US efforts to take control of most of modern-day BC. The name True North came from his daughter, who was then six.

1460 Central Ave.
Grand Forks, BC V0H 1H0
(778) 879-4420
www.truenorthdistilleries.com

FOUNDED **2011**

OWNER **Scot Stewart**

STILLS **Self-designed and fabricated**

PRODUCTS **Absinthe, brandy, gin, muscat, rum, whisky**

AVAILABLE **Onsite, private stores**

NEAREST NEIGHBOURS **Tumbleweed Spirits (page 96) — 1 hr, 30 min**

TASTING NOTES:
BLACK DOG AFTER DARK WHITE RYE
(40% ABV)

A growling dog's hair stands with aggression on the label of this white rye, but the contents will have you as excited as a dog wagging its tail. Ripe apples and wet straw on the nose complement a palate loaded with concentrated rye cereals and grains before a flash of peppery spice opens up to softer grains on the finish.

TUMBLEWEED SPIRITS
OSOYOOS, BC

6001 Lakeshore Dr., #7
Osoyoos, BC V0H 1V6
(778) 437-2221
www.tumbleweedspirits.com

[◎] @Tumbleweedspirits

FOUNDED **2017**

OWNERS **Andrea Zaradic and Mike Green**

STILLS **600-litre HBS copper pot with 12-plate and 4-plate columns; 300-litre HBS pot gin (the stills are named Big Al and Ginger)**

PRODUCTS **Eau-de-vie, brandy, gin, grappa, moonshine, vodka, whisky**

AVAILABLE **Onsite and private liquor stores**

NEAREST NEIGHBOURS **The Dubh Glas Distillery Ltd. (page 76) — 30 min; True North Distillery (page 95) — 1 hr, 35 min.**

TASTING NOTES:
FIREWEED (40% ABV)

Fireweed is one of the first plants to grow after a forest fire. The sweetness of fireweed honey shining through the base grain spirit prepares you for a smooth, sweet ride. But once the spirit coats your mouth, you'll find cinnamon, which kindles an all-out inferno that builds from cinnamon sticks to sticks of dynamite.

The view from Anarchist Lookout on the Crowsnest Highway is so spectacular that it tempts you to strap on a hang glider and soar. If you do, try to land on Lakeshore Drive below, so you can salute your descent at the stand-up bar in Tumbleweed Spirits' tasting room. You will receive a warm welcome that is well worth dropping in for.

Mechanical engineer Andrea Zaradic and contractor Mike Green left Vancouver's rat race to do something together. They were drawn to Osoyoos at the foot of the Okanagan Valley, where Zaradic had built a house a decade earlier. After visiting distilleries in Kentucky, the couple had HBS Copper in Barlow make them two stills. Classic Kentucky, a whisky head above each pot ensures plenty of flavour-generating reflux. These heads, also called hourglasses, are little more than two copper cones welded together. Fermentation tanks are a lot less specialized, so Zaradic and Green hired a local fabricator to make theirs.

Tumbleweed's focus is on grain-based spirits made from malted barley, wheat, rye, and triticale grown 40 minutes up the Crowsnest Highway in Rock Creek. Nevertheless, they also distil Okanagan wine to make eau-de-vie, grappa, and brandy.

REIMAGINING GIN

G in's concept is simple: flavour a neutral base spirit with juniper and other botanicals. But you can trust Canada's distillers to add layers of complexity. If diversity is Canada's strength, then nowhere is this more evident than in our domestically produced gins. The process of developing a botanical recipe can be very complicated, regardless of location. Moreover, because of Canada's vast size, distillers are embracing botanicals distinct to their own regional neck of the woods. What grows on Vancouver Island might be alien to Newfoundland. This natural biodiversity drives innovation in Canadian gin. As Dave Broom points out in his book *Gin: The Manual*, smaller distillers jumped at the opportunity to elevate the spirit just as microbreweries did for beer. Distillers make their gin local, high-calibre, and respectful of tradition while finding ways in which it can reflect the land, as the following examples illustrate.

LONDON GIN

London (Dry) Gin is a protected category strictly defined by process. Juniper must dominate the flavour, but despite the name, it need not be made in London. In the hands of a skilled distiller, this juniper heavyweight is complex and flavourful. In Nova Scotia's Steinhart London Dry Gin (47.5% abv) (pictured here, see also page 282), botanicals leap playfully from a firm juniper foundation chased by deep spices, citrus zest, and spring flowers.

CONTEMPORARY AND MODERN GIN

These gins fit into three broad flavour camps: floral, spicy, or citrus. Juniper takes a back seat to local and specialized botanical flavours, allowing the gin maker to express their true craft. In Toronto, Martha Lowry, a trained botanist, lifts sunshine from her Mill Street Small Batch Citrus Gin (40% abv) (page 194) with citrus peels and citra hops, then balances these with floral tones and earthy spices brightened by juniper.

CLASSIC GIN

This hybrid of London and Contemporary gins has a juniper-forward profile without the protected category's restrictions. In Newfoundland Distillery Seaweed Gin (40% abv) (page 285), juniper lightly connects the dots between the seaweed and herbal savory. This gin finds beauty in its botanical simplicity and complex earthy brine.

SLOE GIN

Traditionally, sloe berries are infused into gin with sugar or honey for this centuries-old liqueur. On Vancouver Island, de Vine Sloe Gin (42% abv) (page 52) is pulling this style out of retirement by avoiding sweetening agents. The berry's natural sweetness and tart plummy notes accent the base gin's abundant classic flavours.

OLD TOM

These botanically intense gins were once sweetened with sugar to hide funky spirit. Column distillation cleaned up the spirit and wound up being the asteroid to take out the Old Tom dinosaurs. They're back, and they're refined. Made in Vancouver, The Liberty Distillery Endeavour Old Tom Gin (45% abv) (page 24) fossilizes for several months in 200-litre French oak barrels. This introduces oak tones to the curvy and semi-sweet palate with a blend of spices that should be jarred and sold on its own.

AGED GIN

Aged gin spends time in contact with wood—either barrels or wood chips. Willibald Gin (43% abv) (page 213), from southwestern Ontario, matures in American oak quarter casks, polishing the juniper and emphasizing spices such as ginger and cardamom, without hiding its citrus peel and floral lavender botanicals.

GENEVER

Genever is arguably the Netherlands' most important contribution to spirits. Unlike gin, genever's base spirit is made by fermenting a mash of cereal grains and malted barley to make a rich malt wine that retains its character after distillation. It is this maltiness that anchors the complex juniper, caraway, pink peppercorn, and woody floral notes of Halifax's Compass Distillers Old Genever (40% abv) (page 273).

QUEBEC TERROIR GIN

Quebec distilleries have taken local ingredients to the heart to create gins that break new ground. The botanicals are unusual, and on the palate they are striking. La Société Secrète's Les Herbes Folles Dry Gin (43% abv) (page 245) is a vacation to the Gaspé Peninsula for your olfactory system. The gin's name translates to "wild grasses" and holds the secret to a proprietary blend of botanicals grown within walking distance of the distillery. Sweet clover and a purple flower called fireweed lend honeyed vanilla and peppery notes layered onto a refined herbaceousness.

JAPANESE GIN

Traditional botanicals blend into Japanese ones such as yuzu, green tea, cherry blossoms, spices, and herbs. Sheringham Distillery Kazuki Gin (43% abv) (page 64), from the Pacific shore of Vancouver Island, illustrates harmony with delicate flavours of sweet floral tea, mild mandarin orange, and soft juniper. ■

YUKON

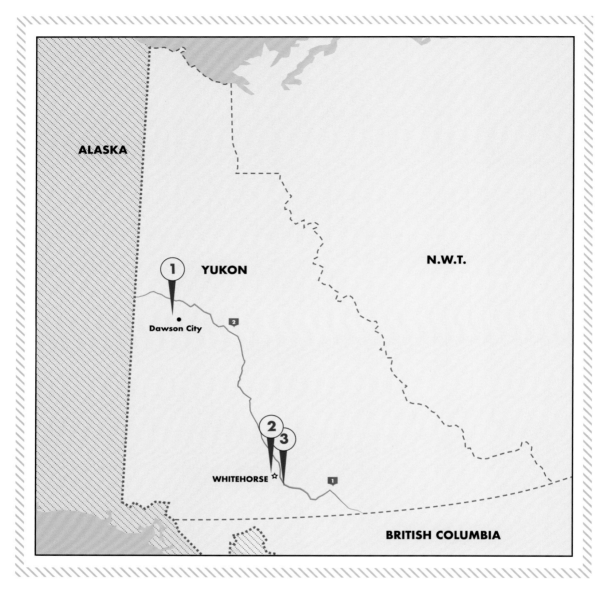

ALASKA

YUKON

N.W.T.

1

Dawson City

2

2
3

WHITEHORSE

1

BRITISH COLUMBIA

YUKON

For a territory with fewer than 40,000 residents, 25,000 of whom live in Whitehorse, Yukon is one happening place. Restaurants here serve a cosmopolitan cuisine prepared by renowned chefs. Even the crummiest-looking dive bar is still reasonably upscale. And a caution: as long as you carry an air horn, there is a pretty good chance you won't encounter a grizzly bear.

Yukon once tried prohibition. On May 1, 1918, in the final months of the Great War and following a wishy-washy referendum, the federal government ordered Yukon to go dry. By September 5, 1921, Yukon residents had abolished prohibition. It was not until 2009, though, that distilling finally became legal there. And even then, the enabling legislation requires distilleries to sell their spirits through the government-owned Yukon Liquor Corporation. Not content to leave well enough alone, in November 2017 the Yukon government ordered large, colourful warning labels to be placed on liquor bottles. Four weeks later, the label program was "paused," only to be revived in a watered-down form. It is often difficult to be a distiller in Canada's North. Nevertheless, distillers find ways to thrive.

Klondike River Distillery (page 104) has been proudly off the grid since it was established in 2008. Its name was raised in the territorial legislature, though, following the goofiest of complaints. Somebody actually worried

that allowing a distillery in the neighbourhood set a precedent that could lead someone else to build something else—erm, yes, a crematorium—there. The things people find time to worry about. Yukon Shine Distillery (page 107) came online a year after the new legislation. A third distillery, Yukon Brewing (page 105), has become the territory's distilling powerhouse, recognized by connoisseurs far and wide as world class.

Yukon Territory is not the arctic wilderness you might expect. It abounds in wildlife, including the wild berries that Yukon Brewing make into brandy on their Two Brewers label, and plump, sweet juniper too overloaded with piney notes to be useful for making gin. It is also a region of pioneers, adventurers, and entrepreneurs.

At the time of the gold rush, Canadian poet Robert Service recorded the eccentricities of Sam McGee, Blasphemous Bill, and a host of other characters he met during his time in the Yukon. Journalist Jim Robb has picked up where Service left off, in a series of books he called *The Colourful 5%*. "Normal is just someone you haven't met yet," as Robb tells it. In a land where the sun stays weeks below the horizon in winter, then shines brightly 24 hours a day in summer, people are bound to have their quirks.

Nevertheless, although Yukon may be small in population, its welcoming spirit is as big as the land. ■

KLONDIKE RIVER DISTILLERY
DAWSON CITY, YT

www.klondikeriverdistillery.com

@KRDistillery

@Klondike_vodka

FOUNDED **2007**

OWNER **Bridget and Dorian Amos**

PRODUCTS **Vodka**

NEAREST NEIGHBOURS **Yukon Shine Distillery (page 107) – 6 hrs, 15 min; Yukon Brewing (page 105) – 6 hrs, 15 min**

Outside of this remote, totally off-the-grid distillery, a caged tube sits mounted on a trailer. It's a trap to catch and relocate bears that come sniffing around for vodka. "All we caught in the bear trap was the neighbour's dog and some lost liquor inspectors," the owners concede. And yes, they are all fine.

Bridget and Dorian Amos know a thing or two about Yukon liquor officials. In 2008 their vodka surmounted bureaucratic obstacles to become the first spirit to be produced and sold legally in Yukon. Real gold flakes added to the black wax–sealed bottle represent the pioneer spirit of the 1898 Klondike Gold Rush.

YUKON BREWING
WHITEHORSE, YT

Walking down Main Street in Whitehorse, it is easy to understand why two Ontario boys on a Yukon canoe trip wanted to bring their families to the North and start a brewery. The city is clean, bright, and friendly, and the surrounding 500,000 square kilometres can only be described as pristine. Bob Baxter and Alan Hansen did exactly that in 1997, the year they launched Yukon Brewing.

In 2009, when the Yukon government legalized distilling in the territory, Baxter and Hansen saw an opportunity and bought a still. "Anything we can make into beer, we can make into whisky," they thought. That includes malted rye and malted wheat. Although they may not be all-barley, their whiskies, which they release on their Two Brewers label, are most assuredly single malts.

Blending whiskies drawn from a variety of barrels adds depth and complexity to a delicate base made from 100% pale malt. They distil specialty malts separately to concentrate the flavours, and then mature them in new and ex-bourbon barrels.

They also use a novel method to season their new barrels. After filling them with spirit, they leave them just a month and then move that spirit into other used barrels. Then they refill the new barrels with more new spirit, so after a few cycles, the barrels are seasoned without making any individual batch too woody. Each release is intended as a one-off, and the variations that this process creates in the final whisky always bring new flavours to the blending table. Batches average between 800 and 1,500 bottles.

Baxter and Hansen are less concerned about the volume of their whiskies than their reputation. "We didn't go into the project expecting to make money," says Hansen, explaining why they do not sell white whisky and why they waited seven years for their first release, rather than the three-year minimum stipulated in law. The partners also make a gin using neutral spirit they have purchased. They do it that way because their malt spirit is all earmarked for whisky. Connoisseurs and critics alike are pleased about this. The whiskies are widely acclaimed, and in 2018 Yukon Brewing was named Artisanal Distillery of the Year at the Canadian Whisky Awards.

(continued)

102 Copper Rd.
Whitehorse, YT Y1A 2Z6
(867) 668-4183
www.twobrewerswhisky.com

 @YukonBeer

 @yukonbeer

FOUNDED **2009**

OWNERS **Bob Baxter and Alan Hansen**

STILLS **400-litre Carl pot; 2,500-litre beer brew kettle with helmet**

PRODUCTS **Beer schnapps, gin, whisky, wild berry brandy**

AVAILABLE **Onsite, private liquor stores in BC and Alberta**

NEAREST NEIGHBOURS **Yukon Shine Distillery (page 107) – 1 min; Klondike River Distillery (page 104) – 6 hrs, 15 min**

TASTING NOTES: TWO BREWERS YUKON SINGLE MALT WHISKY RELEASE 11 (43%)

Canadian single malt has arrived. Release 11 puts Munich Malt in the limelight. Banana and honey segue into a mammoth creamy palate laden with roasted grains and oak spice. Baskets of fall fruit wrapped in heaps of malt glide cleanly into a very long chocolate finish.

YUKON SHINE DISTILLERY
WHITEHORSE, YT

Karlo Krauzig captures the purity and beauty of Yukon in his gin and vodka. In 2012, two years after opening, he pitched a 33% stake in the distillery on the CBC reality show *Dragon's Den*. After capturing Yukon with his spirits, he caught a dragon in Arlene Dickinson, who inked a deal.

Krauzig makes his base spirit by fermenting and quadruple-distilling rye, malted barley, and local Yukon Gold potatoes. Originally, he planned to use Yukon Gold potatoes exclusively, but he added grain to compensate for the potatoes' low alcohol yield. After filtering the spirit through charcoal, he then filters it again, using Yukon gold nuggets (as in the metal, not the spud). He claims the gold's mineral composition contributes a velvety texture without affecting the spirit's flavour. True or not, the clink of gold nuggets sure does beat the clatter of whisky rocks.

137 Industrial Rd.
Whitehorse, YT Y1A 2V2
www.yukonshine.com

 @yukonshine

 @yukonshinedistillery

FOUNDED **2009**

OWNER **Karlo Krauzig**

PRODUCTS **Gin and vodka**

NEAREST NEIGHBOURS **Yukon Brewing (page 105) – 1 min; Klondike River Distillery (page 104) – 6 hrs, 15 min**

THE PRAIRIES

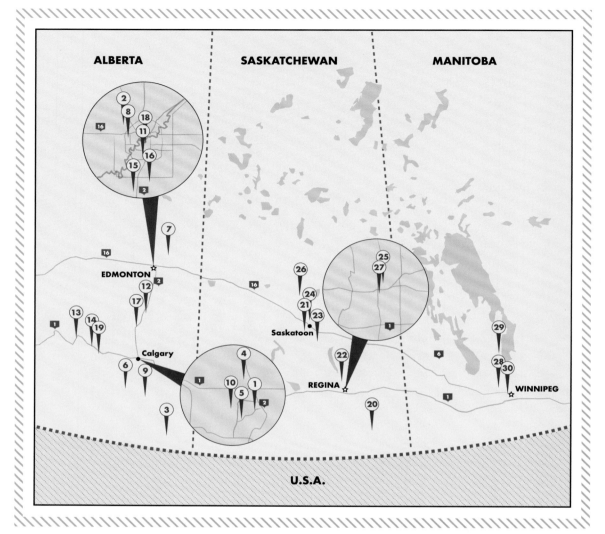

ALBERTA SASKATCHEWAN MANITOBA

EDMONTON

Saskatoon

Calgary

REGINA

WINNIPEG

U.S.A.

THE PRAIRIES

Unless you count illegal stills hidden behind a barn, distilling was not a Prairie tradition. So when prohibition hit the region, it was at best a half-hearted affair. Beginning in 1916, one by one, the Prairie provinces banned liquor sales, then restored them again by 1925. The end of prohibition didn't put a stop to some pretty weird lawmaking, though. In Manitoba, for example, people were permitted to drink liquor at home but had to have it delivered because they were not allowed to transport it themselves. Meanwhile, making spirits for medical and sacramental purposes was fine, a policy that led Harry Bronfman to open his Canada Pure Drug Company in Saskatchewan. From there, he compounded and exported "medical whisky" to Alberta, Manitoba, and the US, grossing up to $390,000 a month.

It wasn't until 1946, nearly two decades after prohibition's collapse, that entrepreneurs Frank McMahon and Max Bell decided to open a distillery in Calgary. The raw materials for making whisky were abundant, but government red tape—provincial *and* federal—halted their progress as they were refused a licence until the distillery was finally equipped. McMahon approached distillers Henry and George C. Reifel, and by 1948 Alberta Distillers (page 113) became the first whisky distillery in the Prairies. It remains the largest producer of 100% rye whisky in the country to this day.

Quebec's Melchers distillery also saw opportunity in the Prairies, and in 1969 acquired Manitoba Distillery Ltd. But after just six years it closed due to the impracticality of such a small distillery. Toronto's McGuinness Distillers also went west and snapped up the smallish Central Canadian Distillery Ltd. of Weyburn, Saskatchewan. The Bronfmans, who had purchased Winnipeg's Bell Hotel in 1912, had moved to Montreal for bigger opportunities in 1917. Then, in 1968, they made their celebrated return to Manitoba when they opened Seagram's Gimli Distillery (page 154)—the house that Crown Royal built.

Gilbey's built the Palliser Distillery (page 115) in Lethbridge, Alberta, in 1973, where it distilled from more than 450,000 bushels of grain annually to quench the thirst for Gilbey's products in western Canada and the States. Their production doubled as annual sales of Black Velvet passed a million cases a few years later.

In 1993 Alberta's star shone brightest when it closed its government stores and became the first province in Canada to introduce private liquor retail. As a result, warehousing and distribution were also transferred to the private sector. Even so, this didn't mean the province was immune to wild distilling laws. Size matters in Alberta, and until 2013 its distilleries were required to produce at least a million litres of spirit each year. Alberta's first microdistillery, Eau Claire (page 118), had to lobby the Alberta government's Gaming, Liquor, and Cannabis authority (AGLC) to remove this minimum requirement before it could open its doors in 2014.

Good thing the prairies are flat. When Saskatchewan peered over the horizon and saw what was happening in Alberta, it, too, introduced private liquor retail. In 2015 the provincial government put 40 of its 75 liquor stores up for sale, and since then, the province has seen about 700 more private stores open.

Today, Alberta and Saskatchewan are experiencing a distilling boom, thanks again to government reform. In 2017 Saskatchewan's Liquor and Gaming Authority (SLGA) introduced a graduated production levy for products not distributed by the SLGA. On the first 50,000 litres, the charge is 70 cents per litre, and the levy rises in steps until distilleries producing between 175,001 and 200,000 litres pay $7.70 per litre. The province also allows distillers to sell samples and cocktails, and to operate one additional offsite retail location. For spirits distributed by the SLGA, expensive markups replace the levy. Shortly thereafter, the AGLC made distilling more profitable when it reduced the liquor markup for small distilleries on their self-distributed products from $13.67 per litre to $2.46.

Although it is a neighbouring province, so far the distilling industry has met with a different fate in Manitoba. In 2016 Capital K Distillery (page 152) became Manitoba's first microdistillery. Since then, staggering provincial government markups have stalled Manitoba's growth in the industry more than in any other province. A distillery producing less than 10,000 litres a year pays a markup of 85%. This then jumps to 105% until the distillery breaches the 50,000-litre mark, when it tops out at 153%. Despite being the home of Crown Royal, the second-bestselling whisky in North America (Jack Daniel's is first), Manitoba lags far behind Canada's other provinces in reaping the economic benefits of the microdistilling boom.

As enthusiasm builds for Canada's microdistilling industry, each of the nation's three Prairie provinces has adopted a different regulatory approach. In the end, it is up to provincial governments to decide how they will leverage vast fields of Prairie grain to the benefit of farmers, entrepreneurs, and consumers alike. ▪

ALBERTA DISTILLERS LIMITED (ADL)

CALGARY, AB

Philanthropic economic development was alive and well in Alberta in the mid-1940s. As oil production tapered off in nearby Turner Valley, two Calgary-based entrepreneurs, oilman Frank McMahon and rancher and publisher Max Bell, developed the idea of establishing a distillery there. Not because they were keen on distilling; they simply wanted to create a market for local farmers to sell their grain.

Although it now distils all five primary whisky grains, Alberta Distillers is best known for using 100% rye grain. The reason? At the time, rye was the grain most suited to the semi-arid climate of southern Alberta. As the farms were growing rye, McMahon and Bell would build a distillery to process it. Since neither of them knew how to distil, they hired George Henry Reifel, a third-generation member of the famed Reifel distilling family. He oversaw the construction and operation of the plant on a 16-hectare plot on what was then the outskirts of Calgary. Ordinarily, rye is a difficult grain to ferment. However, ADL, as it is known, developed a specific enzyme that they grow onsite to break down the rye components that cause foaming and stickiness while at the same time increasing alcohol production.

In 1963, with whisky purchased from Alberta Distillers, an American firm launched Windsor Supreme Canadian whisky. This was the first of many US brands to fill its bottles with Canadian whisky from Alberta Distillers. Today, prominent brands such as WhistlePig, Masterson's, and Jefferson's Rye have all turned to ADL to supply rye whisky.

In 1987, Fortune Brands (now Beam Suntory) bought the distillery and all its brands, but kept the name Alberta Distillers. The distillery is best known for its Alberta Premium brand, a popular mixing whisky that rode to prominence on the basis of being made from nothing but rye. Although it did not set out to be, Alberta Distillers is almost certainly the greatest rye distillery in the world.

1521 34 Ave. SE
Calgary, AB T2G 1V9
www.albertadistillers.com

@AlbertaWhisky

FOUNDED **1946**

OWNERS **Beam Suntory**

STILLS **Custom-made industrial columns and pot still**

PRODUCTS **Vodka, flavoured vodka, whisky**

AVAILABILITY **Widely across North America**

NEAREST NEIGHBOURS **Confluence Distilling (page 118) – 5 min; Last Best Brewing & Distilling (page 123) – 15 min**

TASTING NOTES:
CANADIAN CLUB CHAIRMAN'S SELECT 100% RYE

This first expression of Canadian Club made solely with rye highlights the distillery's expertise with Canada's king of grains. A nose rich in CC's signature fruitiness is complemented on the palate by cloves, peppery allspice, and oak knotted with dusty rye grain. The rye's spices linger from sunup to sundown in this sensational whisky.

BLACK DIAMOND DISTILLERY
ST. ALBERT, AB

16 Renault Cres., #200
St. Albert, AB T8N 4B8
(587) 598-2820
www.blackdiamonddistillery.com

@ @blackdiamonddistillery

FOUNDED 2018

OWNERS David and Andrea Scade

STILLS 200-litre pot still with six-plate column; custom "Frankenstill" with two columns

PRODUCTS Gin, liqueurs, vodka, flavoured vodka, whisky

AVAILABILITY Onsite, farmers' markets, and selected Alberta liquor stores

TOURS Contact distillery

NEAREST NEIGHBOURS Hansen Distillery (page 120) – 15 min; Strathcona Spirits Distillery (page 136) and Lone Pine Distilling (page 124)—both 30 min

When David Scade was planning to propose to his girlfriend, Andrea, a strength and conditioning coach, he remembered that she once told him she would rather have a squat rack than a ring. How romantic! When Scade finally popped the question, on one of her favourite Nova Scotia beaches, he proffered a gorgeous black diamond ring. Her answer made naming the distillery easy.

Black Diamond Distillery makes an impressive lineup of liqueurs, wheat vodka, infused vodkas, gin, and a grain spirit called White Flag, all of them made with local ingredients. These include a rotating stable of seasonal expressions. Of the whisky they have tucked away to mature, one special release is reserved for their son's 18th birthday. "Axel's Whisky will turn 18 in 2035, the same year that he does. It will be up to him to decide what's done with this barrel of 'awesome,'" declares Andrea. "Since sharing this story with our customers, we've had many requests from others for the same thing, and we are excited to be offering them to our community."

The Scades also make custom spirits and labels for special events, especially weddings. Tips on where to buy the best squat rack are free.

TASTING NOTES: WHITE FLAG (40% ABV)

Daphne, the Scades' velveteen beagle, has a white-tipped tail they call a white flag. This unaged three-grain spirit is guaranteed to get that tail wagging. The rich nose exudes cooked corncobs, fresh bread, toasted cereals, and icing sugar. On a glossy palate, creamy, sweet grains and a growling heat soften through the finish.

COCKTAIL: EARL GREY MULE

MAKES 1 COCKTAIL

Handful of ice cubes
3 oz soda water
1½ oz Black Diamond Earl Grey Vodka

1 oz Black Diamond Ginger + Black Pepper Syrup
½ oz fresh lime juice
1 lime wheel, for garnish
1 candied ginger piece, for garnish

In a Moscow Mule mug, combine all ingredients over ice. Garnish with a slice of lime and candied ginger.

(Black Diamond Distillery)

BLACK VELVET DISTILLERY
LETHBRIDGE, AB

What do country singer Tanya Tucker, actor Bruce Willis, and the late comedian George Burns have in common? Early in their careers, each took a turn as the public face of Black Velvet whisky.

In the 1970s, the International Distillers and Vintners (IDV) distillery in Toronto could not meet American demand for the Black Velvet whisky it distilled. IDV needed a second distillery, and they chose to build in Lethbridge, Alberta. Why? Because Lethbridge was closer to the huge market on America's West Coast, which reduced shipping costs. They named the new distillery Palliser, after this region of Alberta.

The 1980s brought a precipitous decline in whisky sales as drinkers switched to vodka. IDV was faced with a decision. Instead of shutting down Palliser, it sold the Toronto facility and moved all production to Alberta.

The Lethbridge distillery, now owned by the US spirits company Heaven Hill Brands, is now called Black Velvet. Its namesake whisky, which is the distillery's primary product, has a legacy that goes back to 1946, when distillers Crosbie Hucks and Jack Napier first distilled it, to much success. Across North America, Black Velvet is best known for its lighter mixing whiskies and its eight-year-old sipper. However, in some parts of Europe it is sought after for its older expressions, such as the rich and succulent Black Velvet Onyx.

Located some distance from other distilleries and in a region with relatively light tourism, the distillery does not have facilities for visitors. Too bad. The reception room alone holds a nostalgic collection of celebrity endorsements from over the years. But times have changed and Telly Savalas no longer encourages us to "Feel the velvet, baby." Instead, the brand has moved on from media celebrities. Where to? Fish! It now sponsors the Bassmaster Elite fishing series.

2925 9 Ave. N.
Lethbridge, AB T1H 5E3

@BVWhisky

FOUNDED **1973**

OWNERS **Heaven Hill Brands**

STILLS **Custom industrial columns and copper pot**

PRODUCTS **Whisky**

AVAILABILITY **Widely in North America and Europe**

TOURS **Not offered**

NEAREST NEIGHBOURS **Highwood Distillers (page 122) – 1 hr, 40 min; Outlaw Trail Spirits Company (page 146) and Sperling Silver Distillery (page 150) – both 6hrs, 15 min east**

TASTING NOTES: BLACK VELVET ONYX 12-YEAR-OLD WHISKY (40% ABV)

Dry rye spices on the nose complement deep caramel and traditional peppery oak spices. The buttery palate moves quickly from sweet vanilla and black cherry to a mid-palate rye spice, then citrus pith. A cleansing finish reveals complex barrel notes that drift into the next sip.

BURWOOD DISTILLERY
CALGARY, AB

4127 6 St. NE, #15
Calgary, AB T2E 6V5
(403) 276-8410
www.burwooddistillery.ca

 @burwoodspirits

@burwooddistillery

FOUNDED 2016

OWNERS Jordan Ramey, Ivan Cilic,
Marko Cilic

STILLS 380-litre HBS pot with column

PRODUCTS Gin, honey eau-de-vie, honey
liqueur, vodka

AVAILABILITY Onsite, online, select private
stores in Alberta

TOURS $10–$15 with tasting; free on
Saturdays; book online

NEAREST NEIGHBOURS Last Best Brewing
& Distilling (page 123) — 17 min; Alberta
Distillers Limited (page 113) and
Confluence Distilling (page 118) — both
15 min

How could anyone know that a SWAT team bursting into Jordan Ramey's garage would kick off a series of events that would lead to the opening of Burwood Distillery?

Like many homeowners, Ramey—who is the head of the brewmaster program at Olds College, north of Calgary—shared a wall with his neighbour. Unlike many, his neighbours turned out to be money launderers. The courts appointed relator Ivan Cilic to dispose of that particular property. As Cilic went about his business—after the dramatic garage scene, of course—he spoke with Ramey and discovered they had a shared interest in small-batch beer and spirits. Cilic's brother Marko had helped with community distillations at home in Croatia and was keen to start his own distillery. By May 2017 the three had distilled their first vodka. Officially, Burwood was the first microdistillery to open after the City of Calgary changed its distilling bylaws in 2016. Today, Ramey jokes that it wasn't that new distilleries opened up; people just started putting signs on what they had long been doing covertly.

The Burwood kit is a combination of a copper HBS still from Kentucky and recycled brewing equipment. Four distillers keep the 93-square-metre distillery running 24 hours a day, seven days a week. Another 140 square metres are given over to a full farm-to-table restaurant serving dinner made with Burwood spirits, raw ingredients from the distillery, and local produce, including meats from a nearby farm. "We put a lot into a little square footage," Ramey declares proudly.

For their vodka, the team begins with Alberta-grown two-row barley. A more unusual spirit, their honey eau-de-vie, is distilled from mead they ferment from 100% Alberta honey. This explains the honeycomb-shaped shelves on the backbar in the Burwood tasting room and cocktail lounge. Ramey still teaches brewing, but it seems he may not have learned one important lesson: Burwood Distillery shares a wall with not one but two adjoining neighbours.

TASTING NOTES: **BURWOOD GIN** (44% ABV)

This gin's bright nose is spring-like with its lemongrass, citrus peels, and peppery coriander all balanced by mild juniper. The palate introduces a new peppery note and a savoury herbal profile. These flavours give way in the finish to an engaging freshly squeezed citrus character.

COCKTAIL: **CRANBERRY THYME GIN AND TONIC**
MAKES 1 COCKTAIL

CRANBERRY SIMPLE SYRUP:
2 cups cranberries
1 cup sugar
1 cup water

COCKTAIL:
Handful of ice cubes
2 oz Burwood Gin
1 oz Cranberry Simple Syrup (see here)
Juice of fresh lime
4 oz tonic water
5 cranberries, for garnish
Fresh thyme sprig, for garnish

For the Cranberry Simple Syrup, combine the cranberries, sugar, and water in a saucepan and bring to a boil, stirring occasionally, over medium heat. Reduce the heat to low and let the syrup simmer for 10 minutes. Strain the syrup into a bowl and let cool. Store unused syrup in a sealed container for up to two weeks.

For the cocktail, in a highball glass with ice, combine the gin, Cranberry Simple Syrup, and lime juice. Stir until combined, then top with tonic water. Garnish with the cranberries and sprig of thyme.

(Burwood Distillery)

507 36 Ave. SE
Calgary, AB T2G 1W5
www.confluencedistilling.ca

NEAREST NEIGHBOURS Alberta Distillers
Limited (page 113) – 5 min; Last Best
Brewing & Distilling (page 123)– 10 min

CONFLUENCE DISTILLING
CALGARY, AB

Confluence: the place where two or more rivers come together as one. Confluence: a Calgary distillery with a philosophy that inspired its name. Founder Ross Alger is creating a confluence of Calgary culture, art, and people into one celebrated community. The flow of his spirits and cocktails help achieve this goal.

For his Manchester Dry Gin, named for Calgary's Manchester district, where the distillery is located, Alger distils each botanical separately before blending them into a modern gin that snaps with floral tones. This gin and Confluence's Headwater Vodka, both distilled from prairie red spring wheat, are on pour in the cocktail lounge, its beautiful bar framed by a picture window that overlooks the glinting stills.

---

113 Sunset Blvd. SW
Turner Valley, AB T0L 2A0
(403) 933-5408
www.eauclairedistillery.ca

 @EauClaireCraft

 @eauclairecraft

FOUNDED 2014

OWNERS David Farran and Larry Kerwin

STILLS Mueller pot with 4-plate and 14-plate columns

PRODUCTS Gin, liqueur, seasonal, vodka, whisky

AVAILABILITY Onsite, Alberta liquor stores, select US states

TOURS $8.50–$18 with tasting; walk in or call ahead

NEAREST NEIGHBOURS Highwood Distillers (page 122)– 30 min; Alberta Distillers Limited (page 113) – 50 min

EAU CLAIRE DISTILLERY
TURNER VALLEY, AB

Without planning to do so, Aunt Polly taught Tom Sawyer a life lesson when she made him whitewash a fence as punishment for some mischief. Sawyer, the engaging hero of Mark Twain's 1876 novel, soon convinced his friends to complete the work on his behalf. David Farran has been known to use the same approach to harvesting grain for his Eau Claire distillery. When harvest time rolls around, he has to act quickly before autumn storms make the ground too wet. The twist, for Farran, is that he does not harvest with a tractor or combine. His farm machines are powered the old-fashioned way, by draft horses, and he is deluged with volunteer helpers when the time comes to bring in the crop.

Farran, a former vice-president of Calgary's Big Rock Brewery, teamed up with long-time commercial brewer and distiller Larry Kerwin in 2014 to launch their own distillery, the first microdistillery in Alberta. At the helm, Caitlin Quinn, with her Heriot-Watt master's degree in brewing and distilling, has the authentic credentials to be called a master distiller.

Although the team is committed to making its spirits from local produce when possible, prickly pear cacti do not grow in southern Alberta, despite its semi-desert environment. For its lusciously sweet prickly pear EquineOx liqueur, the distillery imports cactus berries from the southern US.

Eau Claire is located in the former Turner Valley Movie Theatre and Dance Hall, a building in the heart of the town with a rich history. Built circa 1929, it has also done duty as the town hall, a political rally centre, and a community hangout. The town itself was once a bustling boomtown thanks to the discovery of oil in 1914. Though the boom is now over, Eau Claire has proudly taken the place of moonshine stills behind Whiskey Ridge in the nearby Rocky Mountain foothills. However, Eau Claire's award-winning team just snickers when a wag asks about plans for the building next door to the distillery—a former brothel.

TASTING NOTES: **PRICKLY PEAR EQUINEOX** (40% ABV)

Prickly pear cactus and spring flavours infused into Eau Claire's barley base spirit make a spirit that blossoms with character. The fruitful nose is loaded with pears, watermelon bubble gum, jelly beans, and a crisp strawberry-citrus blend. The palate introduces spice to the fruit and berry medley, toning down the nose's sweetness. This spice leads into a finish that continues to sprout new flavours.

COCKTAIL: **BLONDE FRENCH**
MAKES 1 COCKTAIL

Handful of ice cubes
1½ oz Lillet
1 oz grapefruit juice
¾ oz Prickly Pear EquineOx
½ oz St-Germain
1 dash lemon bitters

Place a coupe in the freezer until chilled, at least one hour. In a cocktail shaker filled with ice, add the Lillet, grapefruit juice, Prickly Pear EquineOx, St-Germain, and lemon bitters. Shake for 10 seconds, then strain into the chilled coupe.

(Eau Claire Distillery)

8818 111 St., Unit 128
Fort Saskatchewan, AB T8L 3T4
www.thefortdistillery.com

NEAREST NEIGHBOUR Black Diamond
Distillery (page 114) – 30 min

THE FORT DISTILLERY
FORT SASKATCHEWAN, AB

Nathan and Kayla Flim brought distilling to the heavy industrial city of Fort Saskatchewan in the fall of 2018. Nathan has a chemistry degree and works as a crop inspector. These two fields of expertise give him practical insight into the distilling process, with the added value of knowing where to go to get the finest locally grown grains. It turns out, that farm is just eight kilometres away. Malted barley and hard red spring wheat are used to make their Prairie Gold Vodka. Gin is also on offer, with many more spirits on the way. Sample them in the distillery's cocktail lounge, where you are encouraged to enjoy food brought in from a neighbouring restaurant.

17412 111 Ave. NW
Edmonton, AB T5S 0A2
(780) 341-0682
www.hansendistillery.com

 @HansenSpirits

@hansendistillery

FOUNDED 2016

OWNERS Shayna Hansen and Kris Sustrik

STILL 1,000-litre DYE pot still with a 25-plate column system

PRODUCTS Gin, moonshine, flavoured spirits, vodka, whisky

AVAILABILITY Onsite, online, private liquor stores in Alberta

TOURS Thursdays–Saturdays; book through the distillery website

NEAREST NEIGHBOURS Black Diamond Distillery (page 114) – 15 min; Strathcona Spirits Distillery (page 136) – 20 min

HANSEN DISTILLERY
EDMONTON, AB

Co-founder Shayna Hansen's great-grandfather Carl left the American Badlands early in the 20th century. He hopped on a train and didn't get off until the tracks ended in the middle of Alberta. There, he met Amanda and started a new life. "They were farmers and did whatever was needed to get by when farming wasn't good," says Hansen. "And that includes making moonshine."

Hansen says her grandparents "adopted the tradition and made spirits for their whole life. They passed it down to my dad." Although she wasn't interested in learning the craft at the time, she felt the tradition shouldn't be lost. Shortly after Hansen met Kris Sustrik, who is now her husband, her father taught him to distil. He spent the next seven years perfecting the craft in his garage. In 2014 Sustrik had sold his welding company and the couple were making a batch of moonshine while discussing what to do next.

"Why aren't we doing this?" Hansen asked.

In 2016 they switched from garage-distilled sugar shine to a licensed distillery, making spirits with Alberta-grown grains and ingredients. They distil triticale for vodka, rye for whisky, and wheat for moonshine. Sustrik also makes gin and flavoured spirits, including the very popular Purple Cow Saskatoon Berry Cream Liqueur.

At the distillery, Hansen proudly displays family distilling artifacts, including her grandparents', father's, and husband's handmade five-gallon milk tank pot stills. Grandma developed her sugar shine recipe on this very still. Hansen didn't plan to distil the family recipe until an unfortunate event marked the time right to release an heirloom classic. In July 2018 Hansen's father, Donald Carl Hansen, passed away. She describes him as a man with a personality that could light up a mountainside. To share his love for the family moonshine, the distillery has released Hansen Sugar Shine, bottled at 55% abv. Proceeds from these sales go to the Little Miracle Fund at Don's favourite radio station, K-97.

TASTING NOTES: BORDER CROSSING RYE (40% ABV)

This rye grain spirit falls into a flavour camp that leans toward the nation of whisky rather than new-make spirit. Rye bread and ripe dark fruits are layered under grassy, floral tones that burst with rye spice on the nose. The palate enjoys a blast of white pepper heat that simmers into lemon peel on a long finish.

COCKTAIL: THE FIXER UPPER

MAKES 1 COCKTAIL

Handful of ice cubes
1½ oz Border Crossing Rye
½ oz Lillet Blanc
½ oz Galliano
2 dashes Fee Brothers Black Walnut Bitters
1 dash Angostura Bitters
Orange twist, for garnish

Place a cocktail glass in the freezer until chilled, at least one hour. Add ice. Pour all of the ingredients except the orange twist into a mixing glass and stir for 10 seconds. Strain into the chilled cocktail glass, then garnish with the orange twist.

(Hansen Distillery)

HIGHWOOD DISTILLERS
HIGH RIVER, AB

114 10 Ave. SE, Box 5693
High River, AB T1V 1M7
www.highwood-distillers.com

 @HighwoodDistill

 @highwooddistill

FOUNDED 1974

STILLS industrial beer still; custom kettle and column still

PRODUCTS Gin, liqueurs, premixed cocktails, rum, vodka, whisky

AVAILABILITY Widely in Canada

TOURS Not offered

NEAREST NEIGHBOURS Eau Claire Distillery (page 118) – 30 min; Black Velvet Distillery (page 115) – 1 hr, 40 min

What's in a name? In 1974 private investors who built this distillery on the outskirts of High River, Alberta, gave it the optimistic, if somewhat bland, moniker Sunnyvale. Perhaps they planned to make energy drinks for senior citizens on the side. In 1985, after Sunnyvale changed hands, the distillery was fittingly renamed for the Highwood River that flows through the town of 13,000.

The two-storey-tall yellow cement-block distillery, with a single square tower to house a column still, does not offer tours. However, if you are a fan of the CBC drama *Heartland* and happen to pass through town, stop by Maggie's Diner, Tack and Feed instead. This 3rd Avenue shop is now a set for the long-running television series.

In 2005, to complement the 100% soft winter wheat it distils on site, Highwood purchased the inventory of Potter's Distillery in Kelowna, BC. This included some older corn whiskies rumoured to have come from McGuinness's long-closed distillery in Weyburn, Saskatchewan. Since Highwood discontinued distilling rye grain several years ago, it now purchases rye spirit from other distillers to mature for its own blends. Although known for its whiskies, vodkas, rum, and gin, the distillery's broad product range now includes everything from liqueurs to single-serve Jell-O shots.

As well as its own successful brands, Highwood sells bulk whisky and also custom-blends and packages spirits for others wishing to launch products without investing in a distillery. This is how Fountana Group of Vancouver came to launch its fabulous Canadian Rockies 35-year-old whisky. Yep, there comes an age where retirement to a place called Sunnyvale begins to feel appropriate.

TASTING NOTES: NINETY 20-YEAR-OLD WHISKY (45% ABV)

A vibrant and creamy whisky nose bristles with peppery mint, balanced baking spice, and sweet dark fruits. The palate's spiced chocolate accentuates the old whisky's creaminess with smoky oak that still snaps. Corn flavours gently disperse wonderful spices through the finish, capping off a true Canadian gem.

LAST BEST BREWING & DISTILLING
CALGARY, AB

In the comfort of his Last Best headquarters in downtown Calgary, Bryce Parsons did something that caught the attention of the *Guinness Book of World Records*. In 2018 he distilled 52 different gins in a single year—a testament to the diversity of Canadian gin. "The biggest reward was that it showed how creative gin can be," says Parsons. "It was an educational tool. The collaboration with local bartenders and chefs resonated the most."

For a distinctly Alberta gin, Parsons worked with an herbalist to grow over 100 botanicals that would thrive there. Gin #52, called Best to Last, uses 16 of them. Fifteen came from a single Alberta herb garden.

Last Best's owners, the Bear Hill Brewing Co., know the brewpub industry's finer points. Distilling and brewing run parallel, making Parsons a beverage structural engineer building bridges between their beer, gin, and whisky programs. "We take some of our core beers and use the unhopped malt recipe as a base to build the whisky wash recipes," says Parsons. For gin, he might ferment beer malts with brewer's yeast and add hops as botanicals.

Bear Hill has now closed its Wood Buffalo Brewing Company in Fort McMurray, in the north of the province, but not without one very special release. On May 3, 2016, a pallet of Baird's peated malt from Scotland was sitting outside when a catastrophic wildfire swept through Fort McMurray. The fire stopped short of the brewery. As the residents evacuated, the abandoned malt became infused with smoke. When all was safe, the Wood Buffalo team returned and distilled it to make a whisky called The Beast—the same name the city's fire chief had given to the inferno. At an auction, The Beast generated record proceeds for the Friends of the Fort McMurray Firefighters Charities. One bottle fetched $10,000, likely a world record for the most ever paid for a single bottle of Canadian whisky.

607 11 Ave. SW
Calgary, AB T2R OE1
(587) 353-7387
www.lastbestbrewing.com

FOUNDED **2014 (brewery) 2016 (distillery)**

OWNER **Bearhill Brewing Co.**

STILLS **500-litre Artisan Still Design pot with 4-plate column, with two gin baskets and two 8-plate copper columns**

PRODUCTS **Aged spirits, gin, whisky**

AVAILABILITY **Onsite, select Alberta liquor stores**

NEAREST NEIGHBOURS **Confluence Distilling (page 118) — 10 min; Burwood Distillery (page 116) — 15 min**

TASTING NOTES: IMPORTER (46.5% ABV)

This hybrid spirit is made from a mash of malted barley, imperial porter, and demerara sugar that is distilled and aged in new oak for three years, then finished in American rye barrels. The nose pulses with chocolate milk, Tootsie Rolls, exotic wood, and timber planks. Bittersweet chocolate, cinnamon, cloves, and caramel top up the rich palate with a finish that introduces rum-like brown sugar.

LONE PINE DISTILLING
EDMONTON, AB

10375 59 Ave. NW
Edmonton, AB T6H 1E7
www.lonepinedistilling.ca

NEAREST NEIGHBOURS Strathcona Spirits Distillery (page 136) — 7 min; Red Cup Distillery (page 131) and Rig Hand Distillery (page 132)— both 20 min

Bryan Anderson was enjoying the view from his cabin and thinking about the as-yet-unnamed distillery he had started with Iain Skinner when he spotted a lone pine tree standing strong on a nearby hill. Anderson was a forest firefighter and knew the lodgepole pine, a common tree in Alberta's mountains and foothills, would stand even after a forest fire. It was a good sign, and he affirmed it by naming his distillery after the solitary tree.

The distillery makes two vodkas, one from corn and a second from wheat, both using local grains. Anderson's dad was a botanist, and Lone Pine's gin releases tap into the history and flavours of native Alberta plants. As well, bourbon-style whisky, rye whisky, and traditional single malt are patiently ageing in new and used barrels.

OLD PRAIRIE SENTINEL DISTILLERY
LACOMBE, AB

Towering grain elevators dot Alberta's landscape, standing watch like sentinels over the land. These elevators, filled with local grain, inspired Rob Gugin to call his distillery Old Prairie Sentinel. Gugin left his job as a brewer for another opportunity, but the art of fermentation never left his blood. He and business partner Steve Dick took fermentation to the next step in 2016 when they launched their distillery. They offer an extensive program of handmade cocktails that feature their Prairie Berry Dry Gin, Barrel Spice Gin, Premium Single Malt Vodka, Pickled Pepper Vodka, and a seasonal Butter Tart Liqueur that flies off the shelves at Christmas. So does a canned Sufferin' Bastard, the classic cocktail they make with gin, ginger, and citrus.

3413 53 Ave., Unit C
Lacombe, AB T4L 0C6
www.opsd.ca

NEAREST NEIGHBOURS **Rig Hand Distillery (page 132) — 1 hr; Stone Heart Distillery (page 134) — 40 min**

PARK DISTILLERY
BANFF, AB

219 Banff Ave.
Banff, AB T1L 1A7
(403) 762-5114
www.parkdistillery.com

 @parkdistillery

 @parkdistillery

FOUNDED 2015

OWNER Banff Hospitality Collective

STILLS 600-litre Kothe pot with two 8-plate columns

PRODUCTS Barrel-aged cocktails, gin, vodka, flavoured vodka, whisky, white rye

AVAILABILITY Onsite, private stores in Alberta, Calgary Airport Duty Free

TOURS Free; daily at 3:30 p.m.; private tours, $30 per person (minimum eight people), daily at 5 p.m. (call three weeks ahead)

NEAREST NEIGHBOURS RAW Distillery (page 130) and Wild Life Distillery (page 138) — both 20 min; Taynton Bay Spirits (page 92) — 2 hrs

When you see his grin as he perches atop a rack of over 100 whisky barrels in the distillery warehouse in nearby Canmore, you know Matthew Hendriks was born to distil. In truth, Hendo, as his friends call him, has been a bartender his whole working life. Tending bar brought the Saskatoon native to work in Banff. His work ethic so impressed the Banff Hospitality Collective—two families that together own 10 restaurants in this busy tourist town—that they asked him to take the lead in opening a distillery. He put in 4,700 hours that first year, 2,000 of them in a basement, learning how to distil.

Meanwhile, the Collective bought a building on the town's main street and converted it into a bar, restaurant, and distillery. "It's the busiest restaurant in Banff," reveals Hendo. "We serve 2,000 meals a day." Then, in the same breath, he announces, "We are a cocktail bar."

If numbers mean anything, this is an understatement. Park Distillery + Restaurant + Bar serves about 110,000 cocktails a year, all of them made with Park Distillery spirits. The pretty part of the 70-square-metre distillery—the stills and shop—is on the ground floor and visible to passersby. Down a few stairs, in a low-ceilinged basement behind, are grain mills, mash tuns, a blending station, and a hand-bottling line.

Today, as head distiller at Park Distillery in this Rocky Mountain tourist haven, Hendo devotes his days to creating "glacier to glass" spirits for others to mix in cocktails. So far, visitors to Banff have also taken more than 100,000 souvenir bottles home to countries around the world. "It's the best advertising we can get," he says. With his success comes a perk. Hendo, his wife, Sarah, and daughter, Piper, are among the very few who qualify to own a home within Banff National Park. And as he tells you this, that happy grin creeps back onto his face again.

TASTING NOTES: PARK GLACIER RYE (40% ABV)
This unaged Alberta rye grain spirit beautifully displays the grain's spicy character while maintaining a polished elegance. The zesty nose counters the palate's sweet, vegetal grain and a slight pinch of heat on the finish. An exceptionally clean and velvety spirit.

(continued)

COCKTAIL: **THE SAWBACK**

MAKES 1 COCKTAIL

½ oz agave nectar
½ oz water
2 handfuls of ice
1½ oz Park Chili Vodka

1½ oz pineapple juice
1 oz fresh lime juice
½ oz triple sec
1 pineapple wedge, for garnish

In a cocktail shaker, add the agave nectar and water and dry-shake until ingredients
are combined (about 10 seconds). Add ice to the shaker along with the vodka,
pineapple juice, lime juice, and triple sec. Shake for 10 seconds, then strain into
a double Old Fashioned glass over fresh ice. Garnish with the pineapple wedge.

(Matthew Hendriks, Master Distiller, Park Distillery)

THIS IS VODKA?

A t the turn of the 21st century, multibillion-dollar liquor conglomerates merrily churned out flavoured vodkas with the authenticity of a get-rich-quick scheme. It got *weird* immediately, with endless novelty flavours: birthday cake, caramel, candy cane, bubble gum, chocolate, and worse. Vodka soon became a punchline. Like most crazes do, the flavoured vodka craze petered out and microdistilleries swept in with their pot stills and short columns, built to capture flavour, not rectify spirit to neutrality. While making "vodka" was often an economic necessity, vodkas with flavourful undertones of their base ingredient were not always simple accidents.

On June 26, 2019, the government of Canada revised its 1959 vodka standard. Vodka no longer must be made from just grain or potatoes and "without distinctive character, aroma or taste." Distilleries that make clear spirit from other agricultural products such as fruit, dairy products, or honey can now call their product vodka. By broadening the standard to include all agricultural products, this revision diminishes regulatory burdens while driving product innovation. Vodka purists may not agree, but these are likely the same people whose 1982 VCRs are still blinking 12:00 a.m. It's time for a change as these newly legal vodkas bring new respect to the spirit.

GRAIN VODKA

One hundred percent neutral vodka still has its place in Canada's spirit lexicon, but Canadian distillers have brought traditional grain vodka's aesthetic into the new millennium by leaving some of the succulent cereal flavours in. Compass Distillers' (pictured here, see also page 273) vodka (40% abv) balances both worlds. Nova Scotia winter wheat, distilled twice through their 28-plate column, has a classic vodka profile. Compass forgoes filtering, and so maintains sweet wheat nuances with mild spice on the finish.

INFUSED VODKA

Unlike the mass-produced, heavily sweetened vodkas that have tarnished the spirit's name, microdistilleries infuse their vodkas with natural ingredients such as chili peppers, berries, dill pickles, or horseradish, while severely cutting back on sugar. Sheringham Distillery's (page 64) seasonal Loganberry Vodka (43% abv) captures the berry's natural wild tartness, yielding an innovative vodka for mixing.

APPLE-BASE VODKA

Ironworks Distillery (page 278) turns Annapolis Valley apples into unfiltered vodka (40% abv) that captures the sweet and tart nuance of the apples, with delicate floral tones and a flare of peppery spice on the finish.

HONEY-BASE VODKA

The bees that make honey for Salt Spring Shine's (page 61) Hive Vodka (40% abv) deserve credit for producing an ingredient that imbues this vodka with a beautifully rich texture and gentle sweetness, while the nose buzzes with delicate layers of honeycomb.

MILK-BASE VODKA

The Dairy Distillery's (page 170) Vodkow (40% abv), which comes in an old-fashioned milk bottle, captures a subtle creamy texture and flavour from its milk base, while the restrained dairy flavour of Yongehurst Distillery's (page 217) Milk Whey Vodka (40% abv) proves milk does a vodka good.

VODKA D'ÉRABLE

Acerum is a spirit made by fermenting and distilling maple sap. The process creates a byproduct that the Distillerie Shefford (page 243) has re-distilled into Vodka d'érable (40%). This vodka style shouldn't be mistaken for maple-flavoured vodka. Instead, expect a full-bodied crystal-clear vodka where maple's essence sparkles with warmth alongside a subtle mineral sugariness. ■

RAW DISTILLERY
CANMORE, AB

810 Bow Valley Trail
Canmore, AB T1W 1N6
(587) 899-7574
www.rawspirits.ca

 @RawspiritsAB

 @rawspiritsab

FOUNDED 2016

OWNERS Lindsay and Brad Smylie, in
partnership with Blake Restaurant

STILLS 100-litre custom pot

PRODUCTS Gin, vodka, whisky, white rye,
white rum

AVAILABILITY Onsite, online, private liquor
stores in Alberta

TOURS $15; book online

NEAREST NEIGHBOURS Park Distillery
(page 126) — 20 min; Wild Life Distillery
(page 138) — 5 min

Like many young boys, when Brad Smylie was growing up near Lake Temiskaming in Northern Ontario, he had a special fondness for his grandmother, Nona Chitaroni. She was fond enough of young Brad to share important knowledge with him—in her case: distilling. Nona, as you might gather, was a bit of a character, enough that a local publishing house published a book about her penchant for moonshining. It turns out that distilling spirits was not her main interest, though. Nona's real obsession was making wine. Distilling rye was incidental, done strictly to keep her wine barrels sweet between batches.

Young Brad clearly learned his lessons well. Now a firefighter, he and his scientist wife, Lindsay, have used those lessons since 2016 to handcraft a range of spirits. In 2019 they moved their distillery to new quarters at BLAKE, an upscale restaurant on the Bow Valley Trail in Canmore.

Real Alberta Whisky (RAW) is their inspiration, made from unmalted Alberta grain in the Headframe Whisky Rocket still they brought up from Montana. Like so many start-ups, the Smylies began with white spirits distilled from wheat and rye while waiting for their whisky to mature. Ironically, their bestseller is 100% unaged rye, a favourite with bartenders looking to increase the rye presence in cocktails.

For their first whiskies, the couple chose to use ex-bourbon barrels, but they have since switched to French oak from nearby Okanagan wineries. All whiskies are finished in former Okanagan Port barrels. Although they now have products in over 400 liquor stores across Alberta, their early days were a real financial challenge.

"Farmers' markets saved us," Brad explains, "because it was the only place we could sell." Their long-term goals include producing a traditional blended Canadian whisky. In the meantime, it's gins, vodka, and white rye that keep their doors open.

TASTING NOTES: SEASONAL RYE UNAGED (40% ABV)

This rye grain spirit has been aged for 24 hours in oak casks that previously contained port wine. A cohesive nose with rye cereals and bold, dry, earthy floral attributes also emanates a distinct fruitiness that dissipates on the palate. A flash of rye spice climbs steadily into a finish of toasted rye grain.

RED CUP DISTILLERY
NISKU, AB

Red Cup Distillery co-owner Rob de Groot is a classically trained opera singer. He's also an aficionado of the Prairies' rich moonshining history. Along with his wife, Barb, he opened the distillery in 2015 to bottle the flavour of Alberta in a spirit that resonates with authentic moonshine traditions. These customs include fermenting 100% malted wheat, traditional sour mashing, and distilling on a homemade still that looks as if it was excavated from an early-20th-century Alberta farm. Their quality Prairie Moonshine also comes in traditional 1,890-millilitre moonshine jugs that are meant to be passed around at family gatherings. Rob may be classically trained, but it's his moonshine that does the singing these days.

3675 44 Ave. E.
Nisku, AB T0C 0V0
www.redcupdistillery.ca

NEAREST NEIGHBOURS **Rig Hand Distillery** (page 132) — 10 min; Strathcona Spirits Distillery (page 136) — 20 min

RIG HAND DISTILLERY
NISKU, AB

2104 8 St., Bay B
Nisku, AB T9E 7Y9
www.righanddistillery.com

 @RigHandSpirits

 RigHandDistillery

OWNERS Geoff and Karen Stewart

FOUNDED 2014

STILLS 1,100-litre custom pot with 4-plate column and 16-plate column; 370-litre Christian Carl still with six plates; 100-litre gin still

PRODUCTS Over 40 spirits, including Brum, cream liquor, gin, grain spirits, flavoured vodka, vodka, and whisky

PRODUCT AVAILABILITY Onsite, online, private Alberta liquor stores

TOURS Daily; call ahead or book online

NEAREST DISTILLERY Red Cup Distillery (page 131) — 10 min; Strathcona Spirits Distillery (page 136) — 30 min

Co-owner Geoff Stewart is a 100-mile-an-hour, hair-straight-back kind of guy who has harnessed his creativity in a distillery. While on a motorcycle trip with his wife and co-owner, Karen, they bumped into two Ohio brothers who operated their own distillery. After Geoff rode his motorcycle through the distillery, they convinced him to take up distilling himself. He listened, and Rig Hand became Alberta's second microdistillery.

Rig Hand Distillery sits in North America's second-largest oil-and-gas industrial park. They have forged an identity with their oil derrick–shaped bottle, a replica of the 1947 Leduc #1 drilling rig that struck oil and thus changed the course of Alberta's history. Each bottle is hand-dipped in black wax, and the liquid inside gushes flavour. Rig Hand makes a staggering 40-plus different spirits. "Because we make such a range of spirits, we appeal to a lot more people," explains distiller and general manager Mike Beile. "One of our goals is to make a product that appeals to everybody. Not everyone likes gin or vodka or whisky, so we distil a variety to get everyone on board."

For their flavoured vodkas, they drop between 13 and 18 kilograms of fruit or berries from local farms into 180 litres of Rig Hand Premium Vodka. After seven to 10 days, this is strained, lightly filtered, and bottled. Stewart moonlights in dental hygiene; perhaps this explains why his spirits are not laced with sugar. For the popular Rig Hand Double Double Coffee Cream, he mixes a rum-and-cream emulsion with a drop of the distillery's Brum—a rum-like spirit made from sugar beets—and blends it with three types of coffee and flavours.

The neighbouring Gruger Family Fungi uses the spent grain mash to grow mushrooms. "He came back with a pink oyster mushroom the size of my head," says Beile. "The biggest smile I've ever seen on anyone's face." Smiles now common on the faces of everyone visiting the distillery.

TASTING NOTES: RIG HAND GARLIC VODKA (40% ABV)

Macerating ten to 12 pounds of flat chopped, Russian red garlic in 180 litres of the distillery's premium vodka produces an aromatic, savoury, and sweet potation with a velvet punch of garlic. More garlic added to the bottle turns it into a garlic snow globe, and perhaps explains Alberta's lack of vampire sightings.

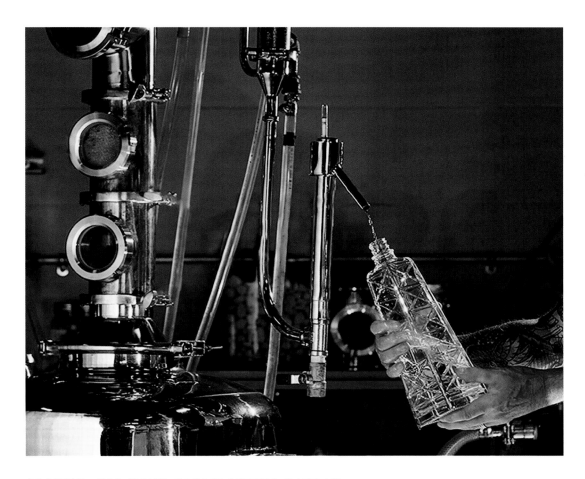

COCKTAIL: **RIG HAND GARLIC VODKA CAESAR**

MAKES 1 COCKTAIL

1 lime wedge
Matt & Steve's Signature Caesar Rimmer
Handful of ice cubes
1 oz Rig Hand Garlic Vodka
1 pinch horseradish

1 dash Tabasco sauce
1 dash Worcestershire sauce
8 oz Clamato
1 pinch celery salt
Matt & Steve's Extreme Bean, for garnish

Rim a 12-ounce Mason jar with lime, then rim with the Caesar rimmer. Fill the jar with ice, add the vodka, horseradish, Tabasco, and Worcestershire sauce, and top with Clamato. Stir until ingredients are combined, then sprinkle with celery salt. Garnish with Extreme Bean.

STONE HEART DISTILLERY
INNISFAIL, AB

**5021 44 Ave., Bay 3
Innisfail, AB T4G 1P7**

NEAREST NEIGHBOURS **Old Prairie Sentinel
Distillery (page 125) — 40 min; Burwood
Distillery (page 116) — 1 hr, 5 min**

"I work full time, plus farm and run the distillery. So I'm pretty busy," says Ian Scott, an oil worker and fourth-generation Albertan farmer. He and his wife, Marnie, were too busy, for example, to operate a tasting room (but they've found time to build one—it's due to open in summer 2020), though not too busy to bring home a gold medal in the 2019 Canadian Artisan Spirit Competition for their vodka. They may be busy, but when it comes to making spirits, they don't take shortcuts. The couple plant their own grains, then nurture them through the growing season until they are ready to be harvested, milled onsite, then fermented and distilled into vodka. Grain to glass? No, it is seed to glass, this time.

TASTING NOTES:
STONE HEART ORIGINAL VODKA (40% ABV)

This vodka shows off wheat's softer side with a clean nose that barely hints at the sweetness of the grain. The palate's tones are mild and sweet, accented by a drop of gentle citrus. This bottle's heart is really made of stone, with the peppery spice flashes late on the palate, but then warms you up again with its incandescent finish.

STRATHCONA SPIRITS DISTILLERY

EDMONTON, AB

10122 81 Ave. NW
Edmonton, AB T6E 1X1
(780) 887-9393
www.strathconaspirits.ca

 @StratSpirits

 @strathconaspirits

FOUNDED **2016**

OWNER **Adam Smith**

STILLS **567-litre custom pot with 4-plate column and 12-plate column; 100-litre Mile Hi pot**

PRODUCTS **Gin, vodka**

AVAILABILITY **Onsite, online, private liquor stores in Alberta**

TOURS **$10 (includes tasting); Thursday, Friday, Saturday (book online)**

NEAREST NEIGHBOURS **Lone Pine Distilling (page 124) – 7 min; Hansen Distillery (page 120) – 20 min**

Adam Smith's interests revolve first and foremost around Edmonton's arts scene. Smith is not the 18th-century Scottish economist, but the man who, for a few years, spent his days working for an Ontario-based brewery before heading over to historic Old Strathcona, the artsy Edmonton neighbourhood south of the North Saskatchewan River. There, in a low, 69-square-metre, grey cement boomtown building, he did his best to run a viable venue for live music called the Baby Seal Club. Although the club developed a loyal cult following, staying solvent was a constant challenge. "I got a street degree in shuffling paper while I was keeping the venue open," Smith laments.

In 2014 a visit to a small West Coast distillery sparked his interest in distilling spirits. The microdistilling community was happy to share its advice, the most common being: "Don't start too small."

When he opened his distillery in 2016, he was limited to the same 69 square metres that had housed the Baby Seal Club. This is why he offers what he calls "point-and-spin" tours. And while the works of the distillery continue within its walls, a red shed out back does duty as a milling station and the place to store supplies.

The distillery has expanded and now includes a farm southwest of the city, and Smith has his eye on a church that he could use for maturing whisky. And since the climate at the farm is half a growing zone warmer than Edmonton, he also grows botanicals there for the gin that he and head distiller Kyle Slipchuk produce.

But how do you explain the beat-up old bush plane that lands in one of the fields, all stickered up with Strathcona Spirits logos? Well, Smith and everyone else at the distillery come from a creative community. This is just their way of having fun while spreading the word about the distillery they reckon remains the tiniest in North America.

TASTING NOTES: BADLAND SEABERRY GIN (44% ABV)
Some of the juniper in this gin comes from the fossil-filled Red Deer River Badlands. Freshly baked orange madeleines, roses, and citrus brighten the nose. These flavours transition to the palate, where the tangy tartness of the seaberry balances the Badlands juniper as it heads into a peppery-spiced finish.

COCKTAIL: **FIDDLER'S GREEN**

MAKES 1 COCKTAIL

CILANTRO AND SALT-INFUSED DOLIN BLANC VERMOUTH:
1 bottle (750 ml) Dolin Blanc Vermouth de Chambery
12 fresh cilantro sprigs
2 tbsp sea salt

COCKTAIL:
2 oz Strathcona Spirits Badland Seaberry Gin
½ oz La Quintinye Vermouth Royal Extra Dry
½ oz Cilantro and Salt-infused Dolin Blanc Vermouth
Handful of ice cubes
2 fresh cilantro sprigs, for garnish

For the infused vermouth, pour the vermouth into a large one-litre jar. Add cilantro and salt, and muddle for 30 seconds. Strain back into the vermouth bottle. Store in the fridge for up to a month.

For the cocktail, place a Martini glass in the freezer until chilled, at least one hour. Add all of the ingredients except the cilantro to a mixing glass with ice. Stir and strain into the chilled Martini glass and garnish with the cilantro. Enjoy!

(Corbin Fredrick Brocks)

WILD LIFE DISTILLERY

CANMORE, AB

105 Bow Meadows Cres., #160
Canmore, AB T1W 2W8
(403) 678-2800
www.wildlifedistillery.ca

 @wldspirits

 @wldspirits

FOUNDED 2017

OWNERS Matt Widmer and Keith Robinson

STILLS 500-litre Hoga pot

PRODUCTS Gin, vodka

AVAILABILITY Onsite, private liquor stores
in Alberta

TOURS $10; 3 p.m. daily

NEAREST NEIGHBOURS Park Distillery
(page 126) — 20 min; RAW Distillery
(page 130) — 5 min

To Matt Widmer and Keith Robinson, wildlife is a lot more than the wolves, eagles, and bison they display on their labels. It also includes surfing in the Pacific Ocean, climbing mountains, and powder skiing in the Bow Valley. That's not unusual, as the outdoor life is in their DNA—Widmer grew up in Banff, and Robinson in Canmore. It comes as no surprise that they forage for all the botanical ingredients for their Alberta Botanical Gin. This may be thought of as work for some, but to these founders, it is a way of life.

In 2017, when the two "friends for life" decided to move beyond hobby distilling and go into business together as distillers, they prepared a special partnership agreement. It was not about who does or gets what, but rather a formal agreement not to let the pressures and strains of business interfere with their friendship. They try to keep financial stresses to a minimum by operating a cocktail bar as well as selling spirits directly from the distillery.

For their vodka, they distil a mash of 70% hard red wheat and 30% malted barley that they mill on site. Their first whisky is made the same way, using 100% malted barley. Its rich new-make spirit exudes cereal notes and creamy sweetness. They also plan to distil rye and malted rye whisky.

Once their mash has fermented, they filter it so they can distil "off the grain," a process they believe gives cleaner grain flavours. This also allows them to dispose of their relatively low volumes of liquid waste in a septic system. At the same time, they have designated their spent grains for yet another wild side of life—feeding bucking bulls at the Rockin R Ranch in Cochrane, Alberta.

TASTING NOTES: WILD LIFE
ALBERTA BOTANICAL GIN 2018 (42.5% ABV)

All of the botanicals in this gin were foraged in Alberta, including cow parsnip, rose hips, thistle, yarrow, and Labrador tea, to name a few. A savoury, peppery character on the nose sits above the tantalizing juniper and floral high notes. The creamy palate screams wild backcountry, locking in carrot-like flavours that taste like they were pulled fresh from the ground.

COCKTAIL: THE CANMORE HOTEL

MAKES 1 COCKTAIL

2 oz Wild Life Gin
1 oz lemon juice
1 oz grapefruit syrup

1 egg white
Handful of ice cubes
2 fresh sage leaves, for garnish

Combine the gin, lemon juice, grapefruit syrup, and egg white into a cocktail shaker and dry-shake vigorously for 15 seconds. Add ice, then shake vigorously for another 20 seconds. Strain into a new cocktail shaker and dry-shake again for 20 seconds. Double strain into a chilled snifter glass. Garnish with sage leaves.

BANDITS DISTILLING INC.
WEYBURN, SK

3A 22nd Ave. SE
Weyburn, SK S4H 3J9
www.banditsdistilling.ca

NEAREST NEIGHBOURS Outlaw Trail Spirits
Company (page 146) —1 hr, 20 min;
Capital K Distillery (page 152) — 5 hrs,
30 min

When the McGuinness distillery closed in 1986, although Weyburn no longer had a distillery, the city's distilling story continued. Weyburn is the largest gathering point for grain in Canada's interior, and grain—lots of it—continued to arrive by train, bound for the city's grain terminals and elevators. Thirty years later, distilling finally returned to Weyburn.

Marnie Gruber is on a bandit's mission to pilfer flavour from the region's bounty. The distillery uses its own homegrown grains, along with those from local farms, to make moonshine, flavoured moonshine, and vodka. Their small-batch Red Coat Gin contains traditional botanicals combined with Saskatchewan specialties such as lilac and birch bud. Whisky is billed as "coming soon."

BLACK FOX FARM & DISTILLERY
SASKATOON, SK

April showers may bring May flowers, but spirits are always available at this flower farm. John Cote and Barb Stefanyshyn-Cote operate a farm they describe as nontraditional. Fields of cut flowers are accented by other fields growing 90% of the ingredients that go into their spirits. This unusual combination is distilling's black sheep, but in Saskatchewan the black fox eats those sheep for breakfast. Barb and John noticed one of these rare black foxes, which are part of the familiar red fox family, playing with a red fox in their fields. It was atypically natural, just like growing flowers and making spirits.

The distillery runs on a geothermal cooling system in which all the by-products of distilling are used to improve the soils in their orchards and fields. The farm's calendula flowers and rhubarb find their way into the gin basket as botanicals to make their Black Fox Gin #3. With all the flowers, bees have moved in, their honey used to sweeten a homegrown raspberry liqueur and honey ginger liqueur.

The farm hosts several festivals and events throughout the year, including a seasonal Wednesday night Gin and Tonic in the Field, where you can enjoy live music, pick flowers with a drink in hand, and maybe catch a glance of a black fox in the distance, cavorting to the music.

245 Valley Rd.
Saskatoon, SK S7K 3J6
www.blackfoxfarmanddistillery.com

NEAREST NEIGHBOURS Lucky Bastard Distillers (page 144) – 20 min; Radouga Distillery (page 150) – 2 hrs, 10 min

TASTING NOTES: BLACK FOX GIN #3 (42% ABV)

The gin's fifteen spices and flowers rhyme the flavours together like a fox in socks. It is cohesive with a fruity berry foundation layering the nose with subtle saffron, juniper and blooming spiced tones. Licorice is lustrous on the creamy palate with fresh citrus and peppery lemon rinds capped with a foxy candied bitter finish.

LAST MOUNTAIN DISTILLERY
LUMSDEN, SK

70 Highway 20, PO Box 736
Lumsden, SK S0G 3C0
(306) 731-3930
lastmountaindistillery.com

 @LMDistillery

@lmdistillery

FOUNDED **2010**

OWNERS Colin and Meredith Schmidt

STILLS 100-litre Artisan Still Design pot with 4-plate and 16-plate columns; 650-litre pot imported from China

PRODUCTS Gin, liqueurs, flavoured moonshine, rum, spiced rum, vodka, flavoured vodka, vodka sodas, whisky, flavoured whisky

AVAILABILITY Onsite, online, private stores in Saskatchewan and Alberta

TOURS $15; Saturdays, 12–5 p.m.

NEAREST NEIGHBOURS Outlaw Trail Spirits Company (page 146) – 30 min; Lucky Bastard Distillers (page 144) – 2 hr, 15 min

Saskatchewan native Colin Schmidt hunts with a bow, ice fishes, and as a student, he completed university on a hockey scholarship. In other words, he is all-Canadian. When Colin and his wife, Meredith, were casting about for a way they could work together, they ran into someone from Hawaii who was making vodka from pineapples. Since they live in the heart of wheat country, why not open a distillery?

In 2010 they approached the Saskatchewan government to inquire about a distilling licence, only to find that the province was in the process of developing new rules and wanted their advice. When the regulations were eventually published, one clause worried them. The province had decided that distillers must produce a minimum of 5,000 litres of alcohol each year. That was an ambitious target for a small start-up with a tiny 1,200-litre hybrid still. "Don't worry about it," came the helpful reply from the Saskatchewan Liquor and Gaming Authority.

The information they dug up in 2010 about microdistilling told them to use corn. They quickly got the knack, and then switched to local wheat. Today, fresh dill pickles that Meredith makes using cucumbers, dill, and garlic from nearby Lincoln Gardens add flavour to Last Mountain's acclaimed Dill Pickle Vodka. Nevertheless, Colin is quick to point out their goal: "We want to be known as a whisky distillery. There is almost more opportunity in Saskatchewan than we can handle."

Now, with 500 barrels maturing, the couple is gearing up for Canada-wide distribution. As their business has grown, the Schmidts have brought on distiller Braeden Raiwet to run their original Artisan Still Design pot and columns and a 650-litre stripping still they imported from China. Several large shipping containers tucked out back add more space to their cozy 750-square-metre distillery. Theirs is a winning set-up, as proven in 2019, when Last Mountain was named Artisanal Distiller of the Year at the Canadian Whisky Awards.

TASTING NOTES: **SINGLE CASK WHEAT WHISKY** (45% ABV)

This three-and-a-half-year-old whisky is rich on the nose with a wheat profile that is like oaked Wheat Chex breakfast cereal. It is sturdy and robust. The palate provides some outstanding barrel spices up front, along with citrus and sweet wheat that is smoky and indulgent. A peppery glow sizzles on the finish, leaving behind traces of oak. Last Mountain is making some of the best wheat whisky in the country.

COCKTAIL: **BLACK FOREST PARALYZER**
MAKES 1 COCKTAIL

Handful of ice cubes
1½ oz Last Mountain Distillery
   Cherry Whisky
4 oz cola
2 oz chocolate milk
2 cherries, for garnish

In an Old Fashioned glass with ice, add the whisky and cola and stir lightly. Top with the chocolate milk and garnish with cherries.

LOST RIVER DISTILLERY
DUNDURN, SK

www.lostriverpermaculture.com

NEAREST NEIGHBOURS Black Fox Farm &
Distillery (page 141) – 30 min; Lucky
Bastard Distillers (page 144) – 30 min

Long before it was a distillery, this property provided water to the Canadian Pacific Railway for its steam locomotives. The aquifer, which locals refer to as the ancient "Lost River," was coveted for its endless supply of crystal-clear water. Owner Shawn Ward is also president of Envirotech CO2, an industrial cleaning company that uses dry ice instead of harmful chemicals. Envirotech built the distillery to expand its agricultural business and to add value to the carbon cycle. For example, a herd of Black Angus cows actively keeps the distillery's pastures grazed and fertilized. "We just love cows!" enthuses Ward.

Saskatchewan wheat is the base for their signature vodka. Wheat whisky ages in 220-litre Canadian virgin white oak barrels, and there are plans to cooper even more casks in their in-house cooperage. The river may be lost, but it has been replaced by a steady flow of crystal-clear spirits.

814 47th St. E
Saskatoon, SK S7K 0X4
(306) 979-7280
www.luckybastard.ca

 @luckybastardSK

@lbdistillers

FOUNDED 2012

OWNERS Cary Bowman, Mike Goldney,
Lacey Crocker

STILLS 300-litre Mueller pot with 4-plate
column; 2,000-litre custom pot

PRODUCTS Gin, liqueurs, malt spirit, rum,
vodka, flavoured vodka, whisky

AVAILABILITY Onsite, online

TOURS Free; hourly, Wednesday–
Saturday; call ahead

NEAREST NEIGHBOURS Black Fox Farm &
Distillery (page 141) – 20 min; Radouga
Distilleries (page 150) – 2 hrs, 10 min

LUCKY BASTARD DISTILLERS
SASKATOON, SK

When your business partner wins the lottery, it's only right that you name your distillery after the lucky so-and-so. In 2010 investment banker Cary Bowman was scanning an in-flight magazine as he and his family headed off on a European vacation. A story about small distillers caught his eye. Once in Europe, he saw how common microdistilling is over there.

"We were surrounded by distilleries," he recalls. On returning to Saskatoon, Bowman did some research and realized how few and far between small distillers were in Canada. His business partners, husband and wife Mike Goldney and Lacey Crocker, were enthusiastic at the possibility of establishing a distillery. The three of them set to work right away planning their new venture, and in May 2012 they were ready to open the doors to Lucky Bastard distillery.

Goldney, a physician, left his practice to run this other kind of operation, while Bowman stayed with the bank until 2014, when it finally made sense for him to turn his full attention to their growing business. The following year, the team moved the distillery to the 1,400-square-metre space they now occupy. Here, they added another still and an automated bottling line to keep 20 full-time and 10 part-time staff hopping. They also run a steadily booked reception centre onsite.

While their sales are focused on Saskatchewan and Alberta, a visit from Canada's ambassador to the Ukraine has led to regular orders from Canada's embassy there. And almost unbelievably, a growing coals-to-Newcastle demand for Lucky Bastard wheat vodka has emerged in Russia. Goldney, the lottery-winning lucky bastard for whom the distillery is named, sees parallels between distilling and his past profession in medicine. Both have a basis in science, he explains, but from his experienced perspective, distilling smells a whole lot better.

TASTING NOTES:
LUCKY BASTARD CHAI VODKA (40% ABV)

Lucky Bastard's 100% Saskatchewan wheat vodka is distilled seven times for good luck, then infused with chai tea spice. This vodka oozes sophistication, enhanced by an exotic blend of spices. Vanilla, cinnamon, and star anise accent aromatics such as cardamom, ginger, and cloves to give this vodka a charisma like no other.

COCKTAIL:
WILD BLUE MOJITO
MAKES 1 COCKTAIL

BLUEBERRY SYRUP:
1 cup blueberry juice
½ cup evaporated cane sugar
1 cup wild blueberries

COCKTAIL:
1 oz Lucky Bastard Knock on Wood Amber Rum
3 lime wedges
5 mint leaves
1 oz Blueberry Syrup (see here)
Handful of ice cubes
5 oz sparkling water
8 fresh blueberries for garnish

For the Blueberry Syrup, in a saucepan add the blueberry juice and evaporated cane sugar and simmer over low heat. Stir regularly until the cane sugar dissolves (about 10 to 15 minutes). Once dissolved, add the wild blueberries. Continue to stir regularly and simmer for an additional 15 minutes. Let the syrup cool. Strain into a clean container. Extra syrup will store in a sealed container for up to three weeks.

In a collins glass, muddle the rum, lime wedges, fresh mint, and Blueberry Syrup. Add ice, then top with sparking water. Garnish with a stir stick skewered with fresh blueberries, and stir well.

OUTLAW TRAIL SPIRITS COMPANY
REGINA, SK

1360 Scarth St.
Regina, SK S4R 2E7
(306) 527-6533
www.outlawtrailspirits.com

 @OutlawTrailSp

 @outlawtrailspirits

FOUNDED 2016

OWNERS John and Charmaine Styles

STILLS 200-litre Mile Hi pot with three-plate and six-plate columns

PRODUCTS Grain spirits, rum, vodka, flavoured vodka

AVAILABILITY Onsite, private liquor stores in Saskatchewan

TOURS $10; Saturday afternoons

NEAREST NEIGHBOURS Sperling Silver Distillery (page 150) – 6 min; Bandits Distilling Inc. (page 140) 1 hr, 20 min

"I must be part raccoon," admits John Styles as he recounts how "all the shiny stuff" he saw when he toured Headframe Spirits in Butte, Montana, got him going. With a 35-year career in oil and gas, Styles understood the basics of distillation. For him, though, the sparkling stills at Headframe were magnets. After selling their last oil company in 2009, Styles and his Montana-born wife, Charmaine, were looking for a retirement project. They had made wine and beer at home; perhaps distilling spirits could be what the two Scotch aficionados were looking for.

Every successful spirit needs an authentic story. Charmaine recalled her family's links to the infamous Outlaw Trail, the route that brought many a notorious cattle rustler north into Saskatchewan. Her grandfather Frank Biggs had been Montana's last cattle-brand inspector. A bit of research revealed that a number of Biggs's most-wanted quarry had followed the Outlaw Trail into Saskatchewan. "It was a legitimate link and something we could reasonably market as a theme."

Once they committed to the project in 2016, the Styleses moved quickly. They wanted to be operational the same year that they began spending money on the distillery they affectionately called The Bomb Shelter. Their first disappointment came when quotes from several long-established still makers came back with 18- to 36-month delivery times.

They switched gears and brought in a hybrid still from Mile Hi Distilling in Colorado. And while John is the main distiller, it was Charmaine who made a recent batch of Olde Foggy Bottom Single Malt, a whisky spirit distilled from malted barley and matured in plastic containers using a product called "inner staves." To keep production moving, for their liqueurs the Styleses purchase grain neutral spirits. John's favourite part of distilling? Thinking up goofy product names—that, and all the shiny stuff.

TASTING NOTES:
OLDE FOGGY BOTTOM
SINGLE MALT (46.2% ABV)

This grain spirit is made from Saskatchewan two-row barley, and it tickles the nose with new-make malt cereal. Pencil shavings intertwine on the nose, but when this spirit hits the palate, it is like a lumberyard full of pristine wood. An herbal spiciness and a note similar to the chocolate marshmallows in Count Chocula cereal stave off the spirit's mineral edge.

COCKTAIL:
OUTLAW SPA WATER
MAKES 1 COCKTAIL

3 mint leaves
Handful of ice cubes
1 oz Outlaw Trail Spirits Climax, SK, Cool Cucumber Vodka
3 oz sparkling lemon water
1 cucumber wheel, for garnish
Fresh mint sprig, for garnish

In a highball glass, muddle the mint leaves. Fill the glass with ice, then add the vodka and sparkling lemon water. Garnish with a cucumber wheel and sprig of mint.

[Charmaine Styles]

THE HOTTEST NAMES FOR YOUR NEW ARRIVAL

Given how people labour over it, naming a distillery certainly seems to be a daunting task. So imagine the challenge of finding just the right sobriquet for your newly arrived still! Will the newest member of the distilling family grow into its moniker, or will the name shape its future? There's serious stuff to consider when making such big life decisions.

Like new parents, distillers proudly display their stills front and centre. True, from time to time, they keep the distiller up late at night, teething for a new part. Or they spit up all over themselves, leaving the distiller to polish them back to their coppery gleam. But that's all part of raising a still. It is only a matter of respect that each still should have a name. On the West Coast, Gillespie's Fine Spirits (page 22) has Sputnik, Junior, and Anna. De Vine Wines & Spirits (page 52) named their still Brünnhilde, after the warrior-maiden from the German Nibelungen saga. The stills at Pacific Rim Distillery (page 57) honour Grandma Patricia and Grandma Judy. Still Fired Distilleries (page 283) use the names Kirby and Morgan. Here are a few of Canada's hottest trends in still names and the stories behind them:

ALL OR NOTHING BREWHOUSE & DISTILLERY (PAGE 163): ELLIE

The Dornan brothers have named some of their fermenters after family, but Ellie just came to them when they first laid eyes on this shiny 5,000-litre Vendome pot still. It's a coincidence that baby books tell us that Ellie means "shining light."

BLACK DIAMOND DISTILLERY (PAGE 114): FRANKENSTILL

It's Alive! Well, not really, lightning didn't bring this still to life. Instead, David and Andrea Scade engineered their 200-litre Frankenstill (pictured here) from scratch. The feed from the still is split to run two columns simultaneously cutting run times in half without sacrificing quality. Frankenbrilliant!

CIRKA DISTILLERIES (PAGE 226): HOMER AND MARIO

Paul Cirka's father, Borden, earned the nickname Homer in university. "It's an homage to my father, who passed away when I was a teenager," says Cirka. Mario was the name of the father of their first investor. "Mario, being Italian, made his cheese, wine, prosciutto, and grappa," explains Cirka. "He would have taken up residence at the distillery if he was still alive."

COMPASS DISTILLERS (PAGE 273): TESS

The distillery can't explain why they named their Vendome still Tess. The name just fit. But digging deeper, Tess is Greek for "harvest," and this still does an excellent job of harvesting flavour from Nova Scotia grains.

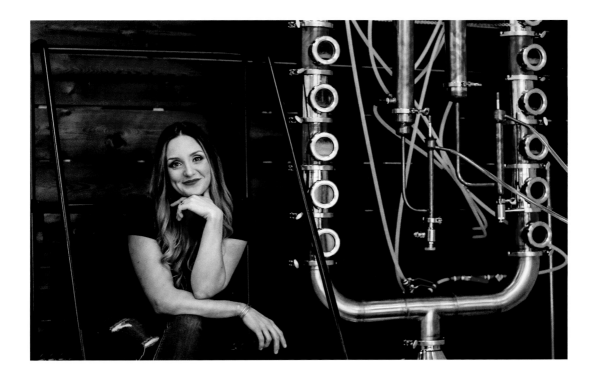

HANSEN DISTILLERY (PAGE 120): THE MISTRESS

Kris Sustrik spends more time with his still than he does with his wife, hence The Mistress.

OKANAGAN SPIRITS CRAFT DISTILLERY (PAGE 88): STILLA

Sometimes it takes time to find a name. This 1,000-litre still began life as just "her" until someone called her Stilla, and it stuck. When a bouncing 2,000-litre still with a monster 50-plate column arrived? What else but Godstilla?

AMPERSAND DISTILLING COMPANY (PAGE 49): DOT AND DASH

This distillery's pot still is Dot, and its column still is Dash. Dot resembles a period and Dash, a hyphen. "Like punctuation, they are the tools that help us shape our spirits into being, so they can be the fullest, most articulate expression," explains Jessica Schacht. "Dash is a bit in jest as well because the column runs are anything but dashed off."

TUMBLEWEED SPIRITS (PAGE 96): BIG AL AND GINGER

Workhorse still Big Al recalls a skinny, retired, chain-smoking trucker the Tumbleweed owners encountered on their path to still discovery. Let's say he's a "backwoods" distiller who gave Tumbleweed some great tips. And it's Ginger who distils their gin. ◼

GIMLI DISTILLERY
GIMLI, MB

19107 Seagram Rd.
Gimli, MB R0C 1B0
www.crownroyal.com

 @CrownRoyal

 @crownroyal

FOUNDED 1969

OWNER Diageo

STILLS Industrial columns and Coffey still

PRODUCTS Crown Royal whisky

AVAILABILITY Widely in North America
and beyond

TOURS Not offered

NEAREST NEIGHBOURS Capital K Distillery
(page 152) and Patent 5 Distillery
(page 155) — both 1 hr, 5 min

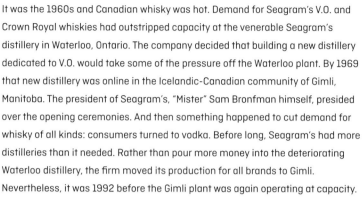

It was the 1960s and Canadian whisky was hot. Demand for Seagram's V.O. and Crown Royal whiskies had outstripped capacity at the venerable Seagram's distillery in Waterloo, Ontario. The company decided that building a new distillery dedicated to V.O. would take some of the pressure off the Waterloo plant. By 1969 that new distillery was online in the Icelandic-Canadian community of Gimli, Manitoba. The president of Seagram's, "Mister" Sam Bronfman himself, presided over the opening ceremonies. And then something happened to cut demand for whisky of all kinds: consumers turned to vodka. Before long, Seagram's had more distilleries than it needed. Rather than pour more money into the deteriorating Waterloo distillery, the firm moved its production for all brands to Gimli. Nevertheless, it was 1992 before the Gimli plant was again operating at capacity.

Seagram's was dissolved in 2000, and global spirits conglomerate Diageo took over the Gimli plant and all its brands. Late in 2018 Diageo sold Seagram's V.O. and several other brands to the Sazerac Company of New Orleans. The distillery, with its almost two million barrels of maturing whisky, is dedicated solely to Canada's bestselling whisky brand, Crown Royal.

Gimli is an unusual Canadian whisky distillery in that it mashes both single grains and US-style mash bills. One mash in particular is most interesting, and people who swear that the percentage of rye determines the flavour should take note. When a fermented mash of 64% corn, 32% rye, and 4% malted barley is distilled in a short column called a beer still, the resulting whisky tastes like bourbon. The very same mash distilled in North America's last remaining Coffey still ends up tasting like American rye whisky. Yes, it is true, in the right hands, the still really can shape the flavour of the whisky.

TASTING NOTES:
CROWN ROYAL LIMITED EDITION (40% ABV)

This whisky captures the harmony of flavours that makes Crown Royal famous worldwide. Clove-studded ripe apples lead straight into a precise nose of bourbon-vanilla notes, grain cereals, and rye spice. The sweet toffee palate is meticulous, with orange pith and peppery ginger spice that refuses to slam on the brakes through the long, creamy finish.

PATENT 5 DISTILLERY
WINNIPEG, MB

In 1869 the Dominion of Canada issued its fifth patent, this one to James Wilson for the "new and useful art of distilling whiskey" with a column still. Luckily for Wilson, his patent has been immortalized in the name of Brock Coutts's distillery.

Coutts has set up shop in the building where the former Dominion Express Company lodged its horses and wagons. Coutts has brought more history into his space by salvaging wood panels from the Oak Room of Winnipeg's once-grand St. Regis Hotel, as well as the three-metre stained-glass doors and chandeliers from its banquet room. They make an impressive backdrop for distilling gin and vodka from Manitoba wheat and barley. The even bigger story, though, is their maturing corn and single malt whisky, making it the first since a whisky-distilling drought hit Winnipeg's downtown. When? Back in 1880.

108 Alexander Ave.
Winnipeg, MB R3B 0L2
www.patent5.ca

NEAREST NEIGHBOURS **Capital K Distillery (page 152) — 15 min; Gimli Distillery (page 154) — 1 hr, 5 min**

ONTARIO

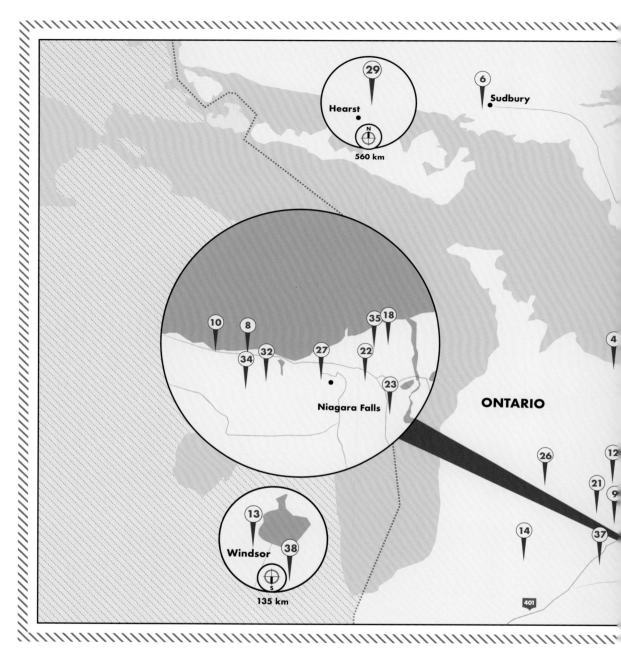

29
Hearst
6
Sudbury
N
560 km

35 18
10
8
34 32
27
22
23
Niagara Falls
ONTARIO
4
26
12
21
9
13
Windsor
38
14
37
S
135 km
401

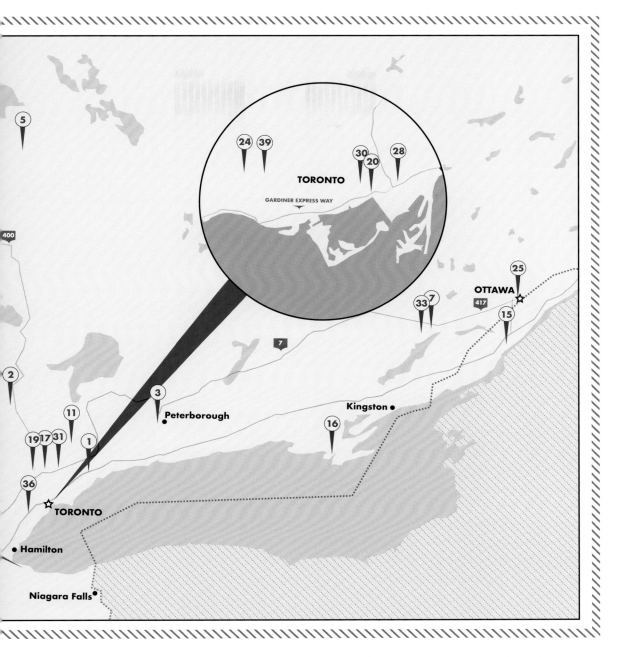

ONTARIO

The lore of Ontario's distilling roots is fraught with supposition, naive analysis, and wishful thinking. People of Scottish heritage often mention proudly that early Scottish settlers "must have" brought tiny pot stills with them. Similarly, some descendants of United Empire Loyalists have boasted how their ancestors "would have" brought distilling to Ontario when they trekked north from a nascent America. Certainly, some of these settlers did, and though small household stills were as commonplace as microwave ovens are today, not a single trace of influence from those early distillations remains. If you peel away the nostalgia, the truth reveals itself.

Distilling as an industry was already well advanced in their homelands by the time settlers began arriving in Canada, and commercial distillers did not start over at square one here. Rather, distilling today is the legacy of well-financed European, British, and American entrepreneurs who saw opportunity in the rapidly growing colony and chose to invest in large milling and distilling operations in what would become Ontario. This began to shape both the political and the economic landscapes when the province was still a British colony. As gristmills popped up, so did licences to distil—51 of them were registered by 1792. These mill-based distilleries became the largest source of government revenues by far, setting the stage for some of the biggest names in distilling's history.

In 1833, while based in Kingston, Thomas Molson ran the largest still in Upper Canada, at 4,000 litres. Four years later, Toronto's Gooderham & Worts added wooden stills, transforming their prosperous milling operation. By the mid-1850s roughly 200 distilleries in Lower and Upper Canada had purchased licences, though some of these were simply home stills. Many more operated without a licence. When an American, Hiram Walker, crossed the Detroit River into Windsor in 1856, he made his mark by launching a distillery (one that eventually would be known for its Canadian Club whisky, which would go on to sell in 155 countries). The following year, Joseph E. Seagram began working at the Waterloo distillery he would ultimately buy. Henry Corby set up shop near Belleville two years later.

Distilling in Ontario continued to see incremental growth. In 1861 Gooderham & Worts expanded from their wooden stills to two 7,000-litre copper pots capable of producing 11 million litres of spirits a year, making theirs the largest distillery on the planet. JP Wiser came on board next, purchasing Charles Payne's distillery in Prescott, and in 1893 he exhibited his Wiser's Canadian whisky at the World's Fair in Chicago. Things were going swimmingly until a series of events spiralled Ontario distilling into the ground.

In 1887 federal legislation introduced ageing requirements for whisky. To give distilleries time to adjust, this began with a minimum ageing requirement of one year in 1889, a condition that increased to two years in

1890. Whisky was the mainstay of distilling, and small operators could not afford to wait two years to see financial returns. This put all but the largest legal distilleries out of business. Prohibition, which occurred in Ontario from 1916 to 1927, and in the United States from 1920 to 1933, was disastrous for the remaining legal distillers. America had been Canada's largest market and, contrary to popular lore, Canadian distilleries struggled as their distribution channels south of the border withered. Corporate takeovers and consolidations were rife.

When the government of Ontario ended prohibition in 1927, it established its Liquor Control Board of Ontario (LCBO), along with tax legislation that further padded the province's wallet at the industry's expense. Conglomerates swallowed up some failing distilleries, while others merely closed. The LCBO had the monopoly on distribution. In 1927 the only legal liquor outlets for the entire province were the 16 stores it owned. By year's end, this had increased to 86. They also introduced a $2 permit that allowed citizens in "good standing" to purchase alcohol for home use. The permit also served a second purpose—data mining. It was a surveillance tool to track who was drinking and how much. If the LCBO suspected—or if anyone reported—that someone was overindulging or couldn't afford to drink, that person was added to a list of people barred from buying or even possessing alcohol. The fact that Indigenous people, women, and members of the lower working classes dominated that list reeks of lingering prohibition-era bigotry.

It wasn't until 1934 that hotels were allowed to sell beer and wine. Public consumption of spirits remained banned until 1947, two years after the end of World War II; only then were bars and lounges finally permitted to sell them. This, along with a booming postwar economy, opened the floodgates.

Canadian whisky was all the rage in the 1950s, 1960s, and 1970s, and under the leadership of Montreal's Seagram's Company, Canadian distilleries thrived. As many as nine large distilleries operated in Ontario—the most in any province. Among these was Brampton's brand new FBM Distillery, a rum distillery built in 1969. It seemed illogical to build a rum distillery in Ontario at the time when Canadian whisky was at a zenith, but there is a story there: shortly after the Cuban Revolution in October 1960, Castro exiled the Bacardi family, including heir Jose Alberto Bacardi. They were forced to abandon their family business—Bacardi rum. However, Jose Alberto resumed distilling his family's iconic brand, this time on Canadian soil, to great success.

During the 1980s, due to declining consumer demands, Ontario went from nine distilleries to three. To save costs, Gilbey's consolidated operations in its newly built Lethbridge, Alberta, distillery in the mid-1980s. The McGuinness distillery in Toronto closed in 1988, and Corby closed its Corbyville (Belleville) distillery in 1989, followed by the Gooderham & Worts distillery in 1990, and Seagram's Waterloo, Ontario, distillery in 1992. FBM became Bacardi-Martini Canada Inc. in 1995, gradually converting its operations from distilling to bottling rum and vodka. Canadian Mist, with its dedicated US market, and Hiram Walker, with its large range of white-spirits brands, hummed away, but no one really noticed.

With the millennium came hope of renewal for distilling in Ontario. Winemaker John K. Hall prepared the way, buying the Rieder Distillery in 1992. By 2003 he was ready for his first whisky release: Forty Creek Barrel Select. Hall began a long, personal marketing campaign that slowly turned Forty Creek (page 176) into the fastest-growing whisky brand in the province, while also making remarkable inroads in the lucrative American market. People were talking about Canadian whisky again, and hopeful entrepreneurs took notice.

In 2009 two Barrys, Bernstein and Stein, founded Still Waters Distillery (page 205) on the outskirts of Toronto to make single malt whisky. In the process they brought microdistilling back from a grave that was now grown over with post-prohibition regulations from the Alcohol and Gaming Commission of Ontario (AGCO). It was a long, discouraging struggle getting through the endless red tape, but they persevered.

Meanwhile, Ontario lawmakers were watching as legislative changes in British Columbia (page 11) created distilling jobs and directed money into the province's agricultural economy. They warmed to the idea, and the pendulum began a slow swing away from these strict regulations. Today, Ontario distilleries still pay a significantly higher tax rate than Ontario breweries and wineries, though new legislation in 2017 did lighten the load. The province now provides up to $4.42 per litre in financial relief, capped at $220,000 per producer. Distilleries can also sell their spirits by the glass, just as wineries and breweries had been doing for a decade. The "tied" house licensing regulation permitted distilleries to market their spirits in their onsite restaurants. And finally, for the first time, the LCBO authorized qualifying microdistilleries to deliver spirits directly to restaurants and bars—until July 4, 2017, they were required to distribute solely through the LCBO.

Although excessive taxes continue to throttle distillery growth compared with provinces such as British Columbia, Alberta, and Nova Scotia (and compared with wineries and breweries), the number of distilleries in Ontario is gradually coming close to matching those the province had back in 1792. Once again, this is thanks to the growth of small distilleries. While large legacy distillers still dominate the market, the small start-ups are setting the stage for the next generation of big-name Ontario distillers. Indeed, Windsor's Hiram Walker & Sons Distillery, the largest in North America, validated this return to small in 2017 when it installed a micro pot still for its own tiny-batch creations. Will microdistilling, a sector that was wiped out by government intervention more than a century ago, finally exert some influence on the spirits Ontarians enjoy? A look at liquor store shelves says, "Yes!" ■

ALL OR NOTHING
BREWHOUSE & DISTILLERY
OSHAWA, ON

In a market dominated by multimillion-dollar breweries, two brothers, Jeff and Eric Dornan, adopted a scrawny underdog of a bare-knuckle boxer named Cornelius as their brewery mascot. Just as Cornelius would have scoured a Charles Atlas bodybuilding course from a comic book in search of tips, the Dornan brothers searched for a way to make high-quality beer that no one could kick sand at. Then, in 2014, they decided to build a brewery. Shovels were ready when they learned that Oakville's Trafalgar Brewery was for sale. The Dornans bought and overhauled it, along with its meadery and distillery.

Their spirits begin with mashed two-row barley, distilled in a 5,000-litre copper pot still named Elie. A touch of unpasteurized honey in their gin adds a subtle sweetness. Their Brewer's Cold Hard Coffee is what puts the muscle in the distillery's lineup. After testing drip coffee vs. French press vs. espresso, the brothers decided that French press yielded the finest flavours. Infusing lightly filtered cold brew coffee with oak-aged Toffee Hammer Moonshine achieves a balance between black coffee and "double double." Late in 2018 All Or Nothing moved to a 1,900-square-metre former beer store in Oshawa. Cornelius notwithstanding, they are underdogs no more.

439 Ritson Rd S.
Oshawa, ON L1H 5J8
(905) 337-0133
www.allornothing.beer

 @AllorNothingBH

@allornothingbh

FOUNDED 2014

OWNERS Jeff and Eric Dornan

STILLS 5,000-litre Vendome copper pot still with 13-plate column

PRODUCTS Gin, flavoured moonshine

AVAILABILITY Onsite, online, LCBO

TOURS Contact the brewery

NEAREST NEIGHBOURS Spirit of York (page 204) and Mill Street Distillery (page 194) – 45 min; Black's Distillery (page 166) – 50 min; Frape & Sons (page 178) – 1 hr

TASTING NOTES:
ONTARIO WILD HONEY GIN BATCH 2 (40% ABV)

It's cold-infused with honey, but don't expect a haymaker of sweetness from this gin. Instead, inhale the honey's delicate floral aromas. Fresh lemon and herbal accents heighten nostalgic flavours of Fun Dip and Lik-A-Stix fruit powder. Subdued juniper on the palate becomes flowing spice tones that match up pound for pound with a finish that pops with a touch of pine.

BEATTIE'S DISTILLERS INC.
ALLISTON, ON

6673 Line 13
Alliston, ON L9R 1V4
(705) 435-2444
www.beattiesdistillers.com

 @Beattiesdistill

@beattiesdistillers

FOUNDED 2016

OWNERS Ken and Liz Beattie

STILLS 5,000-litre Kothe pot with two 42-plate copper columns

PRODUCTS Poitín, potato vodka, sweet-potato vodka

AVAILABILITY Onsite, LCBO

TOURS Informal

NEAREST NEIGHBOURS Frape & Sons (page 178) — 40 min; Barnstormer Brewing & Distilling Co. (page 291) — 45 min; Grand Spirits Distillery (page 179) — 50 min

Heading west down Line 13, just as you pass Beattie's Distillers, the rough road transitions to asphalt. How fitting: this is where potatoes paved the way for fourth-generation potato farmer Ken Beattie's distillery.

Beattie's great-grandfather Roland planted his first crop here in 1876. Lucrative contracts with potato chip companies later turned the farm into one of Canada's largest potato growers. But chipmakers have very specific needs. Every year, they rejected at least 10,000 pounds of potatoes for aesthetic reasons. This scale of waste irked Beattie because he knew that in a still, every potato was equal.

So, Beattie and his wife, Liz, visited the Prince Edward Distillery (page 276) to learn how they make potato vodka. "I gave them a tour, since I split duties between tours and helping the master distiller, Julie Shore," explains Harrison Torr, who went to university in PEI to study the history of alcohol. After graduation, Torr returned to Ontario, and that is when fate intervened. He heard about Beattie's potato vodka and dropped by, looking for an opportunity. "It was when I saw a picture of Ken on the office wall that it all hit me," recalls Torr. Ken and Liz remembered him too, and he landed the gig as Beattie's distiller that day.

Beattie's 5,000-litre Kothe pot still feeds two 42-plate copper columns that resemble NASA rockets ready to launch from the 750-square-metre distillery. "That still is a beast," laughs Torr. "It was a terrifying first run and seemed to last forever." Nevertheless, the 8,000 to 9,000 Dakota Pearl potatoes he fed into that beast came off the still as 95% pure alcohol.

Beattie's has also put Torr's university degree to work distilling a traditional Irish poitín—an aged potato moonshine-like spirit. They have also diversified their vodka lineup to include a sweet-potato spirit and gin, as their whisky ages. All thanks to that fateful first encounter that put a fourth generation of Beatties on the road to another success.

TASTING NOTES:
FARM CRAFTED POTATO VODKA
(40% ABV)

Peeling the potatoes before cooking softens this vodka's earthy flavours, which are instead creamy and buttery in texture. It's brighter than crystal, faintly sweet on the palate, with some beautiful citrus, nutty, and peppery tones. Beattie's Farm Crafted Potato Vodka is a natural for sipping.

COCKTAIL:
THE FIREFIGHTER
MAKES 1 COCKTAIL

Handful of ice cubes
1½ oz Beattie's Farm Crafted
   Potato Vodka
4 dashes Angostura Bitters
5 oz tonic water
1 lemon wedge, for garnish

Place a highball glass in the freezer until chilled, at least one hour. Once chilled, add ice and then the Farm Crafted Potato Vodka, Angostura Bitters, and tonic water. Stir well to combine, then garnish with a lemon wedge.

(Beattie's Distillers Inc.)

BLACK'S DISTILLERY
PETERBOROUGH, ON

99 Hunter St. E.
Peterborough, ON K9H 1G4
(705) 745-1500
www.blacksdistillery.com

@blacksdistillery

FOUNDED 2018

OWNERS Robert Black

STILLS 400-litre hybrid Dye still with two 15-plate columns; 100-litre Dye gin still with rectifying column

PRODUCTS Gin, vodka, unaged barley and rye spirits

AVAILABILITY Onsite, LCBO

TOURS Contact the distillery

NEAREST NEIGHBOURS Persian Empire Distillery (page 291) — 10 min; All or Nothing Brewhouse & Distillery (page 163) — 50 min

Robert Black's fondest memories of his childhood in Peterborough include school trips to Lang Pioneer Village, where he walked in the shoes of the region's first settlers. Among these settlers was one David Fife, who in 1842 introduced Red Fife wheat on his nearby farm. "That stuck with me. It is an important piece of not only Peterborough's history, but of Canadian history," declares Black.

While touring Scotland with his brother recently, the scenic romance of Islay's distilleries inspired Black. "It got a hold of me and I thought it would be really cool to do this, so I set out to learn more about the science behind distilling."

Returning to Canada, he got to work summoning the spirit of Fife. His distillery's connection with the grain is deep-seated. The farmer in nearby Douro who supplies the grain grows it in one of Fife's original fields, and both Black and Fife's ancestries go back to the Scottish Duhb clan.

As well as vodka and gin, he is also maturing whisky, cherry whisky, and a spirit made by distilling maple syrup, all to capture the flavour of Peterborough's illustrious past.

TASTING NOTES:
BLACK'S DISTILLERY GIN (40% ABV)

This gin employs depth and restraint to balance juniper with other botanicals. Within a firm structure, each botanical serves to enhance the velvety Red Fife base. Sparkling ozone is dressed in lemon, citrus, and spiced sweetness. Distinctively aromatic, with many layers merged into an elegant botanical blend.

CANADIAN MIST DISTILLERS
COLLINGWOOD, ON

In the 1960s, Canadian whisky was by far the bestselling whisky style in America. To serve the growing market, Kentucky's Barton Brands decided to bypass the intermediaries and build its own distillery, Canadian Mist Distillers. Encouraged by government incentives, Barton located its new distillery near the shores of Nottawasaga Bay in Collingwood, and Canadian Mist began distilling whisky late in 1967. Although the distillery is better known in Canada for its beefier Collingwood whiskies, the lighter Canadian Mist brand continues to sell briskly south of the border. In 1971 Barton sold Canadian Mist to Brown-Forman, another Kentucky-based whisky company.

A former Great Lakes shipbuilding town, Collingwood suffered when western grain producers switched their grain delivery to eastern markets from lake freighters to rail. Abandoned grain elevators in the once-busy harbour now shelter small recreational vessels from storms off the bay. Canadian Mist relies on local farmers to grow the corn and rye it converts into whisky. When mature, this whisky is blended at cask strength, then shipped to Kentucky in dedicated tanker trucks for bottling.

While Canadian Mist distillery is clean, bright, and well-kept, it is strictly a production facility and does not welcome visitors. Space is tight, and the pair of three-column stills that distil fermented wash "on the grains" are scalding hot. Windowless cement warehouses, connected by a network of covered internal roads, separated by berms and ditches, create the impression of being deep in the bowels of a whisky mine. And sure enough, from time to time a nugget of liquid gold emerges from that mine in the form of special new Collingwood whisky releases.

TASTING NOTES:
COLLINGWOOD CANADIAN WHISKY (40% ABV)

This inimitable whisky can be detected a mile away thanks to its expressive nose of dark cherry and aromatic rose. The palate quenches with a juicy mouthfeel filled with cherry, vanilla, and zesty rye spices. With all the oomph of a sweet sipper, this whisky feels more at home in a classic whisky cocktail.

202 MacDonald Rd.
Collingwood, ON L9Y 4J2
www.canadianmist.com and
www.collingwoodwhisky.ca

@CollingwoodWsky and
@CanadianMist

@collingwoodwhisky and
@canadian_mist_whiskey

FOUNDED 1967

OWNER Brown-Forman Company

STILLS Two custom 3-column stills

PRODUCTS Whisky

AVAILABILITY Widely in Canada and the US

TOURS No

NEAREST NEIGHBOURS Beattie's Distillers Inc. (page 164) — 55 min; Grand Spirits Distillery (page 179) — 1 hr

DAIRY DISTILLERY
ALMONTE, ON

34 Industrial Dr.
Almonte, Ontario, K0A 1A0
(613) 256-6136
www.dairydistillery.com

 @DairyDistillery

@dairydistillery

FOUNDED 2018

OWNERS Omid McDonald

STILLS 1,000-litre Carl with 19-plate column; 2,000-litre pot

PRODUCTS Cream liqueurs, milk spirit, vodka

AVAILABILITY Onsite, online, LCBO

TOURS Drop in

NEAREST NEIGHBOURS North of 7 Distillery (page 200) – 40 min; Top Shelf Distillers (page 208) – 45 min

Omid McDonald began planning his distillery in 2015, with no idea he would become a leading innovator in . . . the dairy industry. It wasn't until he met Neal McCarten, now the director of operations at the distillery, that he learned that permeate—the waste from turning milk into cheese, yogurt, and butter—was rich in lactose, a milk sugar. "Could we make spirits from milk?" they wondered. Conversations with Parmalat, a local company that processes raw milk, confirmed that disposing of permeate from their Winchester plant was a major headache and they'd be happy to have McDonald take it off their hands. Unfortunately, although standard distiller's yeast ferments other sugars into alcohol, it cannot process lactose. After much research, they learned that the inhabitants of the Central Asian Steppes had been fermenting milk into an alcoholic beverage for several millennia.

This led them to Alexandre Poulain, a University of Ottawa biology professor, who told them that in New Zealand a special yeast is used to convert milk waste into fuel alcohol. That same yeast could probably ferment permeate into beverage alcohol, they thought. Poulain asked his student, Jessica Gaudet, if she would like to find out. The result was her master's thesis and, for McDonald, spirits made entirely from milk—a process he now has down pat. After one run through the still, the spirit tastes a lot like high-abv milk. It is perfect for filling into whisky barrels. A second run turns it into an almost creamy vodka-like spirit, dubbed Vodkow. Before you groan at the (albeit witty) pun, you should know the original plan was to house Dairy Distillery in a former church and bottle the spirit as Holy Cow Vodka.

Now that he has proven the concept, McDonald talks of inviting dairy farmers to join him in a cooperative distilling venture that will not only reduce the need to dispose of milk waste, but also generate a new revenue stream for Ontario's dairy industry.

TASTING NOTES: **VODKOW** (40% ABV)

Jack would never trade his dairy cow for magic beans if he knew milk sugar could be made into vodka. The dairy essence of the spirit pops in a fresh, pearly-clean profile. Think of the silky, dreamy aromas of freshly whipped cream. A peppery sizzle late on the palate gently fades into a sparkling-clean finish accented with light traces of condensed milk.

COCTAIL:
MUDDLED MOOSSION
MAKES 1 COCKTAIL

CHAMOMILE TEA AND HONEY SYRUP:
1 chamomile tea bag
½ cup honey

COCKTAIL:
2 strawberries
Handful of ice cubes
1½ oz Vodkow
¾ oz lemon juice

For the Chamomile Tea and Honey Syrup, in a small saucepan, bring ½ cup water to a boil. Add the tea and steep for five minutes. Remove the tea bag. Add the honey and stir until dissolved. Let the syrup cool down. It will keep in the fridge for up to two weeks. To make larger batches, maintain a 1:1 ratio of tea to honey.

For the cocktail, in a shaker, gently muddle one strawberry. Add ice, Vodkow, lemon juice, and the chamomile-tea-and-honey syrup. Shake and strain into a coupe glass. Slice the remaining strawberry into a fan and use as a garnish.

(Jonny Crozier)

DILLON'S SMALL BATCH DISTILLERS
BEAMSVILLE, ON

4833 Tufford Rd.
Beamsville, ON L0R 1B1
(905) 563-3030
www.dillons.ca

 @dillonsdistills

 @dillonsdistills

FOUNDED 2012

OWNERS Geoff Dillon and Dr. Peter Dillon

STILLS 6,000-litre Christian Carl Pot still; 750-litre Christian Carl Pot still with a 23-plate columns; Headframe continuous column still

PRODUCTS Absinthe, bitters, cassis, gin, liqueurs, schnapps, vodka, vermouth, whisky, white whisky

AVAILABILITY LCBO, online, onsite, US

TOURS $5–$30, depending on depth of tour (includes tasting); daily by appointment

NEAREST NEIGHBOURS Tawse Winery and Distillery (page 208) — 5 min; Vieni Estates Inc. (page 209) — 10 min; Forty Creek Distillery (page 176) — 15 min

It's hard to believe that the large building housing Dillon's, which sits in the heart of Niagara wine country, could ever have served a different purpose. But tire marks tattooed into the floor tell the story of its evolution from a truck repair shop, acquired by distiller Geoff Dillon, into a place to tune up your taste buds.

"The dream was to make rye whisky in Canada. I always wanted to take Ontario rye and pot-distil it into whisky," says Geoff. However, since whisky needs time to mature, he started distilling gin in the summer of 2012. He played around with his first botanical mixes, intending to use 100% Ontario rye grain for the base spirit. But the German crew that built his Christian Carl pot still suggested he use readily available local grapes instead. "They kept bringing it up, grapes make the nicest base with a great mouthfeel," says Geoff. "Lucky for us, it did really well and took off. We got into making some fun fruit gins and botanical gins as well as bitters."

While the whisky he distilled early on was ageing, the business continued to change. Influenced by his father, Dr. Peter Dillon, Geoff knew he wanted to make ingredients for cocktails. Dr. Dillon is a bitters maniac with a lab at his hobby farm. His first three bitters sold well, and have since expanded to 25.

The lineup of gins has also proliferated. "That was the fun thing, experimenting and trying to push the boundaries by trying new things," says Geoff. Under the Lab Series label, he also produces a long list of limited-edition spirits, such as Black Walnut Amaro, Pear Brandy, and Cassis. Once his rye whisky matured, it too joined the ranks, followed soon after by a bottled Negroni.

This bottled Negroni marks a new direction: something that is fun and approachable. "We'll see where it takes us," says Geoff, but if the pattern holds, someday a shop will pop up with a lab out back, crafting a range of bottled cocktails in the heart of wine country.

TASTING NOTES:
RYE WHISKY—
SINGLE CASK
BATCH 76 (57.2% ABV)

Dillon's passion for rye parades through this whisky. A mash of 90% rye and 10% malted rye leads to synergies with the sweet oak. Cardamom, cinnamon, and cloves, with wild floral grasses, leap from glass to palate. Assertive with delicate nuances, like a pillow fight, except the pillows are filled with spices.

COCKTAIL:
THE GIN 22
GREYHOUND
MAKES 1 COCKTAIL

1 lime wedge
1 tbsp granulated sugar
1½ oz Dillon's Unfiltered Gin 22
4 oz fresh grapefruit juice
Splash of Aperol
4 dashes Dillon's Lime Bitters
Handful of ice cubes
1 lime wheel, for garnish

Rim a cocktail glass with the lime wedge and then the sugar. In a cocktail shaker, combine Dillon's Unfiltered Gin 22, grapefruit juice, Aperol, and bitters with ice. Shake and strain into the rimmed glass with fresh ice. Garnish with a lime wheel and serve.

(Dillon's Small Batch Distillers)

DIXON'S DISTILLED SPIRITS
GUELPH, ON

355 Elmira Rd. N., #106
Guelph, ON N1K 1S5
(519) 362-1850
www.dixonsdistilledspirits.com

🐦 @dixon_spirits

📷 @ dixonsdistilledspirits

FOUNDED 2013

OWNERS Vicky and JD Dixon, Kevin "Chevy" Patterson

STILLS Custom 2,600-litre copper pot still with a gin column, 4-plate whisky column, and two 8-plate vodka columns

PRODUCTS Gin, gin coolers, moonshine, vodka, vodka coolers, flavoured vodka, whisky

AVAILABILITY Onsite, LCBO, private liquor stores in BC and AB

TOURS Book ahead, or drop by

NEAREST NEIGHBOURS Murphy's Law Distillery Ltd. (page 196) — 25 min; Willibald Farm Distillery (page 213) — 35 min

Dixon's open-concept distillery will have your inner contemporary designer drooling long before you taste their spirits. Barrels of ageing whisky beckon you inside, where you'll find a bottle shop and tasting bar to one side, and the production floor straight ahead, flanked by fermenters and a bottling line for miniatures. Beyond, a 2,600-litre pot still and four columns—one dedicated to gin, one for whisky, and two for vodka—stand at attention, all while the room buzzes with activity.

Vicky and JD Dixon, and long-time friend Kevin "Chevy" Patterson, opened this distillery in 2015. Guelph-area farms supplied the grain, and Dixon's became one of the first distilleries to adopt the now-common practice of making spirits from scratch, using local ingredients.

The distillery established its "creds" with the release of their Ginfusion gin cooler, but it was the cooler's base spirit that attracted the spirits faithful. The trio were not really gin drinkers at the time, so the learning curve to making good gin was pretty steep. It ended up being worth the effort, as their award-winning Wicked Citrus Gin continues to garner accolades for the distillery between its whisky releases.

Patterson credits his development as a distiller to his mentor, Mike Delevante, a distilling legend with 54 years of experience, including time at Toronto's former McGuinness distillery. Patterson's Oatshine is a prime example of his interest in working both within and beyond normal conventions. "We wanted to do something unique," he says. Corn and rye spirit were dedicated to making whisky, so he selected oats for an unaged grain spirit. "The only downfall to the Oatshine is it's a little tougher to ferment. Oats have quite a bit of oil that can trap CO_2 and suffocate the yeast," explains Patterson. It's this willingness to manage such risks while pushing the boundaries that have put Dixon's in the must-try column for Canadian spirits.

TASTING NOTES: WICKED CITRUS GIN (40% ABV)
A pitchfork and forked tail on the label imply a devilish nature, but it's a respectful devilishness when sipping this gin. The refined nose hints at crisp fall spices that come to life on the palate with lemon, grapefruit, black pepper, fresh herbs, and just a touch of juniper. This gin pairs best with sunny days and ice.

FORTY CREEK DISTILLERY
GRIMSBY, ON

297 South Service Rd.
Grimsby, ON L3M 1Y6
www.fortycreekwhisky.com

 @WeAreFortyCreek

@wearefortycreek

FOUNDED 1992

OWNERS Campari Group

STILLS Custom copper pot and column

PRODUCTS Whisky, cream whisky, vodka

AVAILABILITY Widely in Canada and the US

TOURS Free; daily; groups book by appointment

NEAREST NEIGHBOURS Dillon's Small Batch Distillers (page 172) – 10 min; Tawse Winery and Distillery (page 208) – 20 min; Vieni Estates Inc. (page 209) – 20 min; Polonée Distillery Inc. (page 201) – 20 min

Bill Ashburn knows where the good stuff is hidden. He was the distiller at Grimsby's Rieder Distillery in 1992 when John K. Hall purchased the struggling eau-de-vie distillery, turning it first into Kittling Ridge winery, and then into the legendary Forty Creek Distillery. Ashburn worked for Hall for more than two decades as Hall raised the profile of Canadian whisky in Canada and the US. By making his whiskies a little bit more flavourful than those sold by the competition for the same price, Hall established Forty Creek's reputation for quality and built a following so loyal, it verges on being a cult.

When Hall first bought Reider, he and Ashburn did whatever they could to generate income. They made and sold wine, bottled spirits on contract for others, and also made a variety of novelty products. It was a good 10 years before they had whisky that Hall felt was good enough to sell. And it was. Forty Creek became one of the fastest-growing spirits brands of any kind in Canada, and next to Crown Royal, it's the Canadian whisky best known to connoisseurs in the US. All of this because of Hall's vision and his remarkable team to implement it.

In 2014 Hall sold Forty Creek distillery to Italy's Gruppo Campari. Taking the reins at the distillery was none other than Bill Ashburn, the young distiller Hall inherited when he first purchased the plant. A real hands-on type, Ashburn might be carrying bags of grain one day, driving a forklift in a company commercial another, and then sitting in a lab, blending award-winning whiskies, including the ever-so-limited Forty Creek 22-Year-Old Rye, for which he mashed one 50-pound bag of rye flour at a time. Yes, Bill Ashburn has been part of Forty Creek since before day one, and he knows every barrel by heart.

TASTING NOTES: **BARREL SELECT CANADIAN WHISKY** (40% ABV)

A nose rich in vanilla, caramel, and down-to-earth rye defines this scrumptious whisky. Waves of sweet fruits roll on to the palate with dusty rye spices and orange peels, bursting into a finish that is complemented with ginger and cinnamon heat. Hockey and maple syrup should make room for this Canadian whisky staple.

FRAPE & SONS
NEWMARKET, ON

www.frapeandsons.com

🐦 @frapeandsons

📷 @frapeandsons

FOUNDED 2015

OWNERS Justin Frape

PRODUCTS Bitters

AVAILABILITY Onsite, online, LCBO, various Ontario boutique stores

NEAREST NEIGHBOURS Last Straw Distillery (page 190) — 30 min; Still Waters Distillery (page 205) — 30 min; Beattie's Distillers Inc. (page 164) — 40 min

Justin Frape's original Thunder Bay distillery benefited from his background in corporate tax accounting and his love of cocktails. He knew that bitters were classified as non-potable, exempting them from excise tax. With Canada's cocktail movement growing by 2015, the timing was perfect to open an excise tax-free distillery. He infused aromatics into a rum-like spirit he distilled from blackstrap molasses to create seven popular bitters, and now distils single malt barley spirit for an additional three. Since moving his distillery to Newmarket in 2018, Frape has plans for a separate beverage alcohol facility, making alderwood-smoked single malt whisky and gin made with chamomile and Northern Ontario plantain.

GRAND SPIRITS DISTILLERY
GRAND VALLEY, ON

Until Ontario went dry in 1917, hotel taverns such as the Central, Dominion, and Commercial kept the Main Street strip of Grand Valley hopping. Tax-free moonshine from illicit stills in Luther Marsh on the outskirts of town ensured affordable prices. No wonder Grand Valley was the last town in Ontario to enforce prohibition laws.

One hundred years later, Sheila and Jamie Stam revived distilling in this quiet town of 3,000 when they converted an old Main Street school into one of Ontario's first tied houses. They distil spirits onsite and serve them in their adjoining speakeasy-style restaurant. During renovations, they uncovered a curious old school chalkboard hidden in one wall. On it, they saw a math problem calculating cords of wood, not bank interest. How prescient, since their distillery was not funded by bank loans but by community buy-in, with 43 equity shareholders and 340 crowd-sourced founders. Class photos donated by former students now decorate the entrance.

The distillery, bar, and restaurant work in synergy. Spirits from the distillery are served in cocktails and are used by the chef to enhance the cuisine. Try their Grand Valley Gold, a local drink made with barley grain spirit aged in quarter casks for one to three months. It's best if sipped while imagining you've arrived in a time long past, and don't have to solve complex math problems. The class of 1892 has already done that for you.

(continued)

27 Main St. N.
Grand Valley, ON L9W 5S6
(519) 928-9696
www.grandspirits.com

@grandspiritsdistillery

FOUNDED 2017

OWNERS Sheila and Jamie Stam

STILLS 460-litre Still Dragon pot still with 12-plate column

PRODUCTS Gin, grain spirit, vodka, whisky

AVAILABILITY Onsite and online

TOURS Contact the distillery

NEAREST NEIGHBOURS Pepprell Distilling Co. (page 201) — 35 min; Murphy's Law Distillery Ltd. (page 196) — 45 min; Beattie's Distillers Inc. (page 164) — 50 min

TASTING NOTES:
SCHOOL SPIRIT
REAL BARLEY VODKA
(40% ABV)

This is the kind of vodka that would be caught smoking in the boys' bathroom. It replaces excessive polish with down-to-earth cooked barley cereal flavour, marshmallow, and plenty of white-pepper heat. Purists may scoff, but this is one vodka that isn't afraid to settle it old school at recess.

COCKTAIL:
TOFFEE APPLE FAIR
MAKES 1 COCKTAIL

Handful of ice cubes
1½ oz School Spirit Vodka
½ oz Licor 43
5 generous dashes Bittered Sling
   Lem-Marrakech Bitters
Apple slice, for garnish

Add the ice, School Spirit Vodka, Licor 43, and the bitters to a mixing glass and stir until chilled. Strain into a coupe glass, then garnish with an apple slice.

(Jamie Stam)

HIRAM WALKER & SONS DISTILLERY
WALKERVILLE, ON

In 1858 Hiram Walker, a Detroit grocer, whisky rectifier/compounder, and grain dealer, built a flour mill and distillery on 190 hectares of land in what is now Windsor, Ontario. Pro-temperance sentiments in America made distilling a risky investment at home in Detroit. By the time he died, in 1899, Walker had made his fortune selling his Canadian Club whisky right around the world. The town he built to house his employees was named Walkerville, in his honour.

Walker did not live to see Prohibition enacted in the US. However, his grandson, Harrington Walker, who was running the distillery by that time, succumbed to Protestant disdain for alcohol and sold the family-owned distillery to Harry Hatch in 1926. The Hatch family rebuilt and expanded it in the 1950s, leaving the old Florentine palace that was Walker's office as the only remaining original building. Since 2005 Corby Spirit and Wine Ltd. has operated the distillery on behalf of current owner Pernod Ricard.

A renewal of the Hiram Walker blending program, which came with the appointment in 2012 of Dr. Don Livermore as master blender, has helped reinvigorate consumer interest in Canadian whisky (page 185). Each fall, he augments a range of connoisseur whiskies called the Northern Border Collection with high-end limited editions of the core bottlings: Gooderham & Worts, Pike Creek, Lot No. 40, and Wiser's. Rigorous wood-management practices implemented by Livermore, whose doctorate examined the interactions between barrel wood and maturing whisky, have enhanced maturation practices. As well, a move to use only Ontario-grown grain when it is available, and a switch to hybrid rye and commercial enzymes rather than malted rye, have increased consistency without compromising flavour.

With all the excitement about its whiskies, it is easy to forget that Hiram Walker produces a broad range of other spirits, including vodka, gin, and the poolside favourite: coconut-flavoured Malibu Rum. It also distils a number of well-known whisky brands for others, including Gibson's Finest.

(continued)

2072 Riverside Dr. E.
Walkerville (Windsor), ON N8Y 4S5
www.corby.ca

 @CorbySW

@corbysw

FOUNDED 1858

OWNERS Pernod Ricard

STILLS Custom columns, Vendome pots

PRODUCTS Cordials, gin, liqueurs, rum, whisky, vodka

AVAILABILITY Widely in North America and abroad

TOURS Visitor centre

NEAREST NEIGHBOURS Wolfhead Distillery (page 215) — 25 min

TASTING NOTES:
JP WISER'S
18 YEAR OLD (40% ABV)

This rich expression is almost entirely corn whisky. Those rye notes? you ask. They develop sans rye as the whisky slowly soaks up everything the oak has to offer. Immensely intricate on both the nose and the palate, with vanilla, cedar, lumber, peppery rye, prunes, and other dried fruits. A classic citrus pith finish invites another sip.

COCKTAIL: TRINITY
BELLWOODS

MAKES 1 COCKTAIL

4 lemon wedges
6–8 mint leaves
¼ oz simple syrup
2 oz Gooderham & Worts Canadian Whisky
¼ oz Fernet
3 dashes Bittered Sling Lem-Marrakech Bitters
Handful of ice cubes
Crushed ice
Fresh mint sprig, for garnish

Muddle the lemon, mint, and simple syrup in the base of a cocktail shaker. Add the whisky, Fernet, bitters, and a handful of ice. Shake well for five to six seconds, until blended. Add crushed ice to an Old Fashioned glass. Fine-strain the cocktail into the glass, and garnish with a sprig of mint.

[Dave Mitton]

THE DOCTOR IS IN
MEET DON LIVERMORE

When the spirits at Hiram Walker & Sons Distillery need a checkup, they are sent to the doctor's office. Cabinets lined with bottles serve as Dr. Don Livermore's waiting room. Pick one up randomly, and there's a good chance you are holding an award winner—a testament to what the doctor and his blending team have achieved. But it's not the awards and glittering medals that motivate him. Rather, it's a natural curiosity, one that others nurtured in him from a young age.

Schoolwork saved by Livermore's mother points to everyday aspirations such as becoming a firefighter. However, those dreams flickered out in Mr. Weber's Grade 10 biology class. Instead, Weber kindled Livermore's inquisitive nature, guiding him toward a career in microbiology. Then, in 1996, a friend whose father worked at Hiram Walker tipped Livermore off to a lab position there. He applied and got the job. "I got my affinity for Canadian whisky under the tutelage of previous blenders, scientists, and engineers here. I really got into the whisky-making process at that moment," says Livermore.

One of the challenges of distilling at that time was figuring out how to boost alcohol levels in a mash. While attending alcohol school during his freshman year at the distillery, a light bulb went on over his head, like Wile E. Coyote realizing how to catch the Road Runner. Returning to work, he began to analyze the distillery's processes, including tracking fermentation data. Yeast management offered the potential for improvement, he thought, and so he began to work on what would become his proudest accomplishment.

At that time, it was a full day's work to get a complete mock-up analysis of a fermenter. Livermore remembered that while he was attending a conference presentation about a concept straight out of the Acme catalogue: near infrared reflectance, a method used to measure organic material for incoming grain. Connecting the dots, he asked, what if this NIR technology could measure the sugar, alcohol, and acids in fermenting mash? In 1998 he calibrated an NIR machine to do just that, and presto! He was able to analyze a fermenter in 30 seconds. This lightning-quick process made it possible to work on raising alcohol production from 9% to 13%. Today, the distillery is fermenting to between 16% and 17% alcohol. Livermore wrote about his adapted NIR technique in the fourth edition of *The Alcohol Textbook*, and by 2003 it had been adopted by distilleries across the globe.

PhD studies followed at Heriot-Watt University in Edinburgh, where he quantified the ageing process of whisky in wood. After defending his doctoral thesis in March 2012, he was promoted to master blender. It was a good week for Livermore, leading to good years for spirits lovers. "I'm not standing still," he says when asked about the future. "What's driven me is how do you make spirits better and find that perfect blend of science and creativity. That's never going to change."

Thank heavens! ■

JUNCTION 56 DISTILLERY
STRATFORD, ON

45 Cambria St.
Stratford, ON N5A 1G8
(519) 305-5535
www.junction56.ca

🐦 @Junction_56

📷 @junction56distillery

FOUNDED 2015

OWNER Mike Heisz

STILLS Artisan Still Designs hybrid pot-column system with 4-plate whisky column and 16-plate vodka column

PRODUCTS Gin, liqueurs, moonshine, vodka, whisky

AVAILABILITY Onsite and LCBO

TOURS By appointment

NEAREST NEIGHBOURS Pepprell Distilling Co. (page 201) — 45 min; Willibald Farm Distillery (page 213) — 50 min; Murphy's Law Distillery Ltd. (page 196) — 50 min

On June 6, 1939, when King George VI and Queen Elizabeth were touring across Canada, neither royal ventured out to meet the waiting crowd when their train stopped in Stratford. The royal couple was fond of a tipple, and among the regal provisions were two cases of Crown Royal. Perhaps, as Shakespeare once wrote, they had drunk themselves out of their five senses? Whatever their reason, it's too bad. They could have toured the future home of Junction 56 Distillery. Junction 56, founded by Mike Heisz, is named after Stratford's origins around the same railway junction in 1856.

Heisz is no stranger to alcohol. His great-great-great-grandfather owned and operated the former Formosa Brewery. But it wasn't beer that inspired him. "I was at a Canadian whisky tasting, and afterwards I turned to a friend and said, 'We should make a barrel of whisky,'" he explains. "The whole point of opening up a distillery was to move into whisky." When he was scouting locations, he was drawn to the architectural bones of that building along the tracks—as if a 1939 whisky was beckoning.

Like so many others, before he tackled whisky, Heisz began with gin. For four months he went through every botanical, comparing the flavour differences when macerating them versus infusing them in a gin basket. When his attention turned to whisky, Heisz began with a mash bill of corn, wheat, rye, barley, rye malt, and barley malt. He first barrelled it in once-used 56-litre bourbon barrels. Then, after two years, he blended the product with rye whisky he was ageing separately, and transferred this blend into standard 200-litre barrels. When the first 800 bottles were released in November 2018, they sold out faster than a passing train. Fear not: more whisky is ageing, with staggered releases planned until the inventory can support a permanent Stratford brand fit for any passing king and queen.

TASTING NOTES: JUNCTION 56 CANADIAN WHISKY (40% ABV)

Quality grains are on full display as Junction 56 masterfully integrates all those cereal flavours onto a single track. Fresh-cut straw, wildflowers, cereals, doughy bread, a touch of sweet caramel, and some early vanilla oak influence sit on the palate. Rye grain makes a breakthrough on the sizzling finish.

COCKTAIL: BR GIN FIZZ

MAKES 1 COCKTAIL

- Handful of ice cubes
- 2 oz Junction 56 Black Raspberry Gin
- 1 oz lemon juice
- ½ oz simple syrup
- 4 oz club soda

In a collins glass, combine all of the ingredients over ice. Lightly stir to combine.

(Junction 56 Distillery)

KING'S LOCK CRAFT DISTILLERY
JONESTOWN, ON

5 Newport Dr. #1
Johnstown, ON K0E 1T1
(613) 704-2529
www.klcraftdistillery.ca

[O] @kingslock

FOUNDED 2016

OWNERS Laura Bradley and Rob Heuval

STILLS 2,000-litre Koethe with two 29-plate columns; 500-litre Dayou with 4-plate and 20-plate columns

PRODUCTS Gin, moonshine, rum, vodka, flavoured vodka, white whisky, whisky spirit

AVAILABILITY Onsite, online, LCBO, Alberta

TOURS Informal, with tasting

NEAREST NEIGHBOURS North of 7 Distillery (page 200) — 1 hr; Dairy Distillery (page 170) — 1 hr, 10 min

Laura Bradley has a nose for gin. When she and her husband, Rob Heuval, launched King's Lock Craft Distillery in 2016, they quickly learned that when it comes to making great gin, Laura has the knack. She knows exactly when the cut is right, and this is why Rob won't distil gin without her. "The end is so important," says Heuval. "The oils come over at the end." Heuval, on the other hand, has a nose for garlic. They can't keep up with demand for his garlic vodka.

Bradley, an electrical engineer, also understands the science and mechanics, while Heuval, a farmer, has practical experience in land husbandry. Together they decided to open a distillery when they were unable to find organic spirits for sale in Canada. Although they arrived at it from very different directions, they have adopted an ethos of doing what is natural and right for the land. And so their spent grains are spread on fields as fertilizer, they recover their water for heating, and they buy enough solar-generated electricity that the distillery is a completely carbon-neutral operation. Heuval grows organic rye for the distillery on his farm. Other organic grains come from local farms too. Given Canada's climate, they import organic cane sugar for their Thousand Islands Shine and Gold Smuggler's Rum.

King's Lock Craft Distillery is a stone's throw from the St. Lawrence River, across from Ogdensburg, New York, and just down the road from Prescott, where JP Wiser earned his stripes as a whisky maker. There is a long whisky-making tradition in this part of Ontario, as reflected in historical artifacts that Heuval displays in the shop and tasting room. True to tradition, Heuval makes Prescott White and Whiskyjack Ryes. They're tasty and fun, but do yourself a favour and include a dram of Laura's devastatingly scrumptious Conestoga Gin in your tasting flight.

TASTING NOTES: **CANADA'S WHISKYJACK RYE** (40% ABV)
Made from organic rye grain, distilled, then aged on oak chips; so, despite its whisky-like character, this spirit isn't really whisky. Spiced nuts balance toffee accents that lead into a semi-sweet palate where the rye spices take wild flight. Hot cinnamon candy hearts wake up the mouth before the palate shifts to lumber and wood shavings in a long, dry finish.

KINSIP HOUSE OF FINE SPIRITS
BLOOMFIELD, ON

Jeremiah Soucie knows a thing or two about terroir. His Kinsip House of Fine Spirits, in the heart of Prince Edward County, sits squarely in the middle of 45 wineries. No one questions terroir in wine, and Soucie is convinced that by using grain from the 32-hectare distillery farm and its neighbours, his spirits will taste of "The County" too. With an operation as small as Kinsip, he can emphasize characteristics that get averaged out in larger distilleries that buy grain from many sources. "Will we start releasing whiskies with an age statement and also a vintage?" he wonders enthusiastically, noting that he also harvests local juniper berries for his Juniper's Wit Gin.

While they had planned to build their own distillery from scratch, in 2016 Soucie and his wife, Sarah Waterston, her brother Michael Waterston, and his wife, Maria Hristova, instead bought the former 66 Gilead Distillery—a microdistillery founded in 2010 by Toronto physicians Sophia Pantazi and her husband, Peter Stroz. This purchase spared them the aggravation of endless government approvals and allowed them to distil from day one, even as they focused on developing their business. By year two they were putting their own systems and processes in place, and in year three they turned to growth and expansion. Three full-time distillers now keep the distillery running seven days a week. As well, Pete and Marla Bradford have reopened the onsite cooperage.

The bucolic setting of Kinsip, with its one-of-a-kind, First Empire–style brick house and rustic outbuildings, makes a peaceful stop for visitors to Prince Edward County. Sample the full range of spirits in the tasting room, if that is your fancy. If you wander the grounds instead, you may stumble on the Bradfords charring a barrel in a burst of flames. And failing that, you can always count on being entertained by a flock of funky heritage chickens.

66 Gilead Rd.
Bloomfield, ON K0K 1G0
(613) 393-1890
www.kinsip.ca

🐦 @DrinkKinsip

📷 @kinsipspirits

FOUNDED 2009 (as 66 Gilead Distillery)

OWNERS Jeremiah Soucie, Sarah Waterston, Michael Waterston, Maria Hristova

STILLS 1,100-litre Koethe

PRODUCTS Bitters, brandy, cassis, gin, aged gin, rum, shochu, aged shochu, vodka, whisky, maple whisky

AVAILABILITY Onsite, online, LCBO, Quebec, Alberta

TOURS Tasting room, daily, 10 a.m.– 5 p.m. (check winter hours); formal tours Saturday & Sunday (advance booking required)

NEAREST NEIGHBOURS Black's Distillery (page 166) and Persian Empire Distillery (page 291) – both 1 hr, 35 min; King's Lock Craft Distillery (page 188) – 2 hrs

TASTING NOTES: COOPER'S REVIVAL
CANADIAN RYE WHISKY (42% ABV)

Recoopered red wine barrels from Pete Bradford's cooperage next door polish the flavours of this all-Canadian rye. The hefty chiselled bottle pours a whisky that overflows with fresh floral rye, aromatic fruits, and smidgens of fruity grapes. A lustre on the whisky's palate, with its warm maple sugar accents, begs for sipping with a chunk of ice the size of a cooper's biceps.

LAST STRAW DISTILLERY
CONCORD, ON

40 Pippin Rd., #9
Concord, ON L4K 4M6
(416) 564-5971
www.madebyhand.laststrawdistillery.com

 @LastStrawDistil

@laststrawdistill

FOUNDED 2015

OWNERS Don DiMonte, Ana Simoes, Mike Hook

STILLS 600-litre Affordable Distillery Equipment pot still with column; Still Dragon spirit still; 50-litre Genio still

PRODUCTS Blackstrap spirit, gin, moonshine, aged moonshine, rum, vodka, whisky

AVAILABILITY Onsite, online, LCBO, bars

TOURS Monday–Friday, 11 a.m.–6 p.m.; Saturday, 12–5 p.m.; groups by appointment

NEAREST NEIGHBOURS Magnotta Distillery (page 193) — 5 min; Still Waters Distillery (page 205) — 10 min; Nickel 9 Distillery (page 198) — 25 min

Don DiMonte and his wife, Ana Simoes, were busy even before they began distilling. DiMonte ran a construction company and was on call 24/7, while Simoes had a career in law. In 2011, while researching microbrewing, DiMonte's love of spirits steered him to the door of Still Waters Distillery (page 205), where he met distillery co-owner Barry Stein. That visit changed his life.

In 2015 DiMonte, Simoes, their sons, Brandon and Freddie, and family friend Mike Hook opened Last Straw Distillery. There, they produce gin and vodka while exploring innovative ways to make aged spirits. One experiment began with Last Straw lending barrels to the Lake Wilcox brewery to age beer in. "I suggested, why don't they make one of their beers, but not carbonate it," says DiMonte. "I would distil it into a spirit, then put it into a used bourbon barrel and age it into whisky. After it's bottled, I'd give back the barrel so they could age the same beer in it."

Soon, other breweries wanted in. Now, when Last Straw distils brewer's unusable beer into spirit, DiMonte lets the brewery decide whether it should go into a barrel or be made into vodka or gin. Beer that breweries were going to toss now gets a second chance. "It's cool not knowing what these beer spirits will produce; it's adventurous."

It's not all wild-eyed experimentation at Last Straw. DiMonte still lays down rye and malt spirits in a variety of barrels, and he is also working with wheat bran, Argentinian long-grain rice, a combination of rice and rye, and malted and unmalted corn. It may be some time before he can taste the results, but DiMonte is patient; he'll let the barrels guide him as he monitors these spirits while they mature.

TASTING NOTES:
DARKER SIDE CASK 6
(45.5% ABV)

The crew at Last Straw don't cook the corn for this spirit; they bathe it in hot water. It's fermented after adding sugar, distilled, and then aged in oak, all for a sophisticated, resolved palate. Inviting barrel char, buttery maple toffee, roasted cornhusks, boiled cobs, and black pepper transition from the nose to palate. A mellow burn, guaranteed to put a smile on your face, follows a snap of caramelized sugar on the finish.

COCKTAIL:
THE VAUGHAN
MAKES 1 COCKTAIL

Handful of ice cubes
2 oz Darker Side of the Moonshine
¼ oz Fernet-Branca
½ oz dark maple syrup
2 dashes Angostura Orange Bitters
1 lemon twist, for garnish

Place a coupe in the freezer until chilled, at least one hour. Add ice to a mixing glass. Pour in all of the ingredients and stir for 40 seconds. Strain into the chilled coupe glass and garnish with a lemon twist.

(Mike Hook)

LIMITED DISTILLERY
NIAGARA-ON-THE-LAKE, ON

14 Henegan Rd.
Niagara-on-the-Lake, ON L0S 1J0
(289) 272-0611
www.limiteddistillery.com

🐦 @LTDDistillery

📷 @limiteddistillery

FOUNDED 2018

OWNERS Jenna Miles and Danny Keyes

STILLS 660-litre HBS pot with four-plate column; 100-litre HBS pot with six-plate column

PRODUCTS Liqueur, moonshine, flavoured moonshine, white rum

AVAILABILITY Onsite

TOURS Check website

NEAREST NEIGHBOURS Wayne Gretzky Estate Winery & Distillery (page 210) – 5 min; Niagara College Distillery (page 197) – 10 min; Niagara Falls Craft Distillers (page 197) – 20 min; Polonée Distillery Inc. (page 201) – 20 min

TASTING NOTES:
JALAPENO MOONSHINE BATCH 5 (45% ABV)

The LTD crew infused wheat and corn sour mash moonshine with fresh jalapenos to construct this jade-coloured spirit. On the nose, it is as if a loaf of jalapeno cornbread was put through a Jack LaLanne Power Juicer. Sensationally fresh, spicy, bready, and funky, it fully captures every morsel of flavour and heat from the peppers.

Jenna Miles's and Danny Keyes's distillery may be the first on the planet to operate from a record store. The two are proprietors of SRC Vinyl, an online record emporium that runs its brick-and-mortar shop from the distillery. Located in the middle of Ontario's Niagara wine country, there is plenty of wild yeast in the air. Come spring, Miles and Keyes throw the receiving doors open and let siren songs from the record store lure that yeast into open-top Cypress fermenters. There, it ferments a mash that will be distilled into white rum, infused moonshine, or traditional grain moonshine. Small batches of mature rye and rum are next.

MAGNOTTA DISTILLERY
VAUGHAN, ON

The slogan for Canada's Wonderland may be "Thrills Connect," but the real thrills are a 10-minute drive south. Here, you'll find Magnotta Winery's massive production facility, complete with a distillery and its flagship retail store. Rossana Magnotta and her late husband, Gabe, founded their winery in 1988, and only two years later the LCBO notified them that their products would be "delisted" due to a lack of shelf space. Instead of calling it quits, they opened this Vaughan shop, followed by several other Ontario locations so that they could sell their wine themselves. They added the distillery in 1996. Although it isn't open for tours, its spirits are available in the retail shop. For their three luxurious ice grappas, Magnotta thaws the frozen skins of Riesling, Cabernet Franc, or Vidal ice wine grapes, then ferments and distils them in a Charentais-style alembic still. It was Magnotta, incidentally, who bought Kittling Ridge winery from John K. Hall (page 176) in 2013.

271 Chrislea Rd.
Vaughan, ON L4L 8N6
(905) 738-9463
www.magnottadistillery.com

⟨○⟩ @magnottawinery

Founded 1988 (winery), 1996 (distillery)

OWNER Rossana Magnotta

PRODUCTS Brandy, eau-de-vie, gin, ice grappa, vodka

AVAILABILITY Onsite, LCBO

TOURS Daily, by appointment (email events@magnotta.com)

NEAREST NEIGHBOURS Last Straw Distillery (page 190) — 5 min; Still Waters Distillery (page 205) — 15 min

TASTING NOTES: VIDAL ICE GRAPPA (45% ABV)

A fragrant spirit bursting with grappa's distinct fruit-forward signature. Rich Vidal tropical fruits and traces of nail polish on the nose. The palate delivers a burst of sweetness as fruits like lychee come to the forefront. Mild cinnamon hearts devolve into a peppery finish, with floral notes overpowering the tropical fruits.

MILL STREET DISTILLERY
TORONTO, ON

21 Tank House Lane
Toronto, ON M5A 3C4
www.millstreetbrewery.com

 @MillStreetBrew

 @millstreetbrew

FOUNDED Brewery 2002, distillery 2012

OWNERS Labatt Brewing Company

STILLS 1,000-litre and 5,000-litre Kothe water bath pot stills

PRODUCTS Bierschnaps, gin, whisky

AVAILABILITY Onsite

TOURS Tasting room

NEAREST NEIGHBOURS Spirit of York Distillery Co. (page 204) — 2 min (on foot); Reid's Distillery (page 202) — 5 min; Yongehurst Distillery Co. (page 217) — 20 min

In 1831 British immigrants William Gooderham and James Worts built what would become the world's largest distillery in the east end of the Town of York (now called Toronto). When Ontario's prohibition ended in 1927, new owners added another maturing warehouse called Rack House M. The historic distillery closed for good in 1990, as its brands had already moved to Hiram Walker & Sons Distillery (page 181) in Windsor, where they could be produced more economically. Then, in 2003, Mill Street Brewery took up residence amid a dusty mash of reconstruction during a massive "Distillery District" restoration project.

Rack House M is now the Mill Street Beer Hall. There, tucked behind explosion-proof glass, visitors can admire a gleaming distillery. Mill Street installed two Kothe water bath pot stills from Germany and handed the keys to distiller Kaitlin Vandenbosch. If only it were that simple. This was the first time in nearly a century that the City of Toronto had licensed a new distillery, and the red tape was both well entrenched and endless. Finally, on May 1, 2013, the first spirits flowed to make bierschnaps, reviving the district's distilling heritage and bringing a craft back to one of the places where it began.

Current distiller Martha Lowry brewed beer for 18 months before taking on Vandenbosch's role in February 2016. Lowry studied horticulture at the University of Guelph and has developed a sixth sense for how botanicals interact, as demonstrated in Mill Street's first pair of gins. To maintain the brewery aesthetic, Lowry introduced citra hops among the 10 botanicals for her Citrus Gin, and El Dorado hops for her Botanical Gin.

Being in Gooderham's old stomping grounds, Mill Street has also resurrected whisky. Mill Street's annual single-barrel whisky release has also transitioned to Lowry's spirit. She works with a mixture of malts and a variety of yeasts, laying down barrels of whisky in new American oak and ex-bourbon barrels between batches of gin.

TASTING NOTES:
MILL STREET SINGLE MALT CASK SAMPLE
(60.93% ABV)

This two-year-old preview of Martha Lowry's first whisky cask displays promising signs of substance for her Canadian single malt program. Calm spices, balanced by a pinch of confectioner's sugar, accent creamy cereal notes on the palate. Soft and sweet caramel floats dreamily on a bed of young oak.

COCKTAIL:
BICKFORD PARK
MAKES 1 COCKTAIL

Handful of ice cubes
1 oz Mill Street Small Batch Citrus Craft Gin
¾ oz dry vermouth
½ oz Amaro Nonino
½ oz lemon juice
½ oz honey syrup
1 lemon twist, for garnish

Place a coupe glass in the freezer until chilled, at least one hour. Combine the ice, gin, dry vermouth, Amara Nonino, lemon juice, and honey syrup in a shaker. Shake, then strain into the chilled coupe glass. Garnish with a lemon twist.

(Martha Lowry)

MURPHY'S LAW DISTILLERY LTD.
ELMIRA, ON

90 Earl Martin Dr.
Elmira, ON N3B 2P5
(519) 669-2500
www.murphyslawmoonshine.com

🐦 @MurphysLawShine

📷 @murphyslawmoonshine

FOUNDED 2015

OWNERS Ben and Sullivan Murphy

STILLS 1,100-litre Dye pot still with nine-plate column

PRODUCTS Moonshine, flavoured moonshine

AVAILABILITY Onsite, online, LCBO

TOURS By appointment

NEAREST NEIGHBOURS Dixon's Distilled Spirits (page 174) — 25 min; Pepprell Distilling Co. (page 201) — 30 min

There are two traits every moonshiner needs: an excellent nose for proper spirit cuts, and a runner's endurance in case the authorities catch wind. Distillery founder Ben Murphy fostered these skills as a student on a cross-country athletic scholarship at Ohio Valley University in West Virginia. The school was dry, and when Murphy asked members of the track team where he could get beer, a teammate introduced him to moonshine instead. Murphy loved it. The pair went from running laps to running shine. While Murphy spent the next four years studying toward a bachelor of science, he ran a still in his student apartment, earning him an unofficial minor in potable inebriants.

Murphy aspired to a career in law enforcement, but during a boxing match he sustained permanent unilateral hearing loss when he took a punch to the right ear. Trust Murphy's Law! So, when he returned to Canada after graduation, he put his university education to work by partnering with his brother, Sullivan, to open Murphy's Law Distillery.

Murphy's Law focuses on traditional moonshine rather than vodka, gin, or whisky. The Murphys ferment locally grown corn with sugar and then feed the mash straight into the still's columns, running off at 80% abv. From this base spirit, they make about a dozen traditional and flavoured moonshines, including Apple Pie, Maple Cream, and White Lightnin'. The Mason jars they bottle their shine in are emblazoned with a 1948 K-series International Harvester pickup truck. The rugged 1948 K was known for its strong suspension, an important feature when running a moonshine distillery this far north of the Mason-Dixon line. And the quality? There's more than just white lightnin' in the back of that truck. Some of Murphy's moonshine is so indulgent, it warrants a set of whitewall tires on the old pickup.

TASTING NOTES: **WHITE LIGHTNIN'** (40% ABV)

This is the real deal for those looking to be struck by lightnin'. Authentic moonshine that tastes like it's from the backwoods of the Appalachian Mountains, yet refined like the moonshiner has a full set of teeth. The cut includes a drop of tails from the distillation run that amplifies the buttery corn and vanilla top-dressing on the palate. Just when you think it's pretty smooth, a thunderbolt of fiery burn reminds you of its roots.

NIAGARA COLLEGE DISTILLERY
NIAGARA-ON-THE-LAKE, ON

135 Taylor Rd.
Niagara-on-the-Lake, ON L0S 1J0
www.niagaracollege.ca

NEAREST NEIGHBOURS Polonée Distillery Inc. (page 201) — 20 min; Niagara Falls Craft Distillers (page 197) — 20 min

No more teachers, no more books, no more spirits . . . this may be the first time in history that students dread the last day of school. Niagara College opened its Teaching Distillery, the first in Canada in 2018. A small batch of students studied all facets of distilling with the school's distiller, David Dickson, the former head distiller at Dillon's Small Batch Distillers (page 172). Coursework included selling the spirits made in the school's five stills in the college's Wine Visitor and Education Centre.

For the first release, a Gamay Noir from the college's wine program was distilled using three distillation methods to create eau-de-vie. It was a huge accomplishment, and the resulting spirit is already a collector's item, selling out. But fear not: with the next fall semester coming, more school spirit is on the way.

NIAGARA FALLS CRAFT DISTILLERS
NIAGARA FALLS, ON

8699 Stanley Ave.
Niagara Falls, ON L2G 0A9
(289) 477-1022
www.niagarafallscraftdistillers.com

🐦 @NFCraftDistill

📷 @nfcraftdistillers

FOUNDED 2016

OWNERS Chris Jeffries and Ian Kowalchuk

PRODUCTS Gin, vodka, whisky

AVAILABILITY Onsite, LCBO

TOURS Drop in or call ahead

NEAREST NEIGHBOURS Niagara Distillery (page 291) — 10 min; Wayne Gretzky Estate Winery & Distillery (page 210) — 15 min; Limited Distillery (page 192) — 15 min

Still master Chris Jeffries had brewed beer in Niagara Falls for 18 years before he joined his business manager, Ian Kowalchuk, in launching a distillery in 2016. Jeffries knew that 30 million people visit Niagara Falls each year, and typically, they take home a lot of souvenirs. So he includes three litres of Niagara Falls mist in each batch of their whisky and five-times-distilled grain vodka. Extra-thick copper for the custom still ensures longevity, while full automation allows Jeffries to control distillations using an app on his phone. They distil their own products from scratch, while spirits produced on contract for others use sourced grain neutral spirits.

NICKEL 9 DISTILLERY
TORONTO, ON

90 Cawthra Ave. #100
Toronto, ON M6N 3C2
(647) 341-5959
www.nickel9distillery.com

 @nickel9spirits

[IG] @nickel9distillery

FOUNDED 2016

OWNERS Chris Jacks and Harris
Hadjicostis

STILLS Hybrid six-column still; 750-litre
gin still with spirit still

PRODUCTS Apple spirits, bitters,
 brandy, gin

AVAILABILITY Onsite, online, LCBO

TOURS Call

NEAREST NEIGHBOURS Yongehurst
Distillery Co. (page 217) — 10 min; Spirit
of York Distillery Co. (page 204) —
25 min; Mill Street Distillery (page 194)
— 25 min

William Horace Temple, best known as "Temperance Willie," was still a child early in the 20th century when dry communities west of Toronto amalgamated with the larger city. Residents of these neighbourhoods insisted that alcohol sales remain banned. As an adult, Temple founded the Inter-Church Temperance League to fiercely uphold that ban. He died in 1988. By the millennium, Toronto's last dry neighbourhood, the Junction, staggered out of Temple's influence when, by referendum, it finally allowed the sale of alcohol.

Chris Jacks and Harris Hadjicostis started distilling and selling their Junction-made apple spirits on July 1, 2016, as Northern Temple Spirit and Hidden Temple Gin—both respectful nods to Temperance Willie. Jacks and Hadjicostis pump fresh apple juice into fermenters from a tanker, then ferment and distil it into spirits. These include a small-batch brandy called Golden Temple.

Cocktail fans who congregate regularly at the distillery have a special reason to visit during Pride Week. Their Signature Queen Cocktail Series features cocktails that celebrate prominent Toronto drag queens. "Working as a bartender in the Toronto Village, I was surrounded by some of Toronto's most amazing LGBTQ performers," says Nickel 9 representative Michael Pez, who worked with these performers to capture their essences in drinks. The series evokes not only drag queens, but also strong female personas. If Eve was the first to take a bite of the apple, Pez wisely takes what was "pleasant and desirable" fiercely to the next level.

TASTING NOTES: NORTHERN TEMPLE PREMIUM CANADIAN SPIRITS (40% ABV)

A glass-corked bottle is the sanctuary for this stunning spirit brimming with traces of fresh orchard apples and juicy textures. Its softness can also snap on the palate, capturing an apple's crunch with slick vodka-like cleanliness. Although redistilled several times, Northern Temple has not sacrificed flavour to get there.

COCKTAIL:
THE PARTY FOR TWO
MAKES 1 COCKTAIL

SMOKED APPLE SYRUP:
3 McIntosh apples, skins on,
   quartered
4½ cups water
2½ cups sugar
¼ cinnamon stick
⅛ tsp plus ¼ tsp cloves

COCKTAIL:
Handful of ice cubes
1 oz Northern Temple
1 oz Hidden Temple Gin
2½–3 oz ginger ale
1 toasted marshmallow, for garnish

For the Smoked Apple Syrup, smoke the apples with hickory in a wood smoker for two hours. In a large pot, combine the water, smoked apples, sugar, cinnamon stick, and cloves. Over high heat, stir until the sugar dissolves, then bring to a boil. Reduce the heat to medium and simmer for 10 to 15 minutes until the syrup thickens and the apples soften. Remove from heat and let cool. Strain into a sterile, airtight container. The syrup will last up to three weeks in the fridge.

For the cocktail, combine ice, Northern Temple, Hidden Temple Gin, and 1 ounce of the Smoked Apple Syrup in a shaker. Shake, then strain into a highball glass containing fresh ice. Top with ginger ale. Garnish with a toasted marshmallow.

(Syrup by Greg Morrison; cocktail by Michael Pez & Lucy Flawless/Eric Rich)

NORTH OF 7 DISTILLERY
OTTAWA, ON

1733 St Laurent Blvd.
Ottawa, ON K1G 3V4
(613) 627-4257
www.northof7distillery.ca

🐦 @N7Distillery

FOUNDED 2013

OWNERS Greg Lipin and Jody Miall

STILLS Imported from China

PRODUCTS Gin, rum, vodka, whisky

AVAILABILITY Online, onsite, LCBO

TOURS Informal, Monday–Wednesday,
12–5 p.m.; Thursday and Friday,
12–7 p.m.; Saturday, 12–6 p.m.

NEAREST NEIGHBOURS Artist in Residence
Distillerie (page 225) – 25 min; Dairy
Distillery (page 170) – 40 min; King's Lock
Craft Distillery (page 188) – 1 hr; Top
Shelf Distillers (page 208) – 1 hr, 5 min

Enter through the distillery shop and walk back past a finished-goods warehouse and tasting bar into the North of 7 barrel room. There, distillery co-owner Jody Miall stops, points at racks that hold about 150 barrels of whisky, and smiles. "We have enough inventory now to recover our costs if we have to," he affirms, jokingly wiping his brow.

It wasn't always this way. For the first few years, North of 7 survived by making vodka and gin, and sharing space with the original business that Miall and business partner Greg Lipin launched in this suburban strip mall: Coyote Rock Gym. "Every year is better than the year before," says Miall, who credits his wife, Laura, with getting him interested in distilling.

Lipin began researching distillation two years before they installed their still, and that research has paid dividends. Meanwhile, Miall compares his own knowledge of distilling when they started to "that episode of *The Simpsons* where Homer becomes a whisky baron." He appreciates that Lipin never wants to cut corners.

In the beginning, the partners looked to Kentucky for inspiration, making their whisky in traditional bourbon style and maturing it in full-sized barrels. Success with an experimental high-rye mash bill has led to a mix of bourbon and rye-style whiskies and opened the door to other innovations, including single malt whisky. While North of 7 bottles one barrel at a time, they deliberately leave about half their barrels to mature longer than the legally required three years. It's a good strategy. Whiskies that were already quite palatable at three have gained depth and balance as the years have gone by. Meanwhile, their Illuminati Vodka, Triple Beam Gin, and Leatherback Rum have strong followings in the Ottawa area, ensuring the team will never need to liquidate those 150 barrels to recover their investment.

TASTING NOTES: **NORTH OF 7 RYE** (45% ABV)

This four-year-old whisky, made from 95% rye and 5% barley, is persuasively spicy and floral, with enjoyable rye bread overtones. Vanilla and charred oak on the nose surge onto the palate until the rye grain flares with spice and a little chocolate and shaved dry oak. A slightly grassy finish displays tight grain structure. As they fade to the finish, woody barrel notes invite another sip.

PEPPRELL DISTILLING CO.
MOOREFIELD, ON

Josh Cormier discovered his passion for distilling while living on a Halifax street called Pepperell. Along with his roommates, Cormier brewed a lot of beer while at university there. In the winter, they converted one of the bathrooms into a keg fridge by closing the door and opening the window. Today, Cormier, and his former roommates and Nate Reid-Ellis, have converted a building that once housed snowplows into a distillery. Cormier's fascination with the art, chemistry, history, and culture of alcohol is on full display in Pepprell's signature gin. The distillery name is intentionally missing the "e" from that Halifax street so many years ago. Why? Someone else took it!

5 Hillwood Dr.
Moorefield ON, N0G 2K0

@Pepprellspirits

@pepprelldistilling

FOUNDED 2018

OWNERS Josh Cormier, Cameron Curry, Emile McLean, Kyle Cormier, Nate Reid-Ellis

PRODUCTS Gin

NEAREST NEIGHBOURS Murphy's Law Distillery Ltd. (page 196) — 30 min; Junction 56 Distillery (page 186) — 45 min; Dixon's Distilled Spirits (page 174) — 45 min

POLONÉE DISTILLERY INC.
ST. CATHARINES, ON

Adam Szymków was watching people making vodka in a barn in an old Polish World War II movie when he got the idea to open a distillery. "If they could make vodka in such a rustic setting, then I could do something special here," explains Szymków. On Canada's 150th birthday, Szymków and his wife, Patricia, launched what they hope will become Canada's official vodka: Kannuk.

Kannuk blends four distillates to represent Canada's cultural diversity: corn for North America, wheat for Europe, sweet potato for South America and the Caribbean, and wild rice for Asia and Africa. They make each individually before blending them. Kannuk's red label matches the Canadian flag, and it is decorated with a toque, two hockey sticks, a moose, and an Inukshuk to symbolize hope and friendship. The distillery also produces Cytrynówka, a lemon liqueur, and Spirytus, a traditional Polish wheat spirit liqueur for homemade infusions at 95% abv.

380 Vansickle Rd., Unit 450
St. Catharines, ON L2S 0B5
(905) 380-1669
www.polonee.com

@kannukvodka

@kannukvodka

FOUNDED 2017

OWNERS Adam and Patricia Szymków

STILLS Genio G-Still 250; jacketed G-Still 250

PRODUCTS Gin, limoncello, traditional Polish spirits, vodka

AVAILABILITY Onsite, LCBO

TOURS Saturdays, 12–5 p.m. (contact the distillery for rates—reservations recommended)

NEAREST NEIGHBOURS Tawse Winery and Distillery (page 208) — 15 min; Niagara College Distillery (page 197) — 15 min; Wayne Gretzky Estates Winery & Distillery (page 210) — 20 min

TASTING NOTES: KANNUK VODKA (40% ABV)
Kannuk's vodka unites corn, wheat, sweet potato, and wild rice distillates into one integrated flavour profile. Clean suggestions of spirit and pepper mesh with delicate sweet grains in this texturally soft vodka.

32 Logan Ave.
Toronto, ON M4M 2M8
www.reidsdistillery.com

NEAREST NEIGHBOURS Mill Street
Distillery (page 194) — 5 min; Spirit of
York Distillery Co. (page 204) — 5 min

REID'S DISTILLERY
TORONTO, ON

In Leslieville, home to Toronto's studio district, large warehouses have become film studios. Among the lights, cameras, and action, Martin Reid, along with his daughter, Jacqueline, and two sons, Calvin and Graham, explores and harnesses gin's diversity. But don't expect any fancy special effects in Reid's gin, just star-studded flavours. Rather than limiting themselves to local botanicals, Reid searches Canada from east to west to make a truly national gin. "We don't want to do it just for the sake of it; we're doing it to get particular flavours," explains Reid. Take a seat at his bar and discover these flavours in classic and modern cocktails.

6 Highway 583 North, RR 2 #19
Hearst, ON POL 1NO
(705) 362-8263
www.rheaultdistillery.ca

FOUNDED 2009

OWNERS Mireille Morin and Marcel
Rheault

STILLS 250-litre Mueller with columns

PRODUCTS Liqueur, vodka, whisky

AVAILABILITY Onsite, LCBO, BC, Manitoba,
Quebec, overseas

TOURS Monday—Thursday,
10 a.m.–6 p.m.; Friday, 10 a.m.–9 p.m.;
Saturday and Sunday, 10 a.m.–6 p.m.

NEAREST NEIGHBOURS Crosscut Distillery
(page 169) — 6 hrs, 15 min

RHEAULT DISTILLERY
HEARST, ON

Of the six distilleries in the world that make "alpha" vodka, five are in eastern Europe. The lone exception, Rheault Distillery in Hearst, Ontario, is Canadian. How does alpha vodka differ from other vodkas? It contains less than 0.003% methanol, a common vodka congener that some believe contributes to hangovers. Marcel Rheault and his wife, Mireille Morin, gave new meaning to the term "home distilling" when, in 2013, they installed a 250-litre Mueller pot still and two copper columns in their living room. It is the only legal still in Canada in a house. "We are in a non-organized township," explains Morin. "There are no bylaws stopping us."

Nevertheless, government officials who have become aware of the still have advised the couple never to remove it from their house if they want to continue distilling there.

Rheault had been producing English cucumbers hydroponically and researching distilling when he read an article in a New York–based newspaper about alpha vodka. He decided to give it a try and bought a small Portuguese pot still to experiment with.

Today, he ferments starch-rich Ontario Grade #3 spring wheat grown by Hearst-area farmers. He then distils the fermented mash and resulting spirit four times, over a period of about a week. His final distillation is quite unusual in that he takes a page from the books of some sherry and white wine makers by adding whole milk as a fining agent. Casein, a milk protein, helps remove residual impurities from the spirit. "Milk," Rheault points out, "polishes the vodka molecules, but it dirties the still." The resulting vodka, which is meant to be sipped cold, has a meringue-like finish.

Along with Loon Vodka, Rheault produces fruit liqueurs and whisky, which is sold from the distillery, by the bottle or two-litre barrel.

TASTING NOTES: **LOON VODKA** [40% ABV]

This crystal-clear vodka is layered and harmonious with a soft sweetness on the nose that sits firmly on the palate. Earthy tones bring contrast to the palate, giving the vodka's downy texture some very welcome substance.

COCKTAIL: **SINFUL SCREWDRIVER**
MAKES 1 COCKTAIL

Handful of ice cubes
1 oz Sinful Cherry Liqueur
1 oz Loon Vodka
2 oz San Pellegrino Clementina Sparkling Mineral Water
Orange zest twist, for garnish

In an Old Fashioned glass with ice, combine vodka and sparkling mineral water. Stir gently for 5 seconds, then drizzle with the cherry liqueur. Garnish with orange zest twist.

(Rheault Distillery)

SPIRIT OF YORK DISTILLERY CO.
TORONTO, ON

12 Trinity St.
Toronto, ON M5A 3C4
(416) 777-0001
www.spiritofyork.com

🐦 @spiritofyork

📷 @spiritofyork

FOUNDED **2017**

OWNERS **35 shareholders**

STILLS **Three Christian Carl German pots with two 44-plate columns**

PRODUCTS **Aquavit, gin, vodka, whisky**

AVAILABILITY **Onsite, LCBO**

TOURS **Self-guided**

NEAREST NEIGHBOURS **Mill Street Distillery (page 194) – 2 min (on foot)**

In 1861 Toronto's Gooderham & Worts built a brand new stone distillery building. With increased production came a demand for more malt, and the firm added a malt house to satisfy that need. By 1868 the distillery was malting its own barley in the new malt house located at 12 Trinity Street, just steps away from the distillery.

A century and a half later, a new distillery has sprouted in this beautiful building and has become a hot spot for tourists visiting Toronto's historic Distillery District. The distillery has an octagonal tasting bar that sits front and centre, resting beneath a suspended double-decker planter that overflows with herbs. Bartenders serve spirits purchased at the bar from picturesque decanter-style bottles.

A floor-to-ceiling window stretches the length of the distillery and overlooks the production floor, where three Christian Carl pots with the dark patina of working stills are busily making spirits. While they may not be suitable backdrops for tourist selfies, if it's photo opportunities you want, you can head outside, behind the distillery, where explosion-proof glass worthy of a Popemobile encases a pair of three-storey 44-plate column stills.

TASTING NOTES: AQUAVIT (44% ABV)

Big, bright citrus rushes to the nose, making this cleansing aquavit fresh like lemon candies. Caraway plays off hints of rye bread, with dill as a wonderfully restrained side dish to the spirit's creamy mouthfeel. Well-timed spice on the palate's back end completes this enjoyable sipping spirit.

STILL WATERS DISTILLERY
CONCORD, ON

In March 2009 long-time friends Barry Stein and Barry Bernstein kicked off a distilling boom that has seen over 200 new distilleries open across the country. As with many of Canada's first microdistillers, the partners set out to make single malt whisky. Canadian law says grain spirit must spend at least three years in barrels before it becomes whisky, and that's a long time to wait to make a sale. Their solution? Instant sales with Still Waters Single Malt Vodka.

They breathed a sigh of relief when, in 2012, rave reviews from locavores and connoisseurs welcomed their Stalk & Barrel Single Malt. With ample whisky on the shelves, Barry and Barry discontinued their vodka, turning to contract distilling of gin and vodka, along with blending and bottling other distillers' spirits, to provide a second revenue stream.

Still Waters hit the jackpot in 2014 with the release of Stalk & Barrel 100% rye whisky. This wonderfully original dram has Still Waters winning gold medals in head-to-head competition with the major distillers. It caught on quickly, and the team switched more than half of its production to Stalk & Barrel Rye. Traditional Canadian whisky blends, called Stalk & Barrel Blue and Red, were introduced in 2017. That same year, they also doubled the size of the distillery, adding a second maturing warehouse, and in 2018 they installed an automated bottling line. A 2,500-litre pot still for stripping runs followed in 2020.

Stalk & Barrel whiskies are available in 46% abv and natural cask strength versions. Renewed US distribution, beginning in Texas, promises to build on initial enthusiasm in the northern states. Still Waters is a production facility, and though they do not have a visitor centre, you can purchase their full range of spirits onsite in the distillery store.

150 Bradwick Dr.
Concord, ON L4K 4M7
www.stillwatersdistillery.com

🐦 @StalkandBarrel

📷 @stalkandbarrel

FOUNDED 2009

OWNERS Barry Bernstein, Gary Huggins, Barry Stein

STILLS 450-litre Christian Carl pot with column; 2,500-litre pot and column from China

PRODUCTS Whisky

AVAILABILITY Onsite, online, widely in Canada and US

TOURS No

NEAREST NEIGHBOURS Last Straw Distillery (page 190) — 10 min; Magnotta Distillery (page 193) — 15 min

TASTING NOTES: **STALK & BARREL RED BLEND** (43% ABV)

Still Waters shows off how well their rye and barley whiskies complement each other, proving these two grains, though different, can be best friends. The cheerful nose radiates vanilla, floral rye, and a gentle grassiness. Rye spices, especially clove, with a touch of oak and some milk chocolate, punctuate the even, viscous texture of the whisky. Sophistication in a bottle.

THE BARCHEF EXPERIENCE

No one ever accused Hiram Walker's Harry Hatch of being a time traveller, though he made decisions as if he knew what the future had in store. When Ontario's prohibition ended in 1927, spirits were still banned from public places. Hatch's distillery (page 181) entered this new post-prohibition age with ready-to-drink cocktails all set to go when the first LCBO stores opened. Imbibers could take Manhattans and gin Martinis home to enjoy in private. Before long, these ready-to-drink cocktails spread to miniature bottles served on airlines. Then, in the 1970s, as markets shifted to liqueurs and vodka Martinis, these bottled cocktails disappeared like disco's one-hit wonders.

In 2008, almost 30 years after disco died, Frankie Solarik and Brent Vanderveen opened Toronto's BarChef. "Our objective is to challenge the conventional notions and boundaries of the cocktail experience," explains Solarik.

What they have done with cocktails has influenced bartenders across Canada. Peek behind some of the best bars in the country, and there's a chance you'll find a dog-eared copy of Solarik's influential tome, *The Bar Chef*. Late in 2017, they made a move to bring the BarChef experience to customers' homes when they released a ready-to-drink Toasted Old Fashioned. Not just any Old Fashioned, but one stirred on Vanderveen and Solarik's terms. This is not the cocktail served on a 1954 TWA flight from New York to Chicago; it's more like a flight from New York to Jupiter in 2154.

The in-house bitters that Solarik selected exhibit careful craftsmanship in which the various elements of each component lock together like Lego bricks. "All of our bitters are composed so each spice component provides a certain flavour level," explains Solarik. For example, high floral notes click with the toasted chamomile. Chamomile has a floral quality, and toasting it adds depth. Earthy saffron ties into the caraway's mid-tones.

The bitters begin with a 210-litre batch of Stalk & Barrel Red Blend Whisky, which they leave for two months to interact with the spices. During that time, it reduces to roughly 150 litres. They sweeten the cocktail with maple syrup. Stalk & Barrel Red Blend was chosen as the base spirit because of its strong rye spice component. "We emphasize building flavour profiles around the viscosity of the liquid," says Solarik. "This means accenting the whisky's nuances with the bitters' tones and the sweetening component. It was quite the process to make sure we balanced all three of these elements while maintaining the integrity of the composition and showcasing each section."

Cocktails that follow the Toasted Old Fashioned will show the same aesthetic—all made in house and stamped with BarChef's essentials. With more bottled cocktails on the way(!) it's as if Solarik has the keys to Hatch's time machine. ■

3955 Cherry Ave.
Vineland, ON L0R 2C0
(905) 562-9500
www.tawsewinery.ca

STILL 1,000-litre Italian hybrid

TAWSE WINERY AND DISTILLERY
VINELAND, ON

In Burgundy, France, tractors wander from winery to winery, pulling a still. Winemakers run out as if the ice cream truck is coming, carrying fermented grape pomace and ingredients for lunch. The tractor stops, and while the pomace is distilled into marc, steam from the still cooks lunch. The marc will later be aged into a brandy called Marc de Bourgogne. This practice inspired a nostalgic Moray Tawse to install a still in his Niagara Escarpment winery in 2019. Tawse's winemaker, Paul Pender, uses the Italian 1,000-litre hybrid pot still and its two copper columns to distil Canada's first Marc de Bourgogne–like spirit. Pender ages the spirit in used pinot barrels. He also distils a long list of other grape spirits, including vermouth, a batch gin using botanicals from the property's gin garden, and apple brandy from the winery's cider.

14 Warren Cres.
Perth, ON K7H 3P4
www.topshelfdistillers.com

 @TSDistillers

 @tsdistillers

FOUNDED 2014

OWNERS Hanna Murphy and John Criswick

STILLS 600-litre Kothe with two 9-plate columns

PRODUCTS Bitters, gin, liqueur, flavoured moonshine, vodka, whisky

AVAILABILITY Onsite, online, LCBO

TOURS Free at 2 p.m. and 4 p.m.; private tours, $10 (contact the distillery by email tours@topshelfdistillers.com)

NEAREST NEIGHBOURS North of 7 Distillery (page 200) — 1 hr, 5 min; Dairy Distillery (page 170) — 45 min

TOP SHELF DISTILLERS
PERTH, ON

More than a century has passed since the Ontario Temperance Act of 1916 silenced the last copper pot to distil malt spirit in Perth. Although the rest of the province had long since adopted rye as its tipple, malt whisky made sense there in theory, as the settlement initially served as a retirement community for Scottish and other soldiers returning from the Napoleonic Wars. Its location on the River Tay made distilling inevitable.

Years later, in 2014, Perth native Hanna Murphy and her business partner, John Criswick, founded Top Shelf Distillers and revived distilling there. They focused on vodka, gin, moonshine, and flavoured moonshine. But, by 2019 they had succumbed to the allure of whisky and released their first batches of not malt but rye whisky made from rye, corn, and malted barley. Each release sold out in a matter of hours, and based on their robust flavour, that is no surprise. Malt whisky is making something of a comeback among Canada's microdistillers, and according to distiller Garrett Kean, Top Shelf also has some in the works. A line of bitters crafted onsite by Alex Murphy, and moonshine endorsed by Ottawa Valley–born (and now US-based) comedian Tom Green, round out the line.

For the most part, Kean and head distiller Andy Hawkey make their spirit from regional grain. For vodka and gin, they might blend in some purchased grain neutral spirits. They distil gin botanicals in a small gin still rather than the 500-litre German Koethe pot. Kean and Hawkey would like to make more whisky, but they are victims of their own success. "The white whisky (moonshine) is doing so well, we don't have time to make whisky." Nevertheless, about 100 full-sized barrels of Perth whisky, made with traditional River Tay water, are slowly edging toward maturity.

TASTING NOTES:
PERTH CANADIAN WHISKY BATCH #001 (40% ABV)

Perth reclaims its whisky heritage with this splendid dram. An intricate complexity on the nose yields citrus, hints of banana, waxed floors, vanilla, roses, and fresh green bales of hay. The full-bodied palate features slippery peaches that slide into mild peppers on the finish. Very complex and well worth the wait.

VIENI ESTATES INC.
BEAMSVILLE, ON

4553 Fly Rd.
Beamsville, ON L0R 1B2
www.vieni.ca

NEAREST NEIGHBOURS Tawse Winery and Distillery — 5 min; Dillon's Small Batch Distillers — 10 min; Forty Creek Distillery — 20 min

Pasquale Raviele bought this 175-acre estate in 1997 and set to work replacing Concord grapevines with wine varieties. When the first wines were finally ready in 2013, Raviele came out swinging with an Italian 5,000-litre copper pot still to make a grappa-like spirit called Graspa. As they had planned from day one, the winery ferments, then distils fresh pomace left over from the winemaking process, according to Italian traditions. Although they do not invite visitors into the distillery itself, Vieni's spirits are available at the tasting bar, and if you go wild and try them all, an onsite bed and breakfast is the perfect place to stay.

TASTING NOTES: DOLCE PICCANTE GRASPA (43% ABV)

Vieni infuses a grappa-like spirit with maple syrup and hot peppers. The nose exudes maple, fruits, and chocolate mint with a substantial earthy backbone. Searing chili pepper acts as a foil to sweet maple syrup and honeyed vanilla tones. Chili continues to pinch the palate long after the sweet notes have faded from the finish.

WAYNE GRETZKY ESTATE WINERY & DISTILLERY
NIAGARA-ON-THE-LAKE, ON

1219 Niagara Stone Rd.
Niagara-on-the-Lake, ON L0S 1J0
(844) 643-7799
www.gretzkyestateswines.com

 @GretzkyEstates

@gretzkyestates

FOUNDED 2017

OWNERS Wayne Gretzky and Andrew
Peller Limited

STILLS Vendome Pot Still with 8-plate
column; Vendome 15-plate column still

PRODUCTS Wine spirits, whisky, cream
whisky

AVAILABILITY Onsite, widely in Canada
and US

TOURS $30 (book online)

NEAREST NEIGHBOURS Limited Distilley
(page 192) — 5 min; Tawse Winery and
Distillery (page 208) — 5 min; Niagara
College Distillery (page 197) — 10 min

Wayne Gretzky is one of the most celebrated athletes in any sport. Canada's favourite superstar would leave his ego at home on game night, conceding much of his success to the team rather than hogging the glory for himself. The Great One takes the same approach to making spirits. It is his distillery, but distiller Joshua Beach gets all the credit for some astonishingly flavourful spirits. "He doesn't tell me how to play hockey," Gretzky quips, "and I don't tell him how to distil."

For the whisky, either a malted-and-unmalted-rye mash or a 100% corn mash begins with grain that is milled onsite, then cooked and fermented for five days before hitting their Vendome rig. The 15-plate column is tall enough to skip hockey and be drafted into the NBA. Each week, Beach puts away dozens of full-sized barrels to mature. The distillery has earned a reputation for its finishing process, which uses sourced whisky blended by Beach and senior winemaker Craig McDonald's team of winemakers.

Wayne Gretzky No. 99 Red Cask whisky blends corn, rye, and malted rye whiskies finished for four months in American oak red wine casks. No. 99 Ice Cask bumps up the percentage of older whisky and rye in the blend, then finishes it in icewine casks. No. 99 Ninety Nine Proof ramps up the rye content even further, then finishes in ex–Cabernet Sauvignon barrels before it is bottled at 99 proof. Mixologist Zachary Kvas serves cocktails he makes using these whiskies and an assortment of homemade and homegrown shrubs, tinctures, syrups, and infusions in the adjoining tasting room.

It's all good stuff, and Beach could simply have skated down the ice with his budding all-star No. 99 whisky for the easy goal. Instead, he dove into the estate's barrels of high-quality sulphur-free VQA wines and put them through the still. The resulting muscat and Vidal wine spirits were followed by Gamay Noir, together branded as Gretzky Rosé Spirited Wine. Beach further matured the Gamay Noir spirit for three months in Cabernet Franc icewine barrels. Forget Champagne; Gretzky No. 99 spirits are made to be sipped from the Stanley Cup.

TASTING NOTES:
WAYNE GRETZKY NO. 99 RED CASK WHISKY (40% ABV)

The distillery's lumber—wine casks—adds a new dimension to a classic Canadian-style whisky in a blend of individually mashed, fermented, and distilled rye, malted rye, and corn whiskies. Exotic wood, citrus, and sweet spices skate across the palate with rum-like sweetness. Dark fruits, dialed in with the assist of contrasting grape tannins, rack up another point for Gretzky.

COCKTAIL:
THE BOXCAR

MAKES 1 COCKTAIL

1½ oz Wayne Gretzky No. 99 Red Cask Whisky
1 oz Cointreau
½ oz Kvas Northern Maple Old Fashioned Simple Syrup
½ oz lemon juice
1 shake of Angostura Bitters
1 orange twist, for garnish

Place a coupe glass in the freezer until chilled, at least one hour. Fill a shaker with ice. Add all of the ingredients except the Angostura Bitters and orange twist. Shake until too cold to hold and strain into the chilled coupe. Add the Angostura, and garnish with an orange twist dropped in the glass.

(Zachary Kvas)

THE WHITE DISTILLERY
MISSISSAUGA, ON

400 Matheson Blvd. E., Unit 22
Mississauga, ON L4Z 1N8
www.whitedistillery.com

🐦 @whitedistillery

📷 @whitedistillery

FOUNDED **2016**

OWNERS **Kevin Dahi, Tony Salloum, Milo Chebly**

STILLS **1,000-litre Portuguese copper pot**

PRODUCTS **Arak, gin, liqueur, pastis, vodka**

AVAILABILITY **Onsite, LCBO, US**

TOURS **By appointment**

NEAREST NEIGHBOURS **Magnotta Distillery (page 193) — 30 min; Nickel 9 Distillery (page 198) — 30 min**

Handcrafted spirits were an ingrained part of Kevin Dahi's Syrian culture, which is why he was so dismayed, upon arriving in Canada in 2006, to find just two araks available here. Neither of them had the quality he had enjoyed in Syria, where he would make his own. Traditionally, arak is made by fermenting and distilling crushed grapes, with aniseed added for the second of three distillations. In 2016 Dahi and his partners, Tony Salloum and Milo Chebly, imported a 1,000-litre copper pot still from Portugal and set out to make their longed-for Mediterranean spirits. They integrate local fruits, grains, and botanicals following handwritten traditional Syrian recipes, with a contemporary Canadian twist. "They are something different from what everybody else is making in North America," beams Dahi. His triple-distilled Dayaa Arak and Pastis du Hameau begin with Canadian grapes and finish with an authentically Mediterranean flair.

TASTING NOTES: **DAYAA ARAK** (50% ABV)

Brimming with Syrian aniseed on the nose and palate. Sweet, oily, and luxurious, this arak transitions into spiced licorice that drifts through a very long finish.

HOW TO DRINK ARAK

Pour 1½ oz of Arak into a rocks glass. Add 3 oz of room-temperature water. The Arak should turn from clear to cloudy white. Add ice to chill. The ratio of Arak to water for larger drinks is 1:2.

WILLIBALD FARM DISTILLERY
AYR, ON

Richard Willibald Feicht loathed his middle name so much, he struck it from his driver's licence when he arrived in Canada. It was gone for good until his grandchildren, Jordan and Nolan van der Heyden, joined a friend, Cam Formica, to launch the Willibald whisky distillery on the van der Heydens' 100-acre dairy farm. Feicht was horrified! Nevertheless, the old High German name Willibald links the family and land with the region's German heritage. Feicht warmed up to it around the time he was blowing out 88 birthday candles.

They converted a former milking barn into a rackhouse and rehabilitated a cattle barn into the distillery itself. Willibald's herd of Scottish Galloway cattle, housed next door at the neighbours' farm, watched nervously as blueprints for a farm-to-table tied-house restaurant were unveiled. It was perfect . . . unless your name was Bessie.

Willibald Farm Distillery embraces farm-to-table ingredients and aesthetics. The barn's old floorboards were repurposed into gorgeous restaurant tables. On the production side, Nolan built a 4,000-litre Douglas fir wooden washback where he ferments three whisky mash bills—two high in rye and a "birthday mash" of 39% corn, 51% rye, and 10% barley, introduced on Nolan's birthday. Each mash is fermented for four to five days with a flavour-generating Norwegian farmhouse ale yeast called Voss Kveik. It's then double-distilled and aged in 114- and 200-litre new oak barrels. The team is also collecting finishing barrels, including a set of 230-litre French oak red wine barrels previously used for tequila.

Aged gin is where the distillery earned its reputation. Although the plan from day one was to make whisky, that takes time. Ageing their gin in oak quarter casks keeps the distillery rooted in whisky-making fundamentals—fundamentals that would make every Willibald proud to show off his name.

TASTING NOTES: **WILLIBALD SINGLE CASK #7** (63.2% ABV)

Clark Kent should ditch the phone booth and transform into Superman in Willibald's barrel barn instead. This 23-month-old whisky preview is as solid as steel. Made from 60% corn, 35% rye, and 5% malted barley and matured in new oak, it previews big lumber and seasoned char, coming into balance with orchard fruits and earthy grain. Cherries and grassy floral rye leap to the nose with a corn-forward flavour that is spot on and focused.

(continued)

1271 Reidsville Rd.
Ayr, ON N0B 1E0
(226) 556-9941
www.drinkwillibald.com

@ @drinkwillibald

FOUNDED 2017

OWNERS Jordan and Nolan van der Heyden, Cam Formica

STILLS 1,000-litre Kothe Pot Still with three 10-plate columns

PRODUCTS Aged gin, flavoured spirit, whisky

AVAILABILITY Onsite, online, LCBO

TOURS Wednesday–Friday, 5 p.m.–10 p.m., Saturday, 12–10 p.m.

NEAREST NEIGHBOURS Dixon's Distilled Spirits (page 174) — 35 min; Murphy's Law Distillery Ltd. (page 196) — 40 min; Junction 56 Distillery (page 186) — 50 min

COCKTAIL:
WILLIBALD'S
CLASSIC NEGRONI
MAKES 1 COCKTAIL

Handful of ice cubes
1 oz Willibald Gin
1 oz sweet vermouth
1 oz Campari
1 large ice cube
1 orange peel twist, for garnish

In a cocktail shaker, combine ice, gin, sweet vermouth, and Campari. Shake well, then strain into a rocks glass containing a large ice cube. Garnish with an orange peel twist.

(Willibald Distillery)

WOLFHEAD DISTILLERY
AMHERSTBURG, ON

History repeated itself when Tom and Sue Manherz and their partner, Larry Girard, opened Wolfhead Distillery on the property where Tom operates Timberwolf Forest Products. There, he runs a lumber mill, making wooden pallets and crates. It harks back to the 1840s, when John McLeod settled in Amherstburg and opened a lumber mill along the Detroit River. Just like Manherz, McLeod expanded his mill to include a distillery. Except McLeod's story ended when Hiram Walker bought him out in 1874. The Manherz story is only just getting started.

With the Hiram Walker & Sons Distillery (page 181) just up the river, and a former Seagram's distillery in Amherstburg, the Manherz's interest in distilling developed from being surrounded by the business. "I've always loved the industry. Everyone I knew in it, loved it," says Tom. "I already have a lumber mill out back, so how do I go from a mill to a still?" A fortress of Hiram Walker whisky barrels waiting for minor repairs surrounds the distillery, which opens onto a modern building with prohibition-era vehicles on display outside.

When the doors to Wolfhead opened on May 27, 2016, not only were they leading the pack as Ontario's first tied house, but the restaurant—decked out with wooden beams and furnishings milled onsite—had front-row seats to the distilling operations. Chef Girard serves a refined local menu while you watch Wolfhead's beautiful Italian-made Barison copper pot still with its two towering columns and the pièce de résistance—a continuous column still—working together to make whiskies, vodkas, and liqueurs. A mural depicting rum-runners loading a speedboat transitions into the back end of a real boat by the time you reach the checkout. It's an impressive set-up for a team that has gone from pallets to palates.

7781 Howard Ave.
Amherstburg, ON N0R 1J0
(519) 726-1111
www.drinkwolfhead.com

 @DrinkWolfhead

@drinkwolfhead

FOUNDED 2016

OWNERS Tom and Sue Manherz and Larry Girard

STILLS 700-litre Barison pot still with 14- and 18-plate column; 200-litre Barison pot still and continuous column still

PRODUCTS Liqueur, vodka, whisky, flavoured whisky

AVAILABILITY Onsite, LCBO

TOURS Saturday, 1 p.m. and 2 p.m. (call for rates and reservations)

NEAREST NEIGHBOURS Hiram Walker & Sons Distillery (page 181) — 25 min

TASTING NOTES: COFFEE WHISKY LIQUEUR (30% ABV)

Double barrel whisky and cold-brewed Costa Rican coffee blend into this smoky liqueur. Shades of vanilla, rich coffee, and oaky caramel meld seamlessly into a robust spirit with a coffee kick that will put roosters out of business.

(continued)

COCKTAIL: **WOLFHEAD GRAPEFRUIT COSMO**
MAKES 1 COCKTAIL

1 lime wedge
1 grapefruit wedge
½ oz orange simple syrup
2 oz Wolfhead Grapefruit Vodka

½ oz cranberry juice
Handful of ice cubes
1 lemon-peel twist, for garnish

Place a Martini glass in the freezer until chilled, at least one hour. In a cocktail shaker, muddle the lime, grapefruit, and orange simple syrup. Add vodka and cranberry juice, then top with ice. Shake well to combine ingredients, then double-strain into the chilled Martini glass. Garnish with a lemon-peel twist.

(Woldhead Distillery Staff)

YONGEHURST DISTILLERY CO.
TORONTO, ON

Rocco Panacci grew up in a household where the family cured their own meats, grew their own vegetables, and made their own pasta sauce from bushels of fresh tomatoes. "It wasn't out of necessity, it was out of tradition," says Panacci. "As my dad would say, 'doing things the right way.'"

Panacci and cofounder John-Paul Sacco have brought this approach to a lineup of spirits that push the boundaries beyond grain. They use local wild yeast to ferment the mash that makes Harbour Rum, and locally foraged botanicals to make Fiveward Dry Gin. Whatever they can't find in Toronto's backyard, Panacci will grow in his own—"I like the idea of learning about botanicals through physically caring for them."

Yongehurst has also carved out a niche for its experimental releases—a sipping playground of local ingredients inspired by craft beer's seasonal one-offs. "What I love about breweries is that I can taste something different every time I go. Every season, there is something to look forward to," says Panacci. Yongehurst creates this experience with releases such as the nocino he makes with Ontario walnuts, a plum liqueur called umeshu, and many more ageing in a wide variety of oak. "If you can ferment it, we're going to attempt it."

346 Westmoreland Ave. N.
Toronto, ON M6H 3A7
www.yongehurst.com

 @yongehurst

 @yongehurst

FOUNDED 2016

OWNERS Rocco Panacci and John-Paul Sacco

PRODUCTS Gin, liqueurs, rum, white rum, shochu, triple sec, vodka

AVAILABILITY Onsite, LCBO

TOURS Saturdays, 12–5 p.m.

NEAREST NEIGHBOURS Nickel 9 Distillery (page 198) – 10 min; Mill Street Distillery (page 194) – 25 min; Spirit of York Distillery Co. (page 204) – 25 min

TASTING NOTES: HARBOUR WHITE RUM (44% ABV)

As wild Ontario yeast harvested from russet apples ferments organic molasses, it imbues the spirit with its funk-bomb signature. Yongehurst's stills capture a wide spectrum of vegetal flavours and piquant earthiness that balance marshmallow, cotton candy, and cooling menthol on the palate. A grassiness that builds on the nose's dundery foundation adds punch to this already bold rum.

QUEBEC

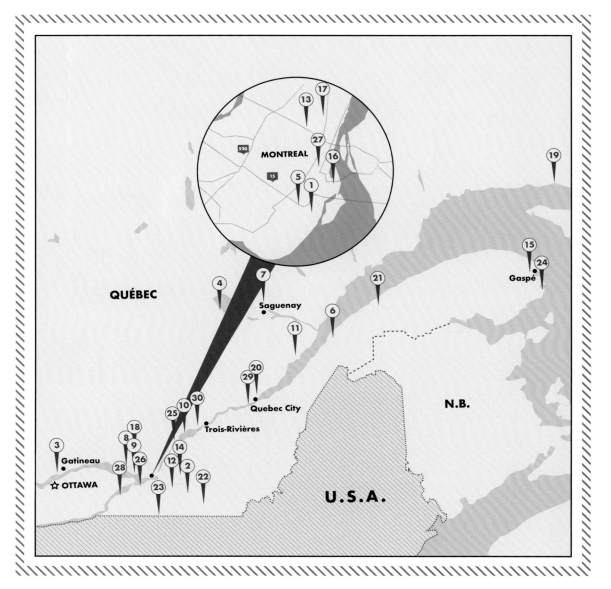

QUEBEC

Although Quebec flirted with prohibition in 1919, a referendum deemed banning beer and wine too radical. Perhaps that is because the church is uniquely influential in Quebec and had let it be known that it saw no problem with people consuming wine and beer. A political compromise resulted in a more precise target: banning spirits alone, and not alcohol in general. And only for a while. Bootlegging became widespread, surprising no one, and by 1922 the government fought back and ended prohibition in favour of government-controlled liquor stores. Quebecers were not required to get a permit to buy alcohol, as consumers were in some provinces, but there was a strict limit of one bottle per person per visit.

This short dry spell hurt Quebec distilleries. Vinegar producer St. Hyacinthe Distillery, for example, had shifted to distilling spirits in 1904 and ramped up production to 500,000 litres of alcohol a year. By the mid-1920s, faced with prohibition, the distillery ceased production altogether, and its brands, such as National Canadian Whisky, faded into obscurity.

It was not all gloom and doom, though. Quebec's rich distilling history began long before prohibition came along. Claims that the still that one James Grant operated in Quebec City around 1769 was Canada's first have entered even the most respectable lore. But who would know? Other stories suggest that, a century earlier, Jean Talon had a still in his "La Brasserie du Roi" in Quebec City, but the evidence remains unclear. However, we do know that, in Montreal, John Molson fired up his pot still

as a trial, but then somehow lost interest. It was a good 20 years before his son, Thomas, began distilling seriously in 1821.

Today's distilleries in La Belle Province have revitalized gin's craft to a fever pitch, but that spirit's cult status in Quebec has its origins late in the 19th century. In 1873 John and Joseph GC Meagher opened Montreal's Meagher's Distillery. Updated in 1920, Meagher's continued making gin until 1976. That was when ownership transferred to other corporations through a complex web of mergers and name changes. The distillery is now home to Sazerac's Old Montreal Distillery (page 234).

In 1875 Jan Melcher opened Melchers distillery in Berthierville after making a name for himself distilling Geneva gin in the Netherlands. This distillery expanded in 1928, when three brothers who worked there bought and modernized the plant. The distillery grew through the late 1960s, until it was capable of handling 5,000 bushels of rye grain a day. It wasn't able to ward off the banks, though, and in 1978 it went bankrupt.

When the Bronfman brothers expanded into Quebec in 1924, they built a new distillery in the Montreal suburb of LaSalle and used equipment they had purchased from Kentucky's Greenbrier distillery. In 1945, when Lewis Rosenstiel bought a former bakery turned distillery in Valleyfield, it was producing industrial alcohol for the war effort, but Rosenstiel quickly rebuilt the plant and shifted to whisky production. He supplied the United States with brands such as Schenley OFC, Golden Wedding, and eventually Gibson's. By 1969 they had produced over a million casks. The Valleyfield Distillery (page 251) is the last of Quebec's legacy distilleries to survive.

Today's provincial government restrictions on how spirits can be sold are not helpful to microdistilleries. That hasn't stopped new distilleries from opening at a steady pace, nor has it prevented government agencies from subsidizing some of these start-ups. Change is coming to Quebec, thanks to a strong distillers' association that clearly has the ear of the government. Almost 100 years after prohibition, distilleries have finally earned the right to sell their own spirits onsite, as of summer 2018. Other older draconian rules are beginning to fade away, too, including the province's dreaded stamp system. Quebec is the last place on the planet to practise this arcane method of inventory control, which requires every bottle of alcohol in a bar to have a stamp on it detailing the date of purchase and the bar's unique permit number. Quebec is moving toward eliminating this stamp system by 2021, and distilleries hope it will open the doors to selling directly to bars and restaurants.

If there is another group that should have a parade for its part in the distilling boom, it's the residents of Quebec. The province's liquor retailer, SAQ (Société des alcools du Québec), promotes Quebec-made products, but behind the curtain, this is all thanks to the people who take pride in locally produced products. The growth of Quebec's gin craze is a result of this consumer pressure. Asking retailers for more Canadian spirits is something every spirit lover in Canada should embrace. ∎

1769 DISTILLERY INC.
VERDUN, QC

Maureen David was concerned. After more than 20 years of marriage and with two teenage sons at home, the successful Montreal television producer worried about her husband, Andrew Mikus. Was he having a mid-life crisis? Mikus was already a partner in a film and television post-production studio. Now? He said he wanted to start a distillery. Yes, David was concerned, though not entirely surprised. For most of their lives together, whenever they travelled, they had taken advantage of opportunities to visit distilleries in Europe and North America.

With David's agreement, Mikus travelled to South Carolina and Washington, where he could work with other distillers and learn the finer points of distilling. When he came back, he started building 1769 Distillery, named for the year that distilling was first recorded in Quebec (and in Canada, for that matter). Fortunately, space was available in the same location as his media business. This allowed him to keep both businesses going until he could distil full time. Today, David runs this urban distillery while the soft-spoken Mikus focuses on production. And with five gins, three Mvodkas (M for Montreal), and a whisky now in SAQ's retail network, and barrel-aged cocktails—delivered barrel and all—in restaurants, that mid-life crisis is beginning to pay off. Like their media production, their spirits have also found their way into the spotlight. In the end, Mikus's new passion turned out to be more of a moment of brilliance.

www.1769distillery.com
(514) 507-1243
@1769distillery
@1769distillery

FOUNDED 2013

OWNERS Andrew Mikus and Maureen David

PRODUCTS Gin, vodka, whisky

AVAILABILITY SAQ

TOURS Not offered

NEAREST NEIGHBOURS Cirka Distilleries (page 226) — 10 min; Old Montreal Distillery (page 234) — 20 min

TASTING NOTES:
MADISON PARK PINK DRY GIN (40% ABV)

Named after the park in New York City, this gin attributes its pink colour to wild hibiscus. What's colourful to the eye is vivid on the palate. The fragrant juniper nose melds into lychee syrup, berries, bright citrus peel, and an herbal spice blend of peppery cinnamon. These slide easily onto the palate, where lavender and black pepper enhance the gin's floral characters. A refreshing entry in the contemporary gin category.

(continued)

COCKTAIL: **PINK LOOKS GOOD ON YOU**
MAKES 1 COCKTAIL

2 large strawberries
Handful of ice cubes
2 oz Madison Park Pink Dry Gin
½ oz simple syrup
½ oz fresh lime juice
3 oz sparkling water
Fresh mint sprig, for garnish

Slice the strawberries, then place in a cocktail shaker and gently muddle. Add ice, gin, simple syrup, and lime juice, then shake vigorously for 10 seconds. Pour all ingredients, including the ice, into a highball glass and top with sparkling water. Garnish with a sprig of mint.

(1769 Distillery Inc,)

800 rue Moeller
Granby, QC J2J 1K7
www.absinthequebec.com

TOURS Contact the distillery by email
info@absinthequebec.com

NEAREST NEIGHBOURS Distillerie Shefford (page 243) — 20 min; Cidrerie Michel Jodoin (page 231) — 30 min; Distillerie Noroi (page 233) — 50 min

ABSINTHERIE DES CANTONS
GRANBY, QC

Jean-Philippe Doyon is passionate about absinthe. So much so that an absinthe tasting event he attended in 2013 inspired him to travel to Switzerland and then on to France to explore the story and the craft of this spirit. Absinthe was the spirit of choice during the Belle Époque, when many Parisian artists attributed their own inspirational muses to the mystical libation. Wormwood plants, which grow in the Eastern Townships, are the crucial botanical in Doyon's traditional white absinthe, named Fleur Bleu. Anise and fennel, along with 10 other botanicals, complete the complex recipe for this absinthe. His traditional green expression, called Joual Vert, is pleasingly bitter when compared with Fleur Bleu. Doyon welcomes visitors and asks that they contact him in advance by email.

ARTIST IN RESIDENCE DISTILLERIE
GATINEAU, QC

Were it not for rows of barrels in the windows, from the outside this ultramodern distillery and bar by the Gatineau airport, just across the river from Ottawa, would resemble a sedate corporate office rather than the "craft distillery for renegades" that it calls itself. When you taste its spirits, though, you quickly realize they belong in a cocktail shaker, not a cubicle. Founder Pierre Mantha travels to Colombia regularly to visit his wife's parents. Friends there encouraged him to diversify beyond his car dealerships and start a distillery. "The main ingredient in spirits is water," he says, "and that's free." When a well he dug behind his truck dealership yielded pure spring water the decision was made. The distillery's four spirits are packaged in unique bottles with beautiful, if quirky labels. AiR, as people call it, adheres to a strict artisanal ethic, and Mantha buys his corn from a nearby farm before grinding it onsite.

243 rue Bombardier
Gatineau, QC J8R 0C6
www.airdistillerie.com

NEAREST NEIGHBOURS North of 7 Distillery (page 200) — 30 min; Dairy Distillery (page 170) — 50 min; King's Lock Craft Distillery (page 188) — 1 hr, 15 min

TASTING NOTES: **WAXWING BOHEMIAN GIN** (41% ABV)

Waxwings are birds that love the flavours juniper berries bring to their mixed-berry diets. Appropriately, forest berries and juniper make up this gin's foundation. An expressive nose yields candied lemon drops, sweet licorice, peppery flowers, tart berries, and wax polish. Peppery evergreen on the palate with sour lemon peel lands this gin in an exciting nest of flavours. And for striking visuals, rosehips lend it a yellow hue that turns vibrant Fanta orange with tonic water.

310 rue Brassard
Roberval, QC G8H 1Z6
www.distilleriebeemer.com

NEAREST NEIGHBOURS Distillerie du Fjord
(page 228) — 3 hrs, 10 min; Menaud
Distillerie et Brasserie (page 231) —
5 hrs, 15 min

DISTILLERIE BEEMER
ROBERVAL, QC

Quebec's beautiful Saguenay–Lac-Saint-Jean region is famous for its cheese and its blueberries. In fact, if you combined all the region's blueberry bushes, they would bury the entire city of Montreal. In 1888 railway contractor Horace Jansen Beemer built a line into this region and opened it up for development.

Distillerie Beemer enjoyed great success with a brewery it opened in 2017, which enabled the company to branch out into distilling. Distiller Philippe Harvey makes his vodka by fermenting and distilling blueberries in a trio of Mueller pot stills. He also distils a gin and blueberry brandy. His eaux-de-vie, made with camerise berries and cranberries, show that Harvey is serious when he says he wants to highlight Saguenay–Lac-Saint-Jean's terroir with 100% regional spirits.

2075 rue Cabot
Montreal, QC H4E 1E2
(514) 370-2075
www.cirka.ca

 @CirkaDistillery

 @cirka_distilleries

FOUNDED 2014

OWNERS Paul Cirka

STILLS 2,300-litre pot still with 4-plate column and 20-plate column; 570-litre pot still with a 4-plate column and gin column with 5 removable botanical baskets

PRODUCTS Gin, vodka

AVAILABILITY Onsite, SAQ

TOURS Contact the distillery

NEAREST NEIGHBOURS Old Montreal
Distillery (page 234) — 15 min; Thompson
Distillery (page 250) — 25 min; Distillerie
de Montréal (page 232) — 30 min

CIRKA DISTILLERIES
MONTREAL, QC

Paul Cirka initially planned on being a whisky maker when he started his distillery. Having studied botany and biology, he was familiar with many of the plants used in distilling, and he was curious about what other interesting ingredients he might find in Quebec. "Early French settlers were fond of making spruce beer from local spruce," he explains. Whisky, of course, takes time, so it's no surprise that one of his first products was a gin made with local botanicals.

A former urban designer and landscape architect, Cirka moved to Montreal to join a high-tech start-up firm. Fifteen years later, he decided he had had enough, and he began to look for something else to do. "I was more of a spirits drinker than beer or wine," he says. "It is amazing what you can pack into a spirit in terms of complexity."

For his biggest seller, Gin Sauvage, Cirka and distiller Isabelle Rochette use a gin basket in the still's vapour stream to integrate the fragrances of 30 different botanicals, many of them local. Some are foraged in old-growth northern boreal forests. "This is genuine terroir," asserts Cirka. As there are no old-growth forests left in Montreal, he employs foragers to harvest these wild botanicals for him. Using gin as a base, he also takes what he calls "a distiller's approach to making vermouth, rather than a winemaker's approach." Cirka's products have Quebec's Agrinature designation on their labels, which means they are about 90% organic.

Although Cirka's gins are wonderfully intricate, he has not abandoned his first interest: whisky. In fact, he now has three different whiskies in barrels, each made from non-GMO grain. One uses 100% corn, another 100% rye, and the third 100% malted barley. He mashes the corn and rye whiskies with commercial enzymes rather than introducing malt. In all, he processes about a tonne of corn a day for whisky. Cirka is very enthusiastic about terroir and strives to make spirits that express the nature of Quebec. Careful selection of all-Quebec ingredients ensures this, and being situated in the heart of Montreal, Cirka also wants his enterprise to contribute to the city's renowned "epicuriosity."

This gin was crafted to celebrate Montreal's 375th anniversary in 2017. Now it's released twice a year as a special edition. The nose has more flavours than candles on Montreal's birthday cake. Tart cranberry, cherry, rose, black tea, and the essence of a forest after rainfall—that flavour geeks call "petrichor"—on the nose. The refreshing, floral palate shows a slight honey-like sweetness. A spicy warmth transitions to cool mint on the finish, making this gin an imaginative entry in Quebec's gin category.

COCKTAIL:
CASSIS DU CANTON
MAKES 1 COCKTAIL

¾ oz lemon juice
½ oz Cirka Gin Sauvage
½ oz Cassis liqueur
½ oz Lillet Blanc
¼ oz simple syrup
Handful of ice cubes
1 mint leaf, for garnish

Place a coupe glass in the freezer until chilled, at least one hour. Combine all of the ingredients except the mint together in a shaker with ice. Shake well for 10 seconds, then strain into the chilled coupe glass. Garnish with a mint leaf.

(Cirka Distilleries)

48 ch. de Price
Saint-David-de-Falardeau, QC
G0V 1C0
www.distilleriedufjord.com

NEAREST NEIGHBOURS Menaud Distillerie
et Brasserie (page 231) — 2 hrs, 30 min;
Distillerie Beemer (page 226) — 3 hrs,
10 min

DISTILLERIE DU FJORD
SAINT-DAVID-DE-FALARDEAU, QC

Saguenay–Lac-Saint-Jean's first distillery draws inspiration from the surrounding
boreal forest. The area's breathtaking scenery includes a glacier-carved fjord that
has left behind 300-metre granite cliffs. The Bouchards—brothers Benoît and
Jean-Philippe and their father, Serge—now make enough gin at their distillery to fill
a fjord. They named their Km12 Monts-Valin Gin after the 12-kilometre marker on
the Mont-Valin road, where naturally pure water flows from the heart of the forest.
The distillery has built a new facility that has expanded production from 50,000 to
100,000 bottles annually. Their plans to add a gin made with blueberry spirit, and a
boreal forest liqueur, are well underway.

TASTING NOTES: KM12 MONTS-VALIN GIN (40% ABV)

A soft floral fragrance highlights this gin's nose with a fluffy, light citrus peel. Fresh
forest evergreen, pink peppercorns, and a gentle sweetness carry over to the fresh
palate. The gin stays in touch with its roots by maintaining mild juniper accents. It
walks the walk and talks the talk, right into a polished finish that struts to its own
delicate subtext.

10291 rang de la Fresnière
Mirabel, QC J7N 3M3
www.intermiel.com

NEAREST NEIGHBOURS Les Vergers
Lafrance (page 229) — 10 min; Distillerie
le Pirate du Nord (page 240) — 30 min

INTERMIEL
MIRABEL, QC

Perhaps nothing symbolizes Canada more than maple syrup. What would happen,
then, if you fermented such a distinctive, sugar-rich liquid? According to Intermiel,
you would make maple wine of about 8–12% abv. And what, then, if you distilled
that wine? Why, you would end up with maple brandy in the range of 60–90% abv.
For Gélinotte, the company's maple brandy liquor, Intermiel does just that. Next,
they blend the brandy with maple syrup and maple wine. After they let the blend
"marry" in a tank, they add natural maple flavours before bottling it at 22% abv. If
this isn't Canada in a bottle, then such a thing does not exist. Intermiel also
produces a similar liquor with the extra flavour of local wild blueberries, along with
a wine-like maple vermouth.

TASTING NOTES: GÉLINOTTE MAPLE BRANDY LIQUEUR (22% ABV)

Fermented maple sap is distilled for a base spirit that is blended with concentrated maple sap, maple wine, additional maple brandy, and natural maple flavours. This dark amber brandy liqueur radiates smoky-sweet maple syrup aromas. The palate is intense, with maple flavours from a stylish sugar shack, including a touch of smoke and a gentle coffee note. Makes an indulgent digestif.

LES VERGERS LAFRANCE
SAINT-JOSEPH-DU-LAC, QC

1473 ch. Principal
Saint-Joseph-du-Lac, QC
(450) 491-7859
www.lesvergerslafrance.com

@VergersLafrance

@ lesvergerslafrance

FOUNDED 1925 (orchard), 2013 (distillery)

OWNERS Éric Lafrance and Julie Hubert

STILLS 800-litre Stupfler Alambic

PRODUCTS Apple spirit, brandy, eau-de-vie, gin, liqueurs, vermouth

AVAILABILITY Onsite and SAQ

TOURS Contact distillery online

NEAREST NEIGHBOURS Intermiel (page 228) — 10 min; Distillerie le Pirate de Nord (page 240) — 30 min

Quebec has long been the "best-kept" secret of Canadian cuisine. While the rest of the country often follows the latest trends in America and Great Britain, Quebecers tend to be more likely to look to France. As a result, whether it is beer, pastry, meat, or cheese, Quebec produce has a personality all its own. So, when third-generation apple grower Éric Lafrance decided to add a still to his thriving cider operation, he turned to the Stupfler family of Bordeaux, who were themselves third-generation still makers. Coincidentally, the Stupflers began making stills in 1925, the same year Lafrance's grandparents founded their orchard (*vergers* in French).

As well as the broad range of apple-based products already produced by Vergers Lafrance, you can now have apple spirits, including gins, vodka, eau-de-vie, brandy, and several vermouths.

TASTING NOTES: PURE LÉGENDE APPLE BRANDY (42% ABV)

The distillery's Stupfler copper pot still masterfully pulls apple flavours from eight varieties that include Cortland, Empire, Geneva, Honeycrisp, McIntosh, Melba, Royal Gala, and Spartan. A medley of apples, rich on the nose, leads to semi-dry spicy heat on the palate. Those spices are subdued into warmth through the finish, with an apple and pear one-two punch.

DISTILLERIE MARIANA
LOUISEVILLE, QC

531 av. Dalcourt
Louiseville, QC J5V 2Z7
www.distilleriemariana.com

NEAREST NEIGHBOURS Distillerie Wabasso
(page 253) – 30 min; Les Distillateurs
Subversifs (page 246) – 1 hr

In 2014, when forest engineer Jean-Philippe Roussy and his uncle André McInnis, also a forester, started their distillery, they looked to the forest for a name. In Latin, the black spruce that grows in every province and territory in Canada is called *Picea mariana*. Hence, Distillerie Mariana.

Early in 2015 Roussy's childhood friend Jonathan Couturier joined the team. Success came quickly, and now Mariana has eight products on SAQ shelves. The team distils a blend of Quebec buckwheat and malt, much of it also local, to produce the base spirit for their vodka, gin, absinthe, and liqueurs. For their dry gin, aptly named Canopée, they go back to the forest to harvest juniper, cedar, maple, oak, and, of course, black spruce. The regional municipality, along with Canada Economic Development and Investissement Québec, has recently demonstrated its support for Mariana with financial contributions which the team has invested in new distilling equipment.

TASTING NOTES: MORBLEU RHUM ÉPICÉ (40.3% ABV)

A whale launching a boat into the air on the label foreshadows what this rum is all about. A soft nose with subdued herbal spices gets hurled onto the palate along with mint, sweet licorice, and a drop of vanilla, all without being sugary. This spiced rum uncharacteristically plays to subtlety instead of overpowering the palate with sweetness.

MENAUD DISTILLERIE ET BRASSERIE
CLERMONT, QC

Félix-Antoine Savard was a Catholic priest and writer who, in 1937, published the classic novel *Menaud, Maitre-Draveur*. This *roman du terroir* (novel of the land) unfolds against the backdrop of Charlevoix's countryside, where a brewery/distillery now not only names itself after the lyrical book, but also embraces the philosophy of its central character—all respect to the heritage and beauty of the region.

Here, in 2018 the partners opened this 1,000-square-metre distillery. They produce Gin de Menaud from a mash bill of 75% wheat and 25% rye and a complex blend of botanicals that "Charlevoisian essence with literary enthusiasm." The team also makes vodka, and to evoke Savard's reverence for the local terroir, vodka infused with herbs harvested in the Charlevoix region.

1 rue de la Riviére
Clermont, QC G4A 1B5
www.menaud.ca

OWNERS Charles Boissonneau, Enrico Bouchard, Grégoire Bluteau, Martin Brisson, Gilles Brouard

NEAREST NEIGHBOURS Distillerie du Fjord (page 228) – 2 hrs, 30 min; Distillerie de Québec (page 241) – 1 hrs, 50 min

CIDRERIE MICHEL JODOIN
ROUGEMONT, QC

Although this Eastern Townships orchard makes half a dozen distilled apple spirits, their first business is apple cider. The farm has been in the Jodoin family since 1901. In 1988, fourth generation Michel Jodoin became one of the first people licensed in Quebec to make apple cider. He has since done his best to raise the bar for artisanal cider across the province and beyond—even travelling to Champage, France, to learn the secrets of creating effervescence. A sip of Jodoin cider, made from red-fleshed Geneva apples, tells you he has learned his lessons well.

In 1999 Jodoin introduced microdistilling to the province by adding a still. He began by making apple spirits for brandy, liqueurs, and vermouth, followed by vodka. What began as a small cidery has grown into a regional tourist attraction with a welcoming reception area and shop, and hiking trails to the top of nearby Rougemont Mountain. It's a lovely ascent, and canine-friendly from Monday to Wednesday. Dogs pay a reduced fee, presumably because they don't imbibe.

1130 rang la Petite-Caroline
Rougemont, QC J0L 1M0
(450) 469-2676
www.micheljodoin.ca

🐦 @cidrerie

📷 @cidreriemicheljodoin

FOUNDED 1988 (cider house), 1999 (distillery)

OWNER Michel Jodoin

PRODUCTS Apple brandy, apple liqueurs, apple vermouth, vodka

AVAILABILITY Onsite and SAQ

TOURS Daily, 9 a.m.–5 p.m. (book online)

NEAREST NEIGHBOURS Distillerie Noroi (page 233) – 25 min; Absintherie des Cantons (page 224) – 35 min; Distillerie Shefford (page 243) – 40 min

DISTILLERIE DE MONTRÉAL
MONTREAL, QC

5447 rue Chapleau
Montreal, QC H2G 2E3
www.distilleriedemontreal.com

NEAREST NEIGHBOURS Brasserie &
Distillerie Oshlag (page 236) — 20 min;
Old Montreal Distillery (page 234) —
20 min; Cirka Distilleries (page 226) —
30 min

Lilian Wolfelsberger comes from a line of French-Alsatian distillers. She and business partner Stéphane Dion have rekindled Wolfelsberger's ancestry in this Montreal distillery. They distil rum in a traditional Charentais pot still made by France's Chalvignac Group. A rare sight in North America, these burgundy beauties have an iconic preheater that at first glance looks more like a cross between a UFO and an onion. The mothership has certainly landed, and it is now distilling gin. Tyler Dyck of Okanagan Spirits Craft Distillery (page 88) collaborated with the wine and spirits agency ReZin and his friend, chef Martin Picard of Au Pied de Cochon in Montreal, to develop two gins under the PDC name. Production of these gins has moved to Distillerie de Montréal to keep up with the incredible demand for them.

TASTING NOTES:
AU PIED DE COCHON GIN DE MATANTE (40% ABV)

This gin's nose balances an enticing fruity sweetness with black peppercorn spice. Satiny sweetness on the palate cushions stewed rhubarb, seasoned with a zesty, late-palate zing. Chef Martin Picard shows that his brilliant reinvention of rich and decadent Quebecois cuisine can also have a delicate and refined layer, just as it does in this gin.

TASTING NOTES:
AU PIED DE COCHON GIN DE MONOCLE (40% ABV)

Chef Martin Picard pays tribute to the liquid in the famous green bottle of DeKuyper gin that traces its lineage to Montreal's Meagher's Distillery. Picard's own green-labelled bottle opens with a juniper-forward nose, balanced by floral violets and licorice. The palate shifts to forest tones with a toasted woodiness. These big flavours are balanced by sweetness and a velvety texture that could only come from a chef's masterful touch.

DISTILLERIE NOROI
SAINT-HYACINTHE, QC

The idea for Distillerie Noroi began to take form when Jonathan Robin found success in an unrelated field. Robin is a construction entrepreneur, and he created Synergia—an office building where notaries, lawyers, and bankers share common services while building their independent practices. What about trying the same approach for start-ups in the agri-food industry? A 1,200-square-metre building owned by his construction firm was available. All he needed were compatible businesses to share the space and to explore the benefits and economies of scale that such a colocation project could provide.

Robin's interest in distilling gin went back to the fall of 2015. He dreamed of creating a gin that captured the full character of its botanicals, a near impossibility with conventional distilling. Not only did the various essences have differing boiling points, but some of them were so fragile that they could not survive in the heat of the still. The answer was an obscure technology called cold distillation. Robin knew that in a vacuum, the temperature at which essences evaporate is greatly reduced. By distilling his botanicals in a vacuum, all their subtleties would be captured, including those heat-sensitive molecules. That's when he turned to Scottish inventor Matthew Pauley for help. The resulting 60-litre glass vacuum still looks like something straight out of the classic sci-fi film *Forbidden Planet*. Cooled with liquid nitrogen, it has become the heart of the Noroi process. Three conventional stills, including a 5,000-litre iStill pot, complement the process, allowing Noroi to distil its less volatile ingredients using traditional methods while reserving the vacuum still for more fragile and delicate botanicals.

With an investment of $2.5 million in economic development funding, Noroi launched early in 2019, using 325 dedicated square metres of the larger space. The distillery also shares space and equipment with a kombucha maker and a brewery that are colocated in the Saint-Hyacinthe building. While the three businesses have separate ownership and operate independently, Robin has taken a partnership interest in each.

6596 boul. Choquette
Saint-Hyacinthe, QC J2S 8E1
(450) 418-8008
www.distillerienoroi.com

@distillerienoroi

FOUNDED 2019

OWNER Jonathan Robin

STILLS 60-litre glass vacuum; 50-litre Still Dragon; 500-litre iStill; 5,000-litre iStill

PRODUCTS Gin, liqueurs, canned vodka soda

AVAILABILITY SAQ

TOURS Contact the distillery

NEAREST NEIGHBOURS Cidrerie Michel Jodoin (page 231) — 25 min; Distillerie de Montréal (page 232) — 45 min; Distillerie Shefford (page 243) — 50 min

6 rue des Cerisiers
Gaspé, QC G4X 2M2
www.odwyerdistillery.com

NEAREST NEIGHBOURS La Société Secrète
(page 245) — 50 min; Distillerie du St.
Laurent (page 241) — 4 hrs, 30 min

O'DWYER DISTILLERIE GASPÉSIENNE
GASPÉ, QC

The forests that blanket the Gaspé Peninsula rise with the mountains and dip with the valleys. Wetlands and sea cliffs fill the gaps in between. The area's geography and climate are perfect for wild mushrooms. Gaspésie Sauvage is a foraging group that sustainably cultivates mushrooms that grow in the wild.

Michael Briand and Frédéric Jacques opened their distillery on this peninsula and include the local mushrooms as a botanical for their Radoune Gin, named after the area between the two mountains where these mushrooms grow in abundance. Wild juniper that flourishes in their backyards is prepared for distilling by drying it with sea salt. The distillery also has plans to distil whisky in the coming years.

TASTING NOTES: **RADOUNE GIN** (43% ABV)
There is a grace to the floral nose that contrasts with damp soil and clear mushroom notes. Juniper and sweetness charge the palate, adding complexity. Citrus, mint, and peppery coriander brighten a savoury mid-palate brine. The gin's sweetness sits long into the uninterrupted finish. This is an iconic Canadian gin.

OLD MONTREAL DISTILLERY
MONTREAL, QC

It took an American firm, the Sazerac Company of New Orleans, to bring distilling back to the former Meagher's Distillery just south of the Lachine Canal in Montreal. Rebuilt at this location in 1920 to make liqueurs and genever, the distillery has been the bottling plant for Sazerac's Canadian whisky portfolio for the past two decades. Over the years, McGuinness (and then Corby) owned the plant before Sazerac bought it in 2011. Located within walking distance of Old Montreal, it is a must-see for visitors to the city's busiest tourist area.

Sazerac is one of the American firms that Seagram's turned to for distribution after Prohibition ended in the US. Although Sazerac is a large company, this is not the largest distillery in Canada. However, with its half-metre diameter, 11-metre-tall Vendome column still, 5,700-litre pot, and 15,000-litre mash cooker, it produces about 18 barrels of whisky spirit a day. Sazerac also has a huge inventory of mature Canadian whiskies purchased from other producers, and the company plans to use Old Montreal as a testing ground for new whiskies. A lot of that experimentation revolves around mash bills. According to master blender Drew Mayville, "The intent is to develop unique, richer, bolder, more complex Canadian whiskies."

Distillery manager Gerry Cristiano began his career in 1990 at the now-defunct Seagram's distillery in LaSalle. From there, he moved over to Corby when Seagram's was dissolved in 2001, and has been at this distillery ever since.

"I love the industry," he exclaims. "You're a fun guy to be around when you are in the liquor industry." He is excited to get back to distilling whisky rather than just blending and bottling it, and he is especially delighted to welcome visitors to this venerable plant.

950 ch. des Moulins
Montreal, QC H3C 3W5
(514) 395-3200

🐦 @SazeracCompany

FOUNDED 1920; recommissioned 2011

OWNERS Sazerac Company

STILLS 11-metre Vendome column and 5,700-litre Vendome pot

PRODUCTS Whisky

AVAILABILITY Across Canada and the US

TOURS Contact the distillery

NEAREST NEIGHBOURS Cirka Distilleries (page 226) — 15 min; Distillerie de Montréal (page 232) — 20 min; Brasserie & Distillerie Oshlag (page 236) — 25 min

TASTING NOTES: **MISTER SAM** (66.9% ABV)

Sazerac's master blender, Drew Mayville, has taken premium American and Canadian whiskies from his whisky library and blended them into a treasure that honours the legendary "Mister" Sam Bronfman, who created several of Sazerac's brands. You may want to sit down before opening this one. The nose dazzles with mature oak, smoke, dark fruits, chocolate, vanilla, and tobacco. The sumptuous palate is loaded with candied dried fruits, cherry, and toasted oak spices, shifting into a honeyed finish that is layered with oaky goodness.

COCKTAIL: **CARIBOU MANHATTAN**

MAKES 1 COCKTAIL

2 oz Caribou Crossing Canadian Whisky
½ oz sweet vermouth
1 dash Peychaud Bitters
1 maraschino cherry for garnish
Handful of ice cubes

In a mixing glass with ice, combine whisky, vermouth, and bitters. Stir for 20 seconds, then strain into a chilled coupe glass. Garnish with maraschino cherry added directly into the cocktail.

BRASSERIE & DISTILLERIE OSHLAG
MONTREAL, QC

2350 rue Dickson, #1400
Montreal, QC H1N 3T1
(438) 387-6500
www.oshlag.com

 @OshlagBrassDist

@oshlag

FOUNDED 2010 (brewery), 2016
(distillery)

OWNER Glutenberg Group

PRODUCTS Gin, ready-to-drink cocktails,
vodka, black whisky

AVAILABILITY SAQ

TOURS Contact the distillery

NEAREST NEIGHBOURS Distillerie de
Montréal (page 232) — 20 min; Old
Montreal Distillery (page 234) — 25 min;
Cirka Distilleries (page 226) — 30 min

In 2010 his sensitivity to gluten led a frustrated Julien Niquet to create Glutenberg, a brewery to specialize in gluten-free beer. Getting that beer to market proved difficult, and he soon sought an alternative. Niquet formed the distribution company Transbroue and started distributing beer for Glutenberg and a number of other microbrewers throughout Quebec. The year 2016 marked a turning point when the firm opened the Oshlag brewery and distillery in Montreal. As a brewer and director of operations at Glutenberg, Jean-François Théorêt was thrilled at this opportunity to distil. He wanted to create spirits that drew their inspiration from brewing, and like many new distillers, he began making vodka. His was vodka with a genuine beer twist, though. After distilling it, he flavoured it with Cascade hops.

Théorêt discovered microdistilling when he was travelling in Germany in 2007. He was intrigued, and soon began studying for a master's degree in the brewing and distilling program at Edinburgh's Heriot-Watt University. Théorêt's first whisky, released in 2019, is a little different. He calls it Black Whisky to reflect the dark colour of the chocolate malt, coffee malt, caramelized malt, and roasted oats he uses for the mash. And curiously, just as early brewers in this neighbourhood had done two centuries earlier, he adds hops to his mash. He matures his whisky in French oak barrels.

And the name Oshlag? That's more history. It refers to the nearby site of an Iroquois settlement that Jacques Cartier visited when he explored the area way back in 1535.

TASTING NOTES: OSHLAG HIBISCUS GIN (40% ABV)

The citrus peel on the nose of this pink gin is incredibly floral and complex. Traditional juniper and earthy coriander-citrus sit high on the palate with bright peppery tones. At the core of this gin's identity are vanilla, citrus pith, and cinnamon, which are accentuated by a tart, lemony cranberry finish. All rest on a complementary base of peppery, piney spices.

COCKTAIL:
HIBISCUS GIN FIZZ
MAKES 1 COCKTAIL

2 cardamom sugar cubes
1 oz lemon juice
2 oz Oshlag Hibiscus Gin
1 egg white
Handful of ice cubes
4 oz soda water
1 lemon wheel, for garnish

Place a highball glass in the freezer until chilled, at least one hour. In a cocktail shaker, add the sugar cubes and lemon juice and muddle until the sugar dissolves. Add the gin and egg white, and dry-shake vigorously for 20 seconds. Add ice, then shake again for 20 seconds. Double-strain into a chilled highball glass, then top with soda water. Garnish with lemon wheel.

LALLEMAND INC.

I t often surprises people that yeast is a key source of flavour in distilled spirits. No less surprising is that one of the world's leading yeast producers is based right here in Canada. Today, nearly 4,000 people around the world work in what was Alsatian immigrant Frédéric-Alfred Shurrer's business venture late in the 19th century. Montrealers called the young man with the broad German accent "l'Allemand"—the German. He liked his nickname, and adopted it for his yeast plant. In 1952 Roland Chagnon acquired the business. Today, Chagnon's grandchildren operate Lallemand from a century-old red campus on Montreal's Préfontaine Street. Yes, the spirits we wax eloquent about all begin with humble yeast.

A microscopic microorganism, yeast—a fungus, really—consumes sugar and turns it into equal amounts of alcohol and carbon dioxide, along with tiny quantities of very potent flavour molecules called congeners. Yeast lives practically everywhere you can imagine. Leave any sweet liquid out for a few days, and yeast will find and ferment it. However, not all yeasts make palatable drinks; distillers must select the best ones. Some long-established fermenting regions simply let nature supply the yeast, but this is not as unmanaged as it sounds. For generations, European winemakers have spread the leftovers from winemaking back into their vineyards, thereby reinoculating them with large quantities of specific yeasts. Consequently, over the centuries they have

Sheets of single strain yeast peeling off a drum dryer (previous page) begin as individual laboratory cultures in Petri dishes.

established favourable wine yeasts as the predominant wild species. Similarly, Belgian brewers have promoted dominance of particular beer yeasts in their breweries.

From an evolutionary perspective, brewing and distilling are relatively new in Canada, so Canadian distillers can't rely on nature. They need a reliable alternative to provide good distilling yeasts. Scientists at Lallemand study how yeast produces congeners and select strains that emphasize desirable characteristics. Distillers can choose from among about a dozen of them for those that will provide the desired flavours.

Lallemand stores frozen samples of these special yeasts in cryovials. When a distiller orders a specific strain, a sample from the cryovial is spread on a growth medium called agar, inside a small tube known as a slant. As it grows, the yeast is transferred to flasks and fed a complex propagation diet: a liquid solution of molasses enriched with oxygen, vitamins, and nitrogen. Rather than making alcohol, this yeast produces more yeast—biomass, as they call it. Ultimately, the contents of the flasks are used to seed large propagation tanks. Finally, massive drums dehydrate the mature yeast before feeding it into extruders to be made into pellets. Within a week, that little dab of yeast that a lab technician took from the cryovial has grown into 16,000 kilograms of dry yeast, to be packaged, ready to ship to our favourite distillery.

Yes, we owe a debt of thanks to the legacy of Frédéric-Alfred Shurrer for many of the spirits we enjoy today. He turned a small start-up yeast plant in Montreal into a global enterprise supplying specialty yeasts to distillers large and small. ■

www.piratedunord.com

NEAREST NEIGHBOURS Intermiel (page 228) — 30 min; Les Vergers Lafrance (page 229) — 30 min

DISTILLERIE LE PIRATE DU NORD
MIRABEL, QC

When he opened his distillery in 2015, André Trudeau's goal was to make rum. He got his sea legs with an oak-and-applewood-finished gin that he called BB3, short for Bootlegger Botanique #3. In 2018 he took a chance and entered BB3 in the New York International Spirits Competition, where it won gold. But what about his passion for rum? New distillers often bemoan the law that says they must age whisky for at least three years. A similar law requires them to age rum for at least one year, so those who do not have deep pockets often begin with vodka or gin, which they can sell right away. Nevertheless, with a gold medal to validate Trudeau's skill as a distiller (and also boost sales), he continues to make the rum that first got him interested, and he has also decided to weigh anchor with whisky. Now *there's* the jaunty confidence of a pirate.

1180 rue du Fer
Havre-Saint-Pierre, QC G0G 1P0
www.distilleriepuyjalon.com

NEAREST NEIGHBOURS Distillerie du Fjord (page 228) — 8 hrs, 50 min; Menaud Distillerie et Brasserie (page 231) — 8 hrs, 40 min

DISTILLERIE PUYJALON INC.
HAVRE-SAINT-PIERRE, QC

Who is Puyjalon? Count Henry de Puyjalon, if you don't mind! In 1888 he was the first lighthouse keeper on the small island of Île aux Perroquets, east of Havre-Saint-Pierre. He was also a geologist and botanist, and he explored the St. Lawrence River's north shore, all the while advocating for the creation of conservation areas. On those same shores, just across from Anticosti Island, the distillery's hometown boasts a long sandy beach with a panoramic view of the gulf. Today, Mario Noël, Caroline Doyle, Fanny Desmeules, and Dany Flowers distil their Betchwan Premium Gin in a nearby barn-shaped building with grey siding and red trim. Let it tickle your toes as you sit in the sand. The crew has plans for vodka, whisky, and rum, and has also been eyeing the region's native cloudberries for future spirits.

DISTILLERIE DE QUÉBEC
QUEBEC CITY, QC

400 rue du Platine, #6
Quebec City, QC G2N 2G6
www.distilleriedequebec.ca

NEAREST NEIGHBOURS Vice & Vertu
Distilleries (page 253) – 30 min;
Distillerie Wabasso (page 253) – 1 hr,
30 min; Menaud Distillerie et Brasserie
(page 231) – 1 hr, 50 min

Christophe Légasse and David Lévesque want to travel back to a time long before prohibition soured the reputation of La Belle Province. Nouvelle-France used to be dotted with small, forgotten distilleries in what is now urban Quebec City. Their spirits continue to pay tribute to this era. Cap-Diamant Vodka recalls the plateau where the St. Lawrence River narrows and Old Quebec still stands strong. It is on these waters where ships filled with goods from around the globe sail into port. The distillery celebrates this history with spirits combining global ingredients and local terroir. Trait-Carré Gin pays homage to the city's historical Charlesbourg district, which was laid out in a star shape for protection and to bring citizens together to a central point. Today, the gin's 14 botanicals may have them converging on another point instead—the distillery. There is other history here that is not celebrated in the distillery's spirits. During prohibition, ships carrying whisky from Seagram's distillery in Montreal, and others, plied these waters on their way to supply American bootleggers.

DISTILLERIE DU ST. LAURENT
RIMOUSKI, QC

327A rue Rivard
Rimouski, QC G5L 7J6
(418) 800-4694
www.distilleriedustlaurent.com

@distilleriedustlaurent

FOUNDED 2015

OWNERS Jean-François Cloutier and Joël
Pelletier

STILLS 2,000-litre Specific Mechanical
still; 1,000-litre pot still

PRODUCTS Acerum, aged gin, gin,
moonshine, whisky

AVAILABILITY Onsite and SAQ—gin is
available internationally

TOURS Monday–Friday (check website)

Jean-François Cloutier traded in a career in naval architecture to pursue distilling with co-owner and brand admiral Joël Pelletier. In 2015 Quebec microdistilling was still in its infancy, making financing difficult. Investors had trouble wrapping their chequebooks around a concept they didn't fully understand or appreciate. "We started really small, with a 400-litre still, and made about 100,000 bottles of gin." These impressive numbers in the first couple of years attracted the kind of financial support that allowed the two to upgrade their distillery. They replaced the small gin still with a 1,000-litre version and brought in a 2,000-litre Specific Mechanical still to make whisky. On December 12, 2018, they filled their 100th barrel.

(continued)

NEAREST NEIGHBOURS Vice & Vertu Distilleries (page 253) — 3 hr, 20 min; Distillerie de Québec (page 241) — 3 hrs, 25 min; O'Dwyer Distillerie Gaspésienne (page 234) — 4 hrs, 30 min

Malheureusement (sadly), when the whisky still arrived from the manufacturer, the instructions were in English. On the still there is a lyne arm (pronounced *line*) that connects the condenser to the column. "We are just a bunch of French guys looking at the box and instructions and pronouncing Lyne like a woman's name," says Cloutier. A name like *bras de jonction* or similar would have been crystal clear. "So we're saying, bring Lyne's arms, bring Lyne's legs as we assembled and mounted the still," laughs Cloutier. "At the end of the day, even though we were looking for a grandiose name, I turned to the team and said, 'We're stuck with "Lyne," guys.'"

Cloutier and Pelletier are inspired by the American way of making whisky and have turned to fermenting two mash bills—a bourbon style with 75% corn, plus rye and malted barley, and a rye mash bill with 80% rye and 20% malted barley. They also have single malt whisky ageing. The Rimouski region is famous for its smoked fish, and drawing on that tradition, the barley malt is smoked with maple wood. "We were inspired by the smokehouses and their 'Let's throw the malt in the smoker and see what happens' attitude. It's cold-smoked barley, which is flavourful without being overpowering," says Cloutier. The region defines who the distillery's people are, and they are proud that the region's character has found its way into their spirits.

TASTING NOTES: **ST. LAURENT GIN** (43% ABV)

This dry gin, inspired by the sea, contains laminaria seaweed hand-harvested in the Bas-Saint-Laurent region. This brings a subtle savouriness to the integrated nose of juniper, pepper, and citrus. The seaweed, nicknamed "the devil's apron," lends the gin a sea-green tinge. On the palate, forest tones and structured spice are seasoned by a pinch of seaweed salt to finish this cultured gin.

COCKTAIL: **LYNE'S MARTINI**
MAKES 1 COCKTAIL

3 oz St. Laurent Gin
¼ tablespoon of olive juice
¼ tablespoon of dry white vermouth
3 pimento-stuffed Manzanilla olives for garnish

Place a martini glass in the freezer overnight along with the bottle of gin and refrigerate the bottle of vermouth. In the chilled glass, combine gin, olive juice, and dry white vermouth. Stir gently and garnish with three skewered Manzanilla olives.

DISTILLERIE SHEFFORD
SHEFFORD, QC

In France, certain spirits categories enjoy designations of origin, which protect tradition, geographical character, and style. Only distillers located in these regions and who follow approved production practices can call their products Armagnac, Calvados, and Cognac. In Mexico it's tequila. In Quebec it's Acerum. Retirees Gérald Lacroix and Josée Métivier of Distillerie Shefford, along with Distillerie du St. Laurent (page 241) and the Domaine Acer maple winery, have pioneered Quebec's first designation for a spirit distilled with maple sap ingredients. This spirit is in its infancy, and like a prodigy in a talent show, it's too soon to know if Acerum will be the next big thing.

Legally, in order to be called Acerum, the spirit must be made solely from Quebec maple sources, fermented, distilled, and bottled at a Quebec distillery, and have a minimum abv of 35%. Distillerie Shefford distils an unaged white Acerum expression and an oak-aged brown expression. Everything has a first; with Distillerie Shefford, that's one small step for Acerum, one giant leap for . . . well, you get the idea.

1125 rue Denison E.
Shefford, QC J2M 1Y6
www.distillerieshefford.com

FOUNDED 2017

OWNERS Gérald Lacroix and Josée Métivier

STILLS iStill 500 NextGen and iStill 100 NextGen

PRODUCTS Acerum, vodka

AVAILABILITY Onsite and SAQ

TOURS For group tours, contact the distillery

NEAREST NEIGHBOURS Absintherie des Cantons (page 224) – 20 min; Cidrerie Michel Jodoin (page 231) – 40 min; Distillerie Noroi (page 233) – 50 min

TASTING NOTES:
DISTILLERIE SHEFFORD ACÉRUM BRUN (40% ABV)

"Acerum" is derived from the Latin for maple trees, and it is *delectamenti*. This oak-aged maple spirit has a nose of caramel, ripe orchard fruits, and pear tarts. Cinnamon-forward oak spices are delicately accentuated by an orange pith, sotolon, and the maple's natural mineral characteristics. Maple sugars scrumptiously accent the finish, ushering in this new class of spirit.

MAISON SIVO
FRANKLIN, QC

1598 ch. de Covey Hill
Franklin, QC J0S 1E0
(514) 773-9460
www.maisonsivo.ca

[instagram] @maison_sivo

FOUNDED 2013

OWNER Janos Sivo

STILLS 250-litre Mueller pot with
400-millimetre 4-plate column

PRODUCTS Aquavit, eau-de-vie, liqueurs,
moonshine, whisky

AVAILABILITY SAQ and My Wines Canada

TOURS Contact the distillery

NEAREST NEIGHBOURS Valleyfield
Distillery (page 251) — 40 min; Thomspon
Distillery (page 250) — 50 min

Janos Sivo retired from the telecommunications industry determined that he would never sit in a rocking chair and let his last and best remaining days drift by. Instead, he started a new career that was already rooted in his family's blood: he opened a distillery.

In socialist Hungary during the 1950s, Sivo fondly remembers families distilling their own spirits. "There were many fruit trees next to roads, in backyards, and at the fields," recounts his son, Zsuzsa Sivo. "First, fruits were picked and eaten, then used to make stewed fruits, and the rest were used to make eau-de-vie, called palinka.

"This was the cheapest way of getting to alcohol. No sugar was added, since that would have cost 'real' money."

Homemade stills were made from two milk cans and from copper pipes "borrowed" from nearby factories. "Distilling was illegal, but it was also common. The village policeman was one of our family's best customers."

Today, if the police drop by Sivo's distillery located in Franklin, it is to pick up whisky, because Sivo makes both rye and malt whiskies. His single malt is a blend of whiskies, aged in several casks, including new oak, Sauternes, and ex-beer casks. He also adds 1% Sauternes wine to the blend to add complexity and texture.

There is also the water to consider. Before the distillery moved in, an entrepreneur planned to build a water-bottling plant on this site. Luckily for Quebec whisky, a referendum decided that this bottled-water boy must move along. "The quality of the water at the foothills of the Adirondacks is outstanding," explains Zsuzsa, adding that this is one of many reasons why his father chose this location. Fresh air is another.

The Sivos are as passionate about horses as they are about making whisky, and include illustrations of horses on many of their labels. Zsuzsa sees them as beautiful, sensitive, and delicate, yet powerful and bold. A poetic perception that says as much about the family's passionate outlook as it does about the character Maison Sivo captures in its whisky.

TASTING NOTES: LE RYE SIVO (42% ABV)

This rye whisky is aged in European oak casks, then finished in port barrels. The nose displays a cornucopia of raisin, orchard fruits, cherry pie, searing pepper, rye spice, and grasses. Oak surges onto the palate, with its trademark spices. Chest-warming rye spices hit the palate with acute precision, along with a touch of malt, while softer oak on the finish nicely integrates straw and sweet port. Sivo Rye is a whisky to watch for.

COCKTAIL: SIVO SIGNATURE

MAKES 1 COCKTAIL

2 handfuls of ice
1¼ oz Maison Sivo Rebel, le Moonshine du Rye
¾ oz Maison Sivo Shámán herbal liqueur
3 dashes forest bitters
¾ oz lemon juice
½ oz simple syrup
Handful of ice cubes
4 cucumber slices
3 oz sparkling water
Fresh thyme sprig, for garnish

In a cocktail shaker with ice, combine Rebel, Shámán, forest bitters, lemon juice, and simple syrup. Shake for 10 seconds. Strain into an Old Fashioned glass containing ice and cucumber slices. Top with sparkling water, then garnish with a sprig of thyme.

(Manu Ruiz)

LA SOCIÉTÉ SECRÈTE
CAP-D'ESPOIR, QC

If God knew about this distillery, he or she would have instructed Noah to use the wood to build a liquor cabinet instead of an ark. That's because Geneviève Blais, Mathieu Fleury, Amélie-Kim Boulianne, and Michaël Côté have saved one of the Almighty's other homes from demolition. St. James Church was built in 1845, and in time it fell into disrepair. The Heritage Foundation of Percé was looking for ways to resurrect and bring occupants into the building. La Société Secrète needed a home and noted that the church's high ceilings would be perfect for their towering column still. What was formerly a place of worship is now where the distillery makes vodka and other spirits, as well as a gin it calls Les Herbes Folles. They infuse this gin with wild local botanicals before ageing it in oak. Its flavours? Heavenly!

1164 Route 132 O.
Cap-d'Espoir, QC G0C 1G0
http://societesecrete.ca

NEAREST NEIGHBOURS O'Dwyer Distillerie Gaspésienne (page 234) — 50 min; Distillerie du St. Laurent (page 241) — 5 hrs

LES DISTILLATEURS SUBVERSIFS
SOREL-TRACY, QC

850 Route 132
Sorel-Tracy, QC J3R 4T9
www.subversifs.ca

 @LesSubversifs

@les_subversifs

FOUNDED 2010

OWNERS Fernando Balthazard, Stéphan Ruffo, Pascal Gervais, Richard Paradis

PRODUCTS Gin, liqueurs, vodka

AVAILABILITY SAQ

TOURS Contact the distillery

NEAREST NEIGHBOURS Brasserie & Distillerie Oshlag (page 236) — 50 min; Distillerie Mariana (page 230) — 1 hr; Distillerie Wabasso (page 253) — 1 hr, 10 min

Our Lady of the Parsnip? With dozens of new gins available to consumers, Fernando Balthazard, Stéphan Ruffo, and Pascal Gervais—and Richard Paradis, who joined them later—were searching for something that would differentiate theirs from the rest. They tried one recipe after another, but none seemed right. They had already named their operation "The Subversive Distillers" and were still searching for something unexpected that had an appealing flavour but at the same time would break the traditional gin mould. Then, one evening, after chatting with a friend who ran an heirloom seed business, Ruffo grated some raw parsnip root into a glass of London Dry Gin. The result was spectacular. The partners had soon developed a recipe for their first product, Piger Henricus Gin. Although Les Subversifs often name their products after disruptive figures from Quebec history, Piger Henricus's honourable name refers to a 19th-century alchemist's oven.

Founded in Longueuil in 2010, Les Subversifs outgrew their quarters, and in 2018 they moved operations to Sorel-Tracy, east of Montreal. There, they found a large vacant space where they could set up shop without running into walls or pillars: the former Marie-Auxiliatrice Church. The only feature that remains from the former occupants is an altar. Other than a large sign on the front of the building and the word "Subversive" painted on the roof, the distillers have promised the city to respect the design of the historic building. And let's not forget that prohibition failed to take hold fully in Quebec in part because the Catholic Church saw nothing subversive about drinking wine and beer. Okay, spirits were forbidden, but back then, no one had thought about making gin out of parsnips.

TASTING NOTES:
PIGER HENRICUS GIN
(43% ABV)

Zesty lemon peel and juniper waft to the nose with the earthy carrot and dill flavour of parsnips. This juniper-forward gin has a spicy floral high note on the palate, with a slight bitterness woven into a late-palate mushroom. A burst of citrus on the finish freshens this distinctive gin.

COCKTAIL:
AVIATION COCKTAIL
MAKES 1 COCKTAIL

2 oz Gin de Marie-Victorin
½ oz maraschino liqueur
¼ oz crème de violette
½ oz lemon juice
Handful of ice cubes
Lemon twist for garnish

Place a coupe in the freezer until chilled, at least one hour. Add gin, maraschino liqueur, crème de violette, lemon juice and ice to a shaker and shake for 10 seconds. Strain into chilled coupe glass. Garnish with a lemon twist.

DIAGEO BLENDING LAB

So, you want to be a master blender? If that means your spirit will be blended as masterfully as Crown Royal, then be prepared to set aside at least eight to 10 years to learn all that's involved. "That's about one full cycle," says blender Joanna Zanin Scandella, referring to how long whisky spirit matures for Crown Royal. The blender must be involved in every step of creating and maintaining their blends. They assess newly distilled spirit, monitor it as it matures, and decide which barrels will be used for which blends.

The human nose, more sensitive than any scientific instrument assures consistency and quality in Canada's bestselling whisky, Crown Royal.

A formal sensory accreditation process ensures that the blender possesses all the skills required for the work. Why? Because blending is an art. In the Diageo Blending Lab in Montreal, where Crown Royal is blended, there are no scientific instruments to measure quality. All evaluation is done strictly by nose. This means the blender must recognize every significant aroma. If they miss just one? Well, they'll find something else to do elsewhere. As well, a formal training program teaches key elements of blending, while a rigorously applied checklist records prospective blenders' progress and ensures they really understand those elements.

Former Seagram's CEO Sam Bronfman, who created Crown Royal, believed that distilling was a science and blending was an art. Bronfman famously said, "When a man goes into a store for a bottle of Coca-Cola, he expects it to be the same today as it will be tomorrow. The great products don't change. Well, our product's not going to change either."

He directed his blenders to figure out how to ensure that it didn't. What they learned has revolutionized the blending of brown spirits—epitomized, of course, in the top-selling Canadian whisky of all time, Crown Royal. "It almost became a religion for us," says long-retired blender Art Dawe, remembering Bronfman's credo.

The company's idea was to create each blend from many different components, so that they could be adjusted to ensure consistency. Crown Royal draws on over 50 different whiskies. When the rye is extra spicy, as it was in 1998, the blender can cut back rye-heavy whiskies in favour of less assertive corn.

The goal of the blender when creating a new spirit is to achieve "robust quality," explains Zanin Scandella. The first thing to look at is whether there is enough whisky to sustain the blend over time. Even with 2.4 million barrels in their warehouses, sales of Crown Royal are massive.

The new whisky begins with test blends. "There are always two or three samples where you say, 'Aha!' And then you tweak it," she continues. Some components are expensive to produce, and that means any tweaks must result in the desired profile while at the same time meeting cost targets. In the end, there is no single master blender; Crown Royal's quality is the result of a team effort. Diageo's head office agrees, naming the Montreal-based blending quality team its "Team of the Year" in 2016.

According to Zanin Scandella, the role of the Canadian whisky blender is "upholding tradition while embracing innovation." This takes the story back to those old blending protocols that were created here in Montreal as far back as the 1930s, and which certainly achieved success then, as they continue to do today. ■

1455 Route 132
Kahnawake, QC J0L 1B0

NEAREST NEIGHBOURS Cirka Distilleries
(page 226) — 25 min; Old Montreal
Distillery (page 234) — 30 min

THOMPSON DISTILLERY
KAHNAWAKE, QC

A proud Indigenous person, Lee Thompson believes he runs the first on-reserve distillery in North America—and likely the first ever to be owned by an Indigenous person. Getting there involves driving along busy Route 132 as it crosses the Kahnawake reserve on the south side of the St. Lawrence River near Montreal, before making a U-turn when you get to Blind Lady's Hill Road. Thompson's distillery, right beside the Mohawk Casino, sits directly across from a tiny business called Rez Smokes. Founded in 2016, the distillery produces vodka, gin, and liqueurs.

www.towerhillroad.com

NEAREST NEIGHBOURS Old Montreal
Distillery (page 234) — 10 min; Cirka
Distilleries (page 226) — 20 min

TOWER HILL ROAD DISTILLERY
MONTREAL, QC

Back in 1926, the neighbours living next to Pierre F. Houpert's Connecticut farm must have thought Houpert had some kind of addiction to baking. A steady flow of sugar was delivered to his Tower Hill Road address, even though he never dropped by with a neighbourly tin of cookies. That was because he was not baking; he was making moonshine. Today, Laurent and Philippe Houpert celebrate their great-uncle's heritage with a vodka they call Houpert & Frère. They make their vodka from corn, the grain of choice for traditional moonshine. And just like their great-uncle, these brothers are running a small operation, but this time distilling their vodka on computer-automated stills called iStills. There's an app for that, which allows the distiller to monitor production over Wi-Fi, which in turn leaves plenty of time to bring cookies to the neighbours.

VALLEYFIELD DISTILLERY
SALABERRY-DE-VALLEYFIELD, QC

The long, slender property where the Valleyfield Distillery is located dates back to the system of land distribution in early Quebec. When rivers were a primary means of transportation, land lots were narrow to ensure that as many of them as possible offered access to the river. The distillery as it exists today was built in 1945 by Lewis Rosenstiel's Schenley Distillers Corporation. In 1990 United Distillers and Vintners, one of the firms that would evolve into Diageo (page 248), bought the distillery, and after a head-spinning series of mergers and acquisitions it was Diageo that finally took it over in 2008.

By mashing primarily Quebec corn 24 hours a day, five days a week, and distilling the fermented mash 24/7, the distillery produces about 28 million litres of alcohol a year in its 1.2-metre column still. With the installation of a 1.8-metre column and a new copper pot still in 2018, Diageo now looks to Valleyfield for its innovation program, as well as to take some of the pressure off their Gimli plant to keep up with demand for Crown Royal. The distillery manager, Martin Laberge, is eager to try some new mash bills, though his first challenge is to replicate, in Quebec, the Gimli profile from Manitoba. Innovation is where the fun is, suggests Laberge, because he does not have to match any existing profile. Valleyfield's warehouses, including a new addition, are at about 95% capacity, with 850,000 barrels resting for the eight to 12 years they need before they are blended into Crown Royal (page 154).

Until the 2018 sale of V.O., Five Star, and Canadian 83 to Sazerac, Valleyfield was responsible for those brands. It's an irony that whisky from this distillery is now part of the growing Crown Royal inventory, given how much Sam Bronfman, who created Crown Royal, detested Lewis Rosenstiel! In addition to distilling, Valleyfield operates a full bottling plant where it bottles all the specialty versions of Crown Royal. Sadly for Crown Royal aficionados looking for a glimpse inside, they do not offer tours.

(continued)

1 rue Salaberry O.
Salaberry-de-Valleyfield, QC J6T 2G9
(450) 373-3230
www.diageo.com

@CrownRoyal

@crownroyal

FOUNDED 1945

OWNERS Diageo

STILLS Custom commercial columns and pot

PRODUCTS Whisky

AVAILABILITY Canada, US, and abroad

TOURS No

NEAREST NEIGHBOURS Thompson Distillery (page 250) — 35 min; Maison Sivo (page 244) — 40 min

TASTING NOTES:
CROWN ROYAL SALTED CARAMEL (35% ABV)

This flavoured whisky features a sweet, rich nose of caramel against a smoky oak-whisky backdrop. The palate is rich and creamy, with maple-dipped caramels oozing with vanilla accented by oak spice. Whisky is reintroduced late on the palate with a pinch of salt that balances out the sweetness and allows oak spices to shine through the incredibly long finish. Slap a crown on this one; flavoured Canadian whisky has a king.

COCKTAIL: BILLION DOLLAR APPLE
MAKES 1 COCKTAIL

GRENADINE:
1 cup unsweetened pomegranate juice
1 cup sugar

COCKTAIL:
¾ oz Crown Royal Apple Whisky
¾ oz Crown Royal XO Canadian Whisky
½ oz sweet vermouth
½ oz grenadine
½ oz fresh-squeezed lemon juice
½ oz cranberry juice
Handful of ice cubes
Maraschino cherry, for garnish

For the Grenadine, add the pomegranate juice and sugar to a saucepan and stir over medium heat until the sugar dissolves. Bring to a boil, then remove from the heat and let cool. Stores in the refrigerator for up to a month in a sealed container.

For the cocktail, place a coupe glass in the freezer until chilled, at least one hour. Add Crown Royal Apple Whisky, Crown Royal XO Canadian Whisky, sweet vermouth, grenadine, lemon juice, and cranberry juice to a shaker and fill with ice. Shake hard for 10 seconds, then double-strain into the chilled coupe glass. Garnish with a maraschino cherry.

(Eric Ribeiro)

VICE & VERTU DISTILLERIES
SAINT-AUGUSTIN-DE-DESMAURES, QC

15 rue de Rotterdam, #11
Saint-Augustin-de-Desmaures, QC
G3A 1S8
www.vicevertu.ca

NEAREST NEIGHBOURS Distillerie de
Québec (page 241) – 30 min; Distillerie
Wabasso (page 253) – 1 hr, 15 min

Dr. Franck Sergerie's passion for spirits and the alchemy behind them inspired him to open this distillery in the fall of 2017. The distillery's name was born out of the contrast between the virtues of life as a radiologist and the (potential) vices he could encourage as a distiller. But his personal combination of "vice" and "vertu" doesn't mean that an angel sits on one shoulder and a devil on the other. In fact, his BeOrigins Gin has its own distinct virtues. For this London Dry Gin, Sergerie uses traditional botanicals, along with blueberry and birch bark, an Indigenous botanical with long-established healing properties. The distillery has expanded to include barrel storage, so the next step will be to fill all its racks with whisky.

DISTILLERIE WABASSO
TROIS-RIVIÈRES, QC

www.distilleriewabasso.com

NEAREST NEIGHBOURS Distillerie Mariana
(page 230) – 30 min; Les Distillateurs
Subversifs (page 246) – 1 hr, 10 min;
Vice & Vertu Distilleries (page 253)
– 1 hr, 15 min

Cofounder Maxime Vincent fell in love with the artisanal side of the business while working at the Microbrasserie Alchimiste, a microbrewery in nearby Joliette. He opened his own distillery in 2018 with business partner Guyaume Parenteau. In 1907, Charles Ross Whitehead founded his Wabasso Cotton Company in Trois-Rivières. By the time it closed in 1985 Wabasso had become an emblem of the city, and Vincent and Parenteau were inspired to maintain that emblem in their distillery. Wabasso is also Ojibwe for "snow-white rabbit," which is why an alabaster bunny now decorates every bottle. Vincent and Parenteau distil their gin in a secondhand 400-litre pot still that Distillerie du St. Laurent (page 241) once used to crank out 100,000 bottles of their own gin. Wabasso distils its small-batch gin using regional botanicals, and also has plans to distil rum and whisky.

ATLANTIC CANADA

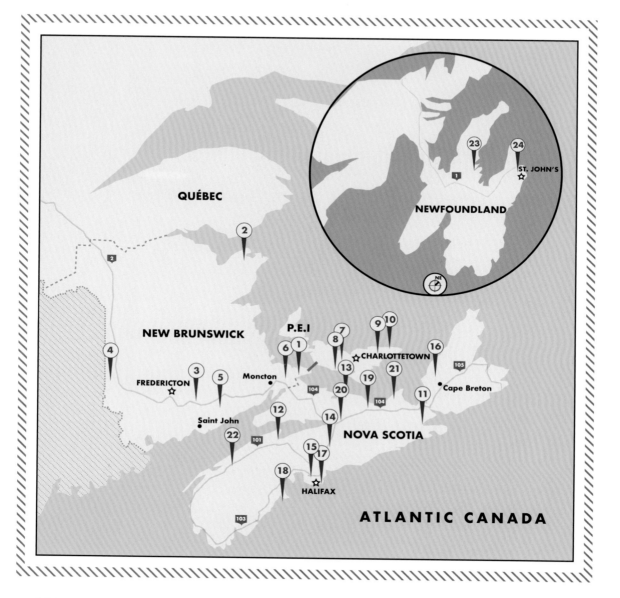

ATLANTIC CANADA

Atlantic Canada may be noted for lobsters, lighthouses, and ocean views, but in the world of spirits, it's the region's love of rum that is legendary. As early as 1787, according to archival records, an unnamed Nova Scotian distillery produced between 15,000 and 20,000 gallons of rum, an astounding amount. West Indies producers complained, but no one listened. The government of the day was too preoccupied with the duties it lost on Caribbean rum that was smuggled into Nova Scotia.

As British North America became Canada in the second half of the 19th century, small distilleries dotted the Atlantic landscape. One of them, McDougall's Distillery in Halifax, employed 22 workers. Business boomed throughout the region until the Atlantic coast went dry. Prince Edward Island was first to introduce prohibition, in 1901. Nova Scotia followed in 1916, then New Brunswick and Newfoundland (still under British control) in 1917.

When America enacted its Prohibition in 1920, the real details of distilling history were washed out to sea, only to be replaced by the fisherman's yarns of marine bootlegging and Rum Runners Row. Certainly, there were moments of intense drama, but most of the time, bootlegging was monotonous work. Nevertheless, thrilling tales of Captain Bill McCoy or John Randell aboard the ship *I'm Alone*, darting in and out of the jagged coastline, all the while dodging bullets, were rampant. And always, these fishy stories included a cast of Al Capone goons waiting on American docks for the ship's precious cargo.

Sometimes the coast guard made hot pursuit, while other times a guy in a canoe rocking in the ship's wake was enough to give rise to a riveting tale of danger and derring-do.

One by one, the Atlantic provinces repealed prohibition—Newfoundland, still British, in 1925; New Brunswick in 1927; Nova Scotia in 1930; and finally Prince Edward Island in 1948. But legal distilling was slow to return. Ontario distiller Larry J. McGuinness planned to establish a rum distillery in the Maritimes, but he could not buy steel because it was needed for the Korean War. Finally, in 1957, he acquired an apple processing plant in Bridgetown, Nova Scotia, and refashioned it into Acadian Distillers Limited, marking the return of distilling to Atlantic Canada.

Acadian Distillers invested in the agricultural economy of Nova Scotia's Annapolis Valley, buying apples and enough local grain to make a million gallons of rye whisky a year. Their prominent brands, such as Port Royal, Four Seasons, Acadian Signature, and Old Canada, were made and bottled in Nova Scotia. And to quench Atlantic Canada's thirst for rum, the distillery blended and bottled 7 Seas Rum and Bluenose Rum. Then, in 1986, Pernod Ricard purchased and closed Acadian Distillers. Atlantic Canada's distilling tradition went dry again.

Until 1990, that is, when Bruce Jardine completed construction of Glenora Distillery on Cape Breton Island and began distilling what was to become Canada's first single malt whisky of the modern era. A year later, Atlantic

Canada's first cottage distillery, Rosswog Farm Distillery, (now Winegarden Estate Ltd., page 265) opened its doors in New Brunswick, selling the first legal microdistilled spirits on the East Coast. Since whisky takes time to mature, this meant Glenora's was not ready to sell for another 10 years.

Today, Nova Scotia is once again paving the way for the other Atlantic provinces. About a dozen small distilleries are taking advantage of recent provincial government policies that benefit small distilleries by providing for favourable margins and reducing markup if all of the distillery's agricultural ingredients are grown in the province.

Yes, prohibition's rum-running stories are still exciting, and so are the spirits being made in Atlantic Canada today. No, this is not a rum-runner's fish story, dreamed up when the coast guard wasn't biting. ■

BLUE ROOF DISTILLERS
MALDEN, NB

If, as you head down the Trans-Canada Highway on the way to PEI's Confederation Bridge, you spot a giant waving potato perched in front of a series of blue-roofed buildings, you have reached Blue Roof Distillers. They call this towering mascot Tater Nate, and with what happens in the buildings behind him, he clearly could kick the fictional Mr. Potato Head's butt.

    Six generations ago, Nathaniel (Nate) Strang planted spuds on the property. "He built a farmhouse and a barn in 1855, and we have been growing potatoes here ever since," says Devon Strang, who, with his father, Richard, began distilling them in 2017. Devon is not the first Strang to fire up a still in the vicinity. Family lore has it that Devon's grandfather Fletcher Strang made moonshine and called it "potato Champagne." That story piqued Devon's interest in turning smaller, unwanted potatoes from the farm into something that everyone wanted: premium vodka.

(continued)

4144 Route 16
Malden, NB E4M 2G1
(506) 538-7767
www.blueroofdistillers.com

FOUNDED 2017

OWNERS Richard and Devon Strang

PRODUCTS Gin, "potato Champagne," vodka

AVAILABLE Onsite, online, ANBL

NEAREST NEIGHBOURS Winegarden Estate Ltd. (page 265) — 20 min

The vodka is labelled as distilled 20 times, with an asterisk pointing to what this means in more detail. "A column still completes our vodka process, and this is a compound still," explains Devon. "This means that we can redirect the flow off the top of the column back into the still, rather than pulling it to the barrel. We do this through the entire process of our run. The still we have is 40 feet tall, and many distillers agree that every two feet of compound distillation is equivalent to one distillation run." So, the vodka is distilled and redistilled 20 times before it finally leaves the column.

Blue Roof also makes a 70% abv spirit called Strang's Original Spirit, created to commemorate Grampa's famed "potato Champagne." Devon testifies that anyone who knows potato shine loves this Russet potato triple distillate. It is legal shine that is made in stills so tall, they would certainly tip off the law to illicit moonshiners.

TASTING NOTES: **BLUE ROOF PREMIUM VODKA** (40% ABV)

A mild mashed-potato nose with a clean and delicate sweetness yields to a buttery texture on the palate, with faint tropical undertones. A welcome hit of heat mid-palate scatters back to the ultra-clean, crisp sweetness that puts this vodka's finish to bed.

COCKTAIL: **BLUE ROOF ROCK**
MAKES 1 COCKTAIL

2 oz Blue Roof Premium 100 Vodka
Handful of ice cubes

A vodka this refined and delicious should be savoured bare every now and again. So, in a rocks glass, simply serve vodka over ice.

(Blue Roof Distillers)

DISTILLERIE FILS DU ROY
PETIT-PAQUETVILLE, NB, AND SAINT-ARSÈNE, QC

Sébastien Roy's eyes flash as he lifts the tall copper head off his Portuguese alembic still. This is old technology, and he is very proud of it. When the still is in operation, the head is attached the old way—glued in place with a paste of rye flour.

Roy plans to be distilling for some time to come. Among stacks of barrels filled with maturing whisky are some bearing dates far in the future. The head on a barrel of malt whisky distilled in 2016 is marked "250 ans du Nouveau-Brunswick en 2034." That's right: he won't bottle that whisky until 2034, to celebrate the 250th anniversary of the founding of New Brunswick. Future bottling years, and the Acadian historical events they commemorate, are noted on about a dozen other barrels. A closer look uncovers two others marked "Whisky Rye tourbe" and "Rye Whisky peated." In 2016 Fils du Roy became one of the few distilleries in Canada peating its own malt in-house.

Roy and a friend enjoyed making beer when they were in school. But it was after he came home from visiting Europe that he and his mother, Diane Roy, founded Distillerie Fils du Roy. Europe opened his eyes to the wonders of distilled spirits and, in particular, to absinthe. It took several years before he was satisfied with the absinthe he produced. Today, Fils du Roy makes a selection of products including that absinthe, most of which incorporate at least some ingredients grown at the distillery. Success breeds success, and in 2015 Sébastien's brother, Jonathan, opened a branch distillery that is also called Fils du Roy, about five hours due west, in Quebec. Currently, carrying alcohol across the Quebec–New Brunswick border is illegal. Solving the problem by establishing a distillery in each province is a stroke of genius for a family business with customers on both sides of the invisible line.

599 ch. Principale
Petit-Paquetville, NB E8R 1G7
(506) 764-2046
and
115 rue de l'Église
Saint-Arsène, QC G0L 2K0
(418) 894-7956
www.distilleriefilsduroy.com

🐦 @FilsDuRoy

📷 @distilleriefilsduroy2011

FOUNDED 2011

OWNERS Sébastien, Diane, and Jonathan Roy

STILLS New Brunswick: two 500-litre Portuguese alembic pot stills for whisky; 3,000-litre Koethe pot with four-plate column and two 300-litre alembic spirit stills for gin/absinthe/pastis; Quebec: two 300-litre Portuguese alembic pot stills

PRODUCTS Absinthe, fruit spirits, gin, grain spirit, molasses brandy, pastis, vodka, aged vodka, whisky

AVAILABLE Onsite, ANBL, SAQ

TOURS Monday–Saturday, 10 a.m.–5 p.m.

NEAREST NEIGHBOURS Blue Roof Distillers (page 259) – 3 hrs; O'Dwyer Distillerie Gaspésienne (page 234) – 5 hrs, 45 min

TASTING NOTES: **GRANDE BAGOSSE** (40% ABV)
Canada's forgotten moonshine remains a cult staple in New Brunswick and eastern Quebec. Grande Bagosse celebrates its pre-prohibition roots with soft, creamy, corn vodka notes and a fine-tuned starchy sweetness that venerates the secret spirit's soul.

GAGETOWN DISTILLERY & CIDERY
GAGETOWN, NB

30 Court House Rd.
Gagetown, NB E5M 1E4
(506) 488-2286
www.gagetowndistillingcidery.ca

FOUNDED 2018

OWNERS Heather Rhymes and Matt
Estabrooks

STILLS 550-litre Affordable Distilling
Equipment stainless steel pot still with
seven-plate copper column

PRODUCTS Apple brandy, gin, moonshine,
vodka, whisky

AVAILABLE Onsite, online, ANBL

NEAREST NEIGHBOURS Sussex Craft
Distilling (page 264) — 1 hr; Moonshine
Creek Distillery (page 263) — 1 hr, 35 min

Alcohol was never Grampa Estabrooks's cup of tea, but to this devoted Baptist, there was a bigger sin: wasting perfectly good apples. He and his son Greg bought this established fruit farm in 1973. Then, when Greg and Mary Lou retired in 2008, their son Matthew and his wife, Heather Rhymes, moved back to Gagetown and took over the farm.

Rhymes is an accomplished culinary and pastry chef. The mature apple trees were so productive that even if she spent every waking hour making jams, jellies, and baked gastronomic delights, the trees still bore too much fruit. So as not to waste the harvest, Estabrooks and Rhymes began making cider. Still, the apples kept coming.

Estabrooks remembered having built a still once, using a teakettle. "If I can do this in a teakettle, I can do it with a pressure cooker," thought Estabrooks, who in winter chopped ice off the front steps to cool the condenser. He decided to take a distilling course at Urban Distilleries and Winery (page 290) in Kelowna, and began distilling apple spirits. The farm commandment "Thou shalt not toss apples" is now no longer broken.

Estabrooks fills ex-bourbon barrels with spirit to make apple brandy, setting one early barrel aside to celebrate the distillery's fifth anniversary. Double-distilled apple spirit is also the base for his Unfiltered Gin 7. Seven botanicals are macerated with the spirit, then bottled, unfiltered, at 45% abv. This London Dry–style gin has a slight apple sweetness with a floral hint of lavender.

With his success making apple spirits, Estabrooks has added triple-distilled vodka using New Brunswick corn. He also has three styles of whisky resting in barrels. Remembering Grampa's penchant not to be wasteful, he referments his leftover vodka mash with granulated sugar to make a 50% abv moonshine. It's his top seller, especially with passengers from the cruise ships visiting Saint John.

TASTING NOTES: **UNFILTERED GIN 7** [45% ABV]

Seven botanicals, macerated with the distillery's apple spirit base, flavour this zesty, floral gin. Draped over a spicy backbone and candy-coated with black licorice, juniper surges forward on the palate to make a perfect candidate for a splendid Martini with hints of the spirit's built-in apple flavours.

COCKTAIL: CLASSIC DIRTY MARTINI

MAKES 1 COCKTAIL

2½ oz Unfiltered Gin 7
½ oz dry white vermouth
¼ oz olive juice
Handful of ice cubes
3 pimento olives, for garnish

Place a Martini glass in the freezer until chilled, at least one hour. In a mixing glass, combine the gin, vermouth, olive juice, and ice and stir for 10 seconds. Strain into the chilled Martini glass. Skewer the pimento olives on a toothpick before garnishing the Martini.

MOONSHINE CREEK DISTILLERY
WATERVILLE, NB

Distilling runs in Jeremiah and Joshua Clark's veins. Officially, their grandfather Marlen Henderson was a barber and butcher. On the side, he also bootlegged alcohol from Maine, rebottled it, and sold it. Henderson always managed to dodge the law, returning home safely to his wife Adeline's famous apple crumble.

Jeremiah's heritage, and the news that he was about to be a father, inspired him to write a business plan for a legitimate distillery. With no legal definition for "moonshine," the brothers opted to name their distillery after it instead, ensuring that their grandfather's legacy would be noted on every bottle they sold.

They double-distil unmalted maritime-grown organic rye and barley in a nine-plate column still. For their flagship Apple Crumble sipping cocktail, they blend clean-cut unaged spirit and sweet New Brunswick apple cider, organic brown sugar, and organic cinnamon. When your grandmother was married to a known bootlegger, it makes perfect sense to serve dessert in liquid form.

11377 Route 130
Waterville, NB E7P 0A5
(506) 375-9014
www.moonshinecreek.ca

@moonshine.creek

FOUNDED 2017

OWNERS Jeremiah Clark and Joshua Clark

STILLS 750-litre steam-jacketed pot still with nine-plate fractional column; 100-litre Portuguese copper pot still for making gin

PRODUCTS Coffee liqueur, grain spirit, flavoured grain spirit, moonshine

AVAILABLE Onsite, ANBL

NEAREST NEIGHBOURS Gagetown Distillery and Cidery (page 262) — 1 hr, 35 min

SUSSEX CRAFT DISTILLERY
SUSSEX CORNER, NB

119 Cougle Rd.
Sussex Corner, NB E4E 2S5
(506) 433-2800
www.sussexcraftdistillery.com

FOUNDED 2017

OWNERS Carmen Blois, Chris Celeste,
Grant Corey, Durck de Winter, Marcus de
Winter, John Dunfield, Rene Hache, Greg
McCollum, Peter Norrad

STILLS 200-litre North copper pot still;
100-litre North flute still

PRODUCTS Liqueurs, rum, rum-based gin

AVAILABLE Onsite, online, ANBL

NEAREST NEIGHBOURS Gagetown Distilling
& Cidery (page 262) — 1 hr; Winegarden
Estate Ltd. (page 265) — 1 hr, 30 min

The town of Sussex took a hit in 2016 when the Potash Corporation suspended its mining operations, putting 430 people out of work. Nine entrepreneurs watched in dismay as countless friends and neighbours lost their jobs. The group had formed an investment club 15 years earlier, and now it was time to put that money to work in a major way. Withdrawing their earnings, they stepped in and opened a distillery.

Such entrepreneurial spirit has been alive in Sussex since the late 1800s, when SH White discovered a well of mineral water. After adding ginger and sugar, he carbonated the water and sold it as Sussex Golden Ginger Ale. During prohibition, dry ginger ale gained popularity as a mixer, eclipsing the stronger-flavoured golden variety. Today, golden ginger ale still has a dedicated following in Atlantic Canada, and Sussex Craft Distillery is ready to spike it.

Master distiller John Dunfield and self-proclaimed "mistress distiller" Gail Fanjoy execute Sussex Craft's mission to make rum from predominantly local ingredients. Their signature maple rum liqueur starts as spirit distilled from Crosby's molasses, which they then age with a spice blend, Steeves maple syrup, and sugar maple hardwood that Fanjoy toasts in a converted kitchen range.

Three other Sussex rums fall under the Wards Creek brand. Wards Creek, for which the rums are named, is a local waterway best known for its covered bridge and its important link to prohibition history. The wooded rural area provided helpful cover for rum-running operations back then. Fanjoy distils Wards Creek Platinum seven times and bottles it at 44% alcohol, while Wards Corner Golden is aged with roasted white oak from southern New Brunswick. One special barrel, filled on Good Friday of one year and bottled on Easter Monday of another, is called Resurrection Rum. It is a fitting name for rum from a distillery doing its part to revive Sussex's spirit for all eternity.

TASTING NOTES:
WARDS CREEK PLATINUM RUM (44% ABV)

Former Wards Creek bootleggers would be proud of this velvety and approachable spirit. Its soft and refined palate reveals slight hints of molasses and toasted sugar cane sweetness, with a touch of heat. A natural fit in a cocktail shaker with tropical fruits.

WINEGARDEN ESTATE LTD.
BAIE VERTE, NB

In 1983 Werner Rosswog left his banking job for a simpler life on a farm. He and his wife, Roswitha, packed their bags, gathered their three children, two dogs, and a cat, and left Germany for New Brunswick. They settled on a farm in Baie Verte, where Werner was soon both baffled and distressed by how much fruit local farmers let go to waste. To him, and the many generations before him, fallen fruit was a windfall for fermenting and distilling. In fact, in 1860 the Grand Duke of Baden granted Werner's ancestor Johannes "Johnny" Ziegler the right to distil fruit spirits, and those rights were passed down through the generations as a legacy to him. However, as popular as farm distilling had long been in Germany, it was unheard of in New Brunswick.

Putting his retirement plans on hold, Werner set out to change that. He petitioned New Brunswick's premier for a licence to operate a distillery, but that was just his first obstacle. Licensing fees were high, the government controlled prices, and its liquor stores had a monopoly on sales. Werner persevered, and in the fall of 1991 the first truckload of apples arrived from a nearby orchard. After juicing them, he pumped the juice into five 12,000-litre fermentation tanks and crossed his fingers. Finally, on December 9, 1991, his federal distillery licence arrived and Winegarden became New Brunswick's first legally certified private distillery. Roswitha was the only woman distiller in North America at the time, and she fired up the stills. Johnny Ziegler Apple Schnaps began to flow.

In 2008 Werner and Roswitha retired, leaving their son Steffen Rosswog, daughter Elke Rosswog Muessle, and granddaughter Tanja Muessle to carry on the Zeigler family distilling tradition. In doing so, they produce the largest range of spirits of any small distillery in Canada.

851 Route 970
Baie Verte, NB, E4M 1Z7
(506) 538-7405
www.winegardenestate.com

⊡ @winegardenestate

FOUNDED 1991

OWNERS Steffen Rosswog and Elke Rosswog Muessle

STILLS 147-litre Guertner copper pot stills

PRODUCTS Bitters, brandy, eau-de-vie, liqueurs, schnapps

AVAILABLE Onsite, ANBL, Ferme Maury Winery

NEAREST NEIGHBOURS Blue Roof Distillers (page 259) — 20 min; Barrelling Tide Distillery (page 270) — 1 hr, 10 min

TASTING NOTES:
JOHNNY ZIEGLER APPLE SCHNAPS (40% ABV)

This crystal-clear apple eau-de-vie captures the sweet core of New Brunswick apples, with orchard apples and floral spring blossoms on the nose and a full-bodied texture that snaps on the palate. Peppery but elegant, with a heavenly crisp apple finish that makes you wonder if *this* is the elusive "angel's share."

DEEP ROOTS DISTILLERY
WARREN GROVE, PE

2100 North York River Rd. (Route 248)
Warren Grove, PE C0A 1H5
(902) 620-1085
www.deeprootsdistillery.com

@DeepRootsPEI

@deeprootsdistillery

FOUNDED 2013

OWNERS Mike and Carol Beamish

STILLS 100-gallon (US) Amphora Society
pot-column combination with two
packed columns

TOURS Call for reservations and rates

PRODUCTS Absinthe, apple brandy, cane
sugar spirit, liqueurs

AVAILABLE Onsite, PEI Liquor,
Charlottetown farmers' market

NEAREST NEIGHBOURS Matos Winery and
Distillery (page 267) — 15 min; Blue Roof
Distillers (page 259) — 50 min

It didn't take a whack on the head from an apple for Mike Beamish to have his eureka moment. Instead, it was the hours he spent in his orchard, picking up the countless victims of Newton's theory. Each year, breezes from the Northumberland Strait would knock 60 to 70% of his apples to the ground. By law, he then had to pasteurize, distil, or discard them. Since Mike had had enough of Mother Nature dropping apples for him to pick up, and since a vat pasteurizer is expensive, he bought a still.

Distilling was not exactly new to PEI. Thirsty backyard distillers had spent the 47 years during which PEI enforced prohibition perfecting their moonshining techniques. One such skill was fermenting cane sugar. Mike's first sugar run passed through the pot still, then he distilled it a second time in a copper-packed column and bottled it as Island Tide, named after the prohibition-era stories of delivering barrels of liquor on the tide.

With sugar moonshine under his belt, Mike was ready to make apple brandy. For this, he ferments four varieties of apples, distils them once in the pot still, then ages them in 60-litre toasted Hungarian-oak barrels. A few barrels of local, organic buckwheat whisky keep company with the maturing brandy. This buckwheat whisky is for limited future release, though Mother Nature has already been banned from the launch party.

MATOS WINERY AND DISTILLERY
ST. CATHERINES, PE

Heather and Jim Matos were drawn to PEI by the prospect of starting a winery. Jim had learned to make wine from his father back home in Pico, in Portugal's Azores islands. In 2007 the couple planted 16,000 French grapevines across four hillside PEI hectares. Three years later they harvested their first grapes. The licence for their Portuguese alembic copper pot still followed in 2012.

Now, after he has fermented Chardonnay and Gamay grapes into wine, Jim can double-distil the remaining fermented pomace to make a spirit base for liqueurs, or grappa-like bagaço. Anisette and orange liqueurs are big sellers, but you can't cross the Northumberland Strait into PEI without trying Matos bagaço. To taste it is to taste the Azores.

TASTING NOTES: **BAGAÇO** (40% ABV)

The dramatic landscapes of Portugal's Azores have nothing on this crystalline PEI-born spirit. An earthy, dry wine core is embellished on the nose with white-pepper heat and a smidgen of straw. Black pepper and an apple nuance are accented on the palate by a touch of honeycomb in this fiery spirit.

3156 West River Rd. (Route 9)
St. Catherines, PE C0A 1H1
(902) 675-9463
www.matoswinery.com

 @MatosWinery

FOUNDED 2012

OWNERS Jim and Heather Matos

STILLS 300-litre Portuguese copper alembic pot still

PRODUCTS Anisette, angelica, apple brandy, bagaço, orange liqueur

AVAILABLE Onsite, PEI Liquor, farmers' markets

TOURS Seasonal

NEAREST NEIGHBOURS Myriad View Artisan Distillery Inc. (page 268) – 1 hr, 10 min; Prince Edward Distillery (page 276) – 1 hr, 15 min

MYRIAD VIEW ARTISAN DISTILLERY INC.

ROLLO BAY, PE

1336 Route 2
Rollo Bay, PE C0A 2B0
(902) 687-1281
www.straitshine.com

FOUNDED 2007

OWNERS Paul and Angie Burrow, Ken and Danielle Mill

STILL 450-litre Christian Carl pot

PRODUCTS Brandy, gin, moonshine, pastis, rum, vodka, whisky

AVAILABLE Onsite and PEI Liquor

TOURS Free

NEAREST NEIGHBOURS Prince Edward Distillery (page 276) — 15 min; Deep Roots Distillery (page 266) — 1 hr

Did an illicit still explode in a basement in Rollo Bay during PEI's moonshining past? *Something* caused a floor beam in a mid-20th-century house on the distillery property to split. Who knows what? But when your business is filled with legend and lore, why not embellish the story? Prohibition did not end until 1948 in PEI, so the beam-cracking story is tenable.

It was 2007 before Paul and Angie Burrow founded Myriad View, with Ken and Danielle Mill joining later as partners. "Work where you live, live where you work," says Mill, and since PEI is traditional moonshining country, it certainly fit the bill. Historically, ships carrying PEI fish and lumber to the Caribbean returned laden with sugar, molasses, and rum. During the province's lengthy prohibition, rum was contraband, but sugar and molasses were not. Islanders began making their own spirits from these imported ingredients, which worked out, since sugar and molasses ferment quickly and taste good. "They have a great shelf life and other (plausible) uses around the house," says distillery partner Ken Mill. "Potatoes . . . well, let's just say Islanders grow millions of them and know that they belong on a plate."

Originally called the Rollo Bay Bootleggers, the partners had to change the name to get a distillery and excise licence. Calling their product moonshine was also a problem. Instead, they just named it Strait Shine, and for the label they crafted a shadowy moon behind the name. Regardless of names, this spirit is their biggest seller and the reason people seek out the distillery.

Myriad View also makes other spirits, including Strait Lightning, bottled at a beam-splitting 75% alcohol. It's their summer Dandelion Shine that you should watch for, though. Mill makes it from fermented dandelions and matures it in ex-bourbon barrels. It's a nostalgic process, given that he was just a teenager the first time he observed this method of making shine.

TASTING NOTES: **STRAIT SHINE** (50% ABV)

Steeped in tradition, Strait Shine disciplines its alcohol heat with a slight caramel sweetness. It's a new chapter in PEI's hushed but shiny moonshine past.

NOVA SCOTIA

AUTHENTIC SEACOAST DISTILLERY & BREWERY
GUYSBOROUGH, NS

People in Guysborough are pretty happy that a vacationing stranger named Glynn Williams rode into town on a bicycle some 30 years ago and fell in love with the charming little town and its picturesque seascapes. Success in Toronto's financial market afforded Williams the freedom to make personal investments with yields that are as much human as they are financial. By 2016 that commitment to investing included a distillery to complement his coffee shop, brewpub, and several inns in Guysborough. Generating employment and nurturing a 400-year-old local craft tradition found a home among Williams's goals.

Williams was well aware of Nova Scotia's long rum tradition, so he imported rum from the Caribbean and launched his flagship Fortress Rum before the distillery came into existence. Fortress Rum matures for at least two years in barrels placed inside the historic Fortress Louisbourg on the Atlantic shores of Cape Breton. After the rum has matured, the barrels are refilled with 12-year-old Canadian whisky; there, for the next eight months, it accumulates the gentle nuances of the rum. If Fortress is a whisky lover's rum, then Glynnevan Cabot 12-year-old Triple Barrel whisky is certainly the whisky for rum lovers. "I think we've cracked the code on blends," says distillery manager John Stapleton with a knowing smile.

One side of the distillery is reserved for blending, the other for distilling. Before the stills were installed, rum and whisky purchased from other distillers were matured and blended onsite. Authentic Seacoast now distils Annapolis Valley spring wheat for vodka, local corn and rye for whisky, and Crosby's molasses for Seafever Rum. Fortress Rum still comes from the Caribbean. In all, about 350 barrels of rum and 500 barrels of whisky are maturing at Louisbourg and in Guysborough. A $1.4 million automated Italian bottling line keeps four people busy filling 1,200 bottles each hour. Despite significant computerization, though, this is still a hands-on operation. In the still house, Stapleton watches the readouts, but in the end he makes his cuts by taste.

80 Main St.
Guysborough, NS B0H 1N0
(902) 533-2078; 1-855-533-2499
www.authenticseacoast.com

🐦 @AuthenticCoast

📷 @authenticseacoast

FOUNDED 2016

OWNER Glynn Williams

STILLS 2,000-litre Vendome with 19-plate column

PRODUCTS Rum, vodka, whisky

AVAILABLE Onsite, government liquor stores across Canada, abroad

TOURS Contact the distillery

NEAREST NEIGHBOURS Glenora Inn and Distillery (page 275) – 1 hr, 30 min; Steinhart Distillery (page 282) – 1 hr, 10 min

TASTING NOTES:
GLYNNEVAN DOUBLE BARRELLED CANADIAN RYE (43% ABV)

Born in western Canada, then rebarrelled at the seaside distillery. A spicy nose slowly discloses maple sugars, oak caramels, and dill pickle brine. The succulent spiced palate finishes clean, in a wave of citrus pith.

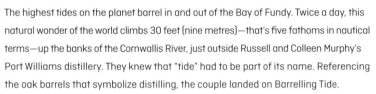

BARRELLING TIDE DISTILLERY
PORT WILLIAMS, NS

1164 Parkway Dr.
Port Williams, NS B0P 1T0
(902) 542-1627
www.barrellingtidedistillery.com

 @BarrellingTide

 @barrellingtidedistillery

FOUNDED 2016

OWNERS Russell and Colleen Murphy

STILLS 400-litre Mueller pot

PRODUCTS Fruit liqueurs, gin, rum, vodka

AVAILABLE Onsite, online, NSLC

NEAREST NEIGHBOURS Halifax Distilling Company (page 276) and Compass Distillers (page 273) – 1 hr, 5 min; Iron Works (page 278) – 1 hr, 15 min

The highest tides on the planet barrel in and out of the Bay of Fundy. Twice a day, this natural wonder of the world climbs 30 feet (nine metres)—that's five fathoms in nautical terms—up the banks of the Cornwallis River, just outside Russell and Colleen Murphy's Port Williams distillery. They knew that "tide" had to be part of its name. Referencing the oak barrels that symbolize distilling, the couple landed on Barrelling Tide.

The Murphys built Barrelling Tide Distillery on a vacant riverfront property. The hefty, ocean-blue, white-trimmed building houses production facilities, a tasting room, and a barrel loft for ageing spirits. Their German Mueller pot still, with its signature sparkling helmet, imbues the space with fragrant aromatics as the distillers hand-tune its seven-plate reflux column to suit the character of each specific spirit.

As a youth, Russell worked on local farms that now supply ingredients for the distillery's spirits. With his trained chef's palate, he captures these familiar local flavours in Barrelling Tide's growing portfolio of spirits and liqueurs. Not surprisingly, the distillery's top seller is the appropriately named 5 Fathom Dark Rum, an East Coast stalwart with a strong enough footing that it won't be swept away in Fundy's tidal bore.

TASTING NOTES: 5 FATHOM DARK RUM (42% ABV)

Rich and complex molasses, caramel, toasted brown sugar, and smoky char on the nose lead into a molasses-sweet, wood-smoked palate with a pleasing salted caramel note. A beautifully balanced set-up to a long and easy molasses-rich finish.

COCKTAIL: CHERRY GIN SOUR
MAKES 1 COCKTAIL

2 handfuls of ice cubes
1½ oz Barrelling Tide Gin
¾ oz Barrelling Tide Cherry Liqueur
¾ oz fresh-squeezed lime juice

½ oz simple syrup
½ oz egg white
3 dashes Pernod
1 cherry, for garnish

Place a cocktail glass in the freezer until chilled, at least one hour. In a shaker filled with ice, pour all of the ingredients except the cherry. Shake, then strain into the chilled glass. Garnish with a fresh cherry.

(Barrelling Tide Distillery)

CALDERA DISTILLING
RIVER JOHN, NS

In 1878 James Stuart built the Glenrothes distillery in Speyside, Scotland. In 2013, a hundred and thirty-five years later, James's distant descendant Jarret Stuart built his own distillery, this one in the tiny Nova Scotia community of River John. It was James who sent Jarret's great-great-grandfather to find his fortune in Canada, where he settled in Mission, BC.

If Jarret comes by his distilling chops through family lineage, it is fitting that much of the grain he distils comes from his wife's family farm. Tracy's parents bought the 70-hectare property when they retired. Incidentally, in 2008, before she was a farmer, Tracy Cannon won a bronze medal for rowing at the Beijing Olympics.

Using grain from the same farmland year after year means each batch of Hurricane 5 and Champlain whisky is slightly different from the one before. Why? The weather! Some years, the grain is plump and rich with starch; other years, it is less so. Then there is harvesting. By the time Stuart's Gazelle spring rye is ready to harvest in the fall, rain has set in, and sometimes it is just too wet to harvest. A switch to winter rye, which matures earlier in the year, is in the offing.

River John is a sleepy little town today. Nevertheless, it has seen several boom periods, each one brought on by wars in Europe. The attendant need for oceangoing vessels brought waves of people to River John to work in shipbuilding. One of the largest of these ships was the three-masted wooden ship *Caldera*, completed in 1884. After a late night of testing recipes, the Stuarts decided to adopt the ship's name for their new distillery. A vicious 1939 storm, notated in pencil on the wall of the distillery barn, inspired Hurricane 5 whisky. A newer addition to the lineup, Champlain whisky, pays tribute to Samuel de Champlain and his birthplace in the Cognac region of France by blending in 6.8% Cognac.

TASTING NOTES: CALDERA HURRICANE 5 BLENDED CANADIAN WHISKY (40% ABV)

Whisky from grain grown on the family farm is blended with Alberta rye to make Hurricane 5. The eye of this whisky storm is fruit-laden with buttery caramel, barrel char, radiant peppery spice, and enough baking spices, including ginger and cloves, to cook up a storm.

65 River John Rd.
River John, NS B0K 1N0
(902) 456-7348
www.caldera.ca

🐦 @calderadistill

📷 @caldera_distilling

FOUNDED 2013

OWNERS Jarret Stuart and Tracy Cannon

STILLS 1,000-litre custom combo pot and four-plate column

PRODUCT Whisky

AVAILABLE Online, widely across Canada, abroad

NEAREST NEIGHBOURS Nova Scotia Spirit Co. (page 280) — 35 min; Raging Crow Distillery Inc. (page 281) — 45 min

COLDSTREAM CLEAR DISTILLERY
STEWIACKE, NS

87 Main St. W.
Stewiacke, NS B0N 2J0
(902) 639-9030
www.coldstreamclear.com

 @coldstreamclear

 @coldsteamclear

FOUNDED 2015

OWNER Riley Giffen

STILLS 100-litre Dye still

PRODUCTS Liqueurs, rum, spirit, vodka, vodka soda

AVAILABLE Onsite, online, Nova Scotia liquor stores

NEAREST NEIGHBOURS Halifax Distilling Company (page 276) and Compass Distillers (page 273) — both 50 min; Raging Crow Distillery Inc. (page 281) — 25 min

Early in the 1990s, someone discovered mastodon bones near Milford, Nova Scotia. Local legend says the beast died of thirst waiting for Riley Giffen to open his distillery in neighbouring Stewiacke. Well, the story isn't passed around that much, but wouldn't it be great if it were?

Riley's original Canadian ancestor, Simon Giffen, brought his distiller's trade to Halifax from Ireland in 1749. Despite this connection, young Riley discovered distilling through unconventional means: making essential oils from orange peels in organic chemistry class. An eager student, he decided to transfer his skills to making vodka and rum in a homemade still. Alas, his first corn, molasses, and sugar spirits tasted more like traditional East Coast–style moonshine. But they still managed to inspire his father.

Riley returned home from a summer job one year to discover milk crates filled with Mason jars. His father's handwritten labels said "Cold Stream Clear"—local jargon for quality moonshine. Now it was Riley's turn to be inspired. He went legit.

Today, Coldstream Clear Distillery makes vodka and rum, along with liqueurs and vodkas flavoured with natural ingredients. An old-fashioned unaged rum-like spirit called 1749 Original Spirit pays tribute to Great-Great-Grandpa Simon's success 270 years ago.

And the mastodon has returned. Perched atop neighbouring Mastodon Ridge, its trunk pointing to the sky, it stands with its mouth open. Surely, this time Coldstream Clear Distillery will not let it go thirsty.

COMPASS DISTILLERS
HALIFAX, NS

Residents of Halifax have long suffered from a severe phobia of invasion. Back in 1749 they built the Citadel, a military installation, to protect their city from French invaders who, as history tells us, never appeared. Nevertheless, they upgraded the fort to protect the city during the American Revolution, the French Revolutionary Wars, and the War of 1812, and again in 1856 to stop Americans invading by land. Still, no raiders ever arrived until a grey-bricked tower with copper siding on Agricola Street brought invaders of another sort: spirits lovers visiting Compass Distillers and returning home with liquid booty some of it aged in the Citadel.

Compass Distillers thrives on the energy of a revitalized North End neighbourhood that embraces local spirits and the distillery's small-scale, creative approach to making them. Founders Joshua Judah, David LaGrand, and Graham Collins were school chums who played Dungeons and Dragons until LaGrand's family moved to Grand Rapids, Michigan. He grew up and opened Long Road Distillers there. During a visit back to Halifax, the three rolled a 100-sided dice and decided to capitalize on LaGrand's experience by opening a distillery in Halifax.

With its north–south alignment, and the cardinal compass points on the exterior, their tower home incorporates a compass theme. This reflects their distilling philosophy—follow a true path with full transparency and with no shortcuts. Hence, the team has chosen to make every drop they sell from scratch.

The tower also houses a shop and tasting room. There, you can sample Compass Rhumb, a brown-sugar-and-molasses-based spirit, bottled straight off the still. Canadian law requires rum to be barrel-aged for a minimum of one year, so they call their unaged spirit "rhumb," while their fully aged rum is named Nauss' Reserve after the Nauss bicycle shop that used to occupy the property. A two-bedroom Airbnb atop the tower provides a vantage point from which phobic visitors with a sense of history can keep watch for the next wave of intruders heading for the Citadel.

(continued)

2533 Agricola St.
Halifax, NS B3K 4C4
(902) 446-0467
www.compassdistillers.ca

@CompassDistills

@CompassDistillers

FOUNDED **2017**

OWNERS **Joshua Judah, David LaGrand, Graham Collins**

STILLS **500-gallon (US) Vendome hybrid still with 20-plate column**

PRODUCTS **Aquavit, gin, moonshine, rum, rhumb, whisky, vodka**

AVAILABLE **Onsite, online, Nova Scotia liquor stores**

NEAREST NEIGHBOURS **Halifax Distilling Company (page 276) — 5 min; Coldstream Clear Distillery (page 272) — 45 min**

TASTING NOTES:
SPRING GINS BATCH
NO. 1 [45% ABV]

The first gin made entirely from
Nova Scotia ingredients rejuvenates
your palate with spring flavours,
savoury kelp, tart cranberries, fresh
cucumber, blooming elderflower,
and fragrant chokeberry blossoms,
all infused with juniper and spruce
tips. Beautifully balanced and
distinctly flavourful.

COCKTAIL: THE LOST
AND FOUND

MAKES 1 COCKTAIL

2 sage leaves, plus extra for
    garnish
½ oz Nova Scotia honey
1½ oz GiNS
¾ oz lemon
¼ oz Lillet Blanc
Handful of ice cubes

In a shaker, muddle two sage leaves
with honey. Add the rest of the
ingredients and shake vigorously.
Fine-strain into a coupe glass and
garnish with a sage leaf.

[Compass Distillers]

GLENORA INN AND DISTILLERY
GLENVILLE, NS

No one knew it at the time, but the founding of Glenora Distillery 30 years ago marked Canada's entry into the new age of microdistilling. Glenora was the dream of Bruce Jardine, a retired public servant. He thought that Nova Scotia's deep Scottish roots required that the province have a whisky distillery, just as they have in Scotland. Jardine began with high hopes but sketchy financing. He managed to secure, secondhand, two 5,600-litre copper pot stills that Bowmore Distillery in Scotland had purchased, after they had served ceremonial duty in a royal celebration. Bowmore provided training, and everything looked rosy. But early distillations were disappointing. As a result, the first whisky released in 2000, ten years after the distillery was founded, was only eight years old.

Before they finally got on track, Jardine became ill, and in 1994 he sold the distillery to Lauchie MacLean. Jardine died in 1999 without seeing any of Glenora's whisky bottled. However, 21 years after he bought the distillery, MacLean paid tribute to the founder by releasing Bruce Jardine Special Reserve 25 Year, a whisky Jardine himself helped distil in 1990.

In part, economic development funds from the provincial government supported Glenora to create employment for about 50 people to work in the distillery and an onsite inn and restaurant. The inn attracts about 12,000 tourists annually, many visiting from overseas. Reflected in a 3,785-kilolitre holding pond, and with the Mabou Highlands in the background, the low, white distillery building provides visitors with an Instagram-ready backdrop. Although in the beginning it generated income by selling white whisky—dubbed Kenloch Silver—after 30 years operation, Glenora has settled on Glen Breton single malt whiskies as its sole product. There is one interesting twist, though. Glenora is the first distillery to finish some of its whisky in icewine barrels. These come from a local winemaker, bringing sweet, fruity touches to a whisky that is well known for its floral nature.

13727 Route 19
Glenville, NS B0E 1X0
(902) 258-2662
www.glenoradistillery.com

@GlenBreton

@glenoradistillery

FOUNDED 1990

OWNER Lauchie MacLean

STILLS Two 5,600-litre Forsyths pots

PRODUCTS Single malt whisky

AVAILABLE Onsite, widely across Canada, bars, abroad

TOURS $7; on the hour, mid-May to late October

NEAREST NEIGHBOURS Authentic Seacoast Distillery & Brewery (page 269) — 1 hr, 35 min; Steinhart Distillery (page 282) — 1 hr, 55 min

TASTING NOTES:
GLEN BRETON RARE 10 YEAR OLD [43% ABV]

A vast nose with traditional mellow Scottish single malt spices. Bright and floral on the palate, with vanilla-soaked pipe tobacco, malt, refined oak, and brisk spices. The back palate packs a wallop of pepper and ginger, subsiding eventually to a calm, honeyed fruitiness.

HALIFAX DISTILLING COMPANY
HALIFAX, NS

1668 Lower Water St.
Halifax, NS B0J 2C0
(902) 431-0505
and Prince Edward Distillery
9984 Route 16
Souris, PE C0A 2B0
(902) 687-2586
www.halifaxdistillingco.ca,
www.princeedwarddistillery.com

 @HalifaxSpirit

@hfxdistillingco

FOUNDED 2007 (Prince Edward Distillery),
2016 (Halifax Distilling)

OWNERS Arla Johnson and Julie Shore

STILLS 650-litre German copper pot
(Halifax)

PRODUCTS White, gold, spiced, black, and
cream rums (Halifax); vodka, wild
blueberry vodka (Prince Edward)

AVAILABLE Onsite, online NSCL, Halifax
airport

TOURS 1 p.m., 3 p.m., and 5 p.m.
(Halifax); contact the Prince Edward
Distillery for seasonal hours

NEAREST NEIGHBOURS Halifax: Compass
Distillers (page 273) – 5min; Coldstream
Clear Distillery (page 272) – 45 min;
Prince Edward Island: Myriad View
Artisan Distillery Inc. (page 268) –
20 minutes

For too long, distilling has been the domain of men. Today, women commonly assume senior roles in major distilleries, and establish and operate distilleries of their own. Julie Shore and Arla Johnson are proud of their place in this change, even as their JD (Julie Diane) Shore rum carries on a paternal Shore family tradition of handcrafted spirits made in small batches in a copper still.

The North Carolina natives relocated to Canada in 1997 to operate an inn on Prince Edward Island. But Julie, the great-great-great-great-granddaughter of the legendary North Carolina distiller IC Shore, saw PEI's famed potato crop not as dinner for her guests, but as fine dining for yeast. In 2007 the couple established Prince Edward Distillery, making potato vodka, gin, and wild blueberry vodka.

Business was good, but what drinkers in Canada's Atlantic provinces really wanted in large volumes was rum. Despite this demand, not one distillery in the region made much of it. Nevertheless, Arla and Julie believed that Maritimers would embrace a rum they could call their own. They began exploring the potential to distil it on the famed Halifax waterfront. Then, in 2014, the government of PEI decided to establish a wind farm near the couple's distillery. They were not pleased, but neither were they ready to give up. Instead, Arla and Julie hired staff to keep Prince Edward Distillery operating while they accelerated their plans to open a second distillery in Halifax.

Halifax Distilling Company opened in 2016, making rum from premium ingredients, such as Canada fancy molasses. After distillation in a small copper still, a dash of Caribbean rum was added to the final blends. As the two had predicted, their JD Shore rum is a hit with locals and visitors to Halifax, the economic hub and tourism capital of Atlantic Canada.

TASTING NOTES: JD SHORE GOLD RUM (40% ABV)

Celebrates Nova Scotia's rum-running history by blending the distillery's Canadian rum with Caribbean rum, fusing vanilla and molasses sweetness with caramel-covered fruit. Fragrant and vaguely floral, this toothsome rum is best in rum-forward cocktails—shaken or stirred.

COCKTAIL: **STORMY WEATHER**
MAKES 1 COCKTAIL

Handful of ice cubes
1½ oz JD Shore Black Rum

2 oz Propeller ginger beer
½ oz fresh-squeezed lime

Pour the JD Shore Black Rum into a highball glass filled with ice. Top up with Propeller ginger beer and a slush of fresh lime.

(Halifax Distilling Company)

IRONWORKS DISTILLERY
LUNENBURG, NS

2 Kempt St.
Lunenburg, NS B0J 2C0
(902) 640-2424
www.ironworksdistillery.com

 @Ironworks_NS

@ironworksDistillery

FOUNDED 2009

OWNERS Lynne MacKay and Pierre Guevremont

STILLS 220-litre wood-fired Mueller pot; 500-litre Genio hybrid column

CAPACITY 50,000+ bottles annually

PRODUCTS Apple brandy, fruit liqueurs, gin, pear eau-de-vie, rum, vodka

AVAILABLE Onsite, online, Nova Scotia government and private liquor stores, Halifax airport, Newfoundland, Alberta

TOURS 3–4 p.m. daily in summer

NEAREST NEIGHBOURS Halifax Distilling Company (page 276) and Compass Distillers (page 273) — 1 hr, 5 min; Barrelling Tide Distillery (page 270) — 1 hr, 15 min

Lynne MacKay and Pierre Guevremont were puzzled. No one in Nova Scotia was using that province's rich bounty of fruits to make spirits. Then, in 2009, opportunity knocked. Walters Blacksmith Shop in Lunenburg—a small, photo-friendly community rich in folklore and tourists—had become vacant.

The shop had been in the Walters family for 112 years. Given its Maritime location, the Walterses did shipsmithing for shipbuilders Smith and Ruhland, just around the corner on Montague Street. Smith and Ruhland built one of the most celebrated sailing vessels in Canada: the *Bluenose*, with ironwork by Walters Blacksmith Shop. In addition to its maritime history, Lunenburg was a major player during American Prohibition, serving as a staging port for rum-runners. How fitting, then, that this former ironworks became the perfect location for a now-legal distillery.

Being careful to protect the building's heritage, MacKay and Guevremont installed stills and fermenters, and by 2010 they were ready to open the doors to Ironworks Distillery. The name, of course, is a nod to the ironworks (blacksmith shop) formerly housed here. It has to be one of the most beautifully located distilleries in Canada.

Its bestselling Bluenose Rum comes by its name honestly. MacKay and Guevremont ferment Crosby's molasses, distilling it twice in their Mueller copper pot still. Then they do something that is only possible near water: they age their rum in barrels in a floating warehouse, *Black Beauty*. The tides gently rock the rum into maturity.

On January 4, 2018, a vicious winter storm ripped *Black Beauty* from its moorings and washed it ashore 100 metres from the distillery. MacKay and Guevremont managed to salvage 24 barrels and turned their contents into a "shipwrecked edition" of their rum. Today, a fully repaired *Black Beauty* continues to rock Rum Boat Rum to maturity.

TASTING NOTES: **BLUENOSE RUM** (42% ABV)

This stout, gorgeous dark rum builds on a solid wood foundation. Precise molasses notes on the nose and palate stop on a dime, then transition into rich, caramel-soaked raisins and vanilla. The finish balances complex spices with bittersweet undertones. Of Canada's rums, Bluenose is the Queen of the Atlantic.

COCKTAIL: SPRING GIN PUNCH

MAKES APPROXIMATELY THIRTY 4 OZ COCKTAILS

ROSEMARY SIMPLE SYRUP:
1 cup white sugar
1 cup water
4 fresh rosemary sprigs

PUNCH:
750 ml (1 bottle) Ironworks Gin
6 cups cranberry juice
1 cup fresh-squeezed lemon juice
2 cups cold water
4 cups cold sparkling water
4 limes, cut into coin slices for
    garnish

For the Rosemary Simple Syrup, add sugar and water to a small saucepan and stir over medium heat until sugar dissolves. Turn off heat and add rosemary. Allow to cool. Strain syrup through a fine strainer. Refrigerate extra syrup in a clean, sealed jar for up to two weeks.

For the punch, in a punch bowl, mix together one cup of the rosemary syrup, gin, cranberry juice, lemon juice, and water. Chill for at least 30 minutes until quite cold. (This can be done a day ahead and chilled in the fridge until ready.) Before serving, add sparkling water and top the punch with lime coin slices. Ladle into a punch glass.

(Steven Cross)

NOVA SCOTIA SPIRIT CO.
STELLARTON, NS

230 Foord St.
Stellarton, NS B0K 1S0
(902) 600-2160
www.nsspiritcompany.com

 @nsspiritco

@insspiritco

FOUNDED 2015

OWNERS Alex Rice and Evan MacEachern

STILLS 1,000-litre custom copper multi-column system for grain neutral spirits or vodka; isolated column for gin, with a bypass for whisky and rum

PRODUCTS Gin, rum, vodka, canned vodka soda

NEAREST NEIGHBOURS Caldera Distilling (page 271) — 40 min; Steinhart Distillery (page 282) — 35 min

I scream, you scream, but the town of Stellarton does not scream for ice cream. In 2013 Nova Scotia's milk surplus led the Scotsburn Dairy Group to close its Stellarton factory, ending the town's long-standing tradition of ice cream making. Enter Alex Rice and Evan MacEachern. They were looking to move their small Trenton distilling operations, and the deserted dairy factory was a perfect fit. They removed the dairy tanks and replaced them with fermenters and a still.

Riffing off seabound coast culture, the partners have named their spirits with a particularly baited hook: Fisherman's Helper Rum, Willing to Learn Gin, and Blue Lobster Vodka. Catching a rare blue lobster is a sign of good fortune. Naming their vodka after this unusual crustacean has given them some seriously tight lines. The company has become one of Canada's top start-ups. Its motto is "Small town, small batches, tall tales."

A small but growing full-time crew and several part-timers keep the old dairy plant humming, but with a new purpose. Rice and MacEachern have also expanded the 2,800-square-metre space to house the Painted Boat Brewing Company, where the distillery cans its all-natural Blue Lobster vodka soda. It's a big hit during the summer months, though sadly for some, this product is lactose-free.

COCKTAIL: BLUE LOBSTER LEMON LIME VODKA SODA IN A CAN
MAKES 1 COCKTAIL

Handful of ice cubes
355 ml (1 can) Blue Lobster Lemon Lime Vodka Soda

Place can in the fridge until cold. In a highball glass, add ice. Pull back tab until you hear a "pshtt" sound. Pour over ice.

RAGING CROW DISTILLERY INC.
NORTH RIVER, NS

Jill Linquist was strolling through her Goose Landing Vineyard, trying to come up with a name for her new distillery, when she noticed the property was alive with crows. These clever, resourceful, and inquisitive creatures truly embodied the qualities that she sought in her spirits.

Linquist and her friend Kris Pruski had renovated a barnlike building for the distillery before realizing that North River was, in fact, a dry community. This meant they could distil and sell spirits but were prohibited from offering tastings. Five months before their grand opening, the crow raged and almost 90% of the community voted in favour of lifting this archaic zoning law. They say crows are a bad omen, but this time luck was on their side. The province acquiesced, eliminating tasting bans in all of Nova Scotia's formerly dry communities.

The two use natural local ingredients when possible. Their bestselling El Cuervo Furioso (Raging Crow in Spanish) coffee liqueur is made from locally roasted cold-brewed coffee from the Aroma Maya roastery, just five minutes away. For Spruce Tip Gin, Jill and Kris picked spring spruce tips from the distillery and neighbouring property, while their triple-distilled Nazdrowka Potato Vodka was the first potato vodka produced in Nova Scotia. And thanks to a crow who raged for change, you can taste all of Raging Crow's spirits onsite.

592 Route 311
North River, NS B6L 6H2
(902) 890-6460
www.ragingcrow.com

@ragingcrowdistillery

FOUNDED 2017

OWNERS Jill Linquist and Kris Pruski

STILLS 200-litre North Stills pot and 400-litre flute column with 12 plates

PRODUCTS Dark rum, gin, liqueurs, vodka, flavoured vodka

AVAILABLE Onsite, online, farmers' markets

NEAREST NEIGHBOURS Caldera Distilling (page 271) – 45 min; Coldstream Clear Distillery (page 272) – 25 min

STEINHART DISTILLERY
ARISAIG, NS

5963 Route 245
Arisaig, NS B2J 2L1
(902) 863-5530
www.steinhartdistillery.com

 @SteinhartDistil

@steinhartdistillery

FOUNDED 2014

OWNER Thomas Steinhart

STILLS 1,200-litre and 300-litre Holstein pots

PRODUCTS Gin, liqueurs, vodka

AVAILABLE Onsite, online, Nova Scotia liquor stores, somelio.de (Europe)

NEAREST NEIGHBOURS Nova Scotia Spirit Co. (page 280) – 35 min; Caldera Distilling (page 271) – 1 hr, 5 min

Thomas Steinhart travelled all over the world as a mechanical engineer. However, it was a vacation in Halifax that changed his life: he fell in love with a local woman and was attracted to the slower pace of Maritime life. He left his native Germany, invested in two Holstein stills—as his grandfather had done back home—and opened Steinhart Distillery on a heritage farm that dates back to the 18th century.

Before he was old enough to drink spirits, Thomas washed bottles for his grandfather and fed logs into the wood-fired stills. In time, "Opa" had him running the still. Aromas of grain, cooking mash, spices, and fruity spirit are etched into his internal flavour library.

Today, Steinhart produces a classic London Dry Gin and something new and truly Canadian: maple vodka. Some of the botanicals for London Dry Gin are not native to Nova Scotia, but what are plentiful are local hops, lavender, blueberries, and hopsack. Steinhart combines Old World and New World botanicals in his double-distilled winter wheat spirit. When he was invited to join England's Gin Guild as a "warden rectifier" in 2017, Steinhart became the first North American distiller to receive this honour.

COCKTAIL:
THE CANADIAN
MAKES 1 COCKTAIL

Large handful of ice cubes
4 oz milk
1 oz Steinhart's Maple Vodka

Fill an eight-ounce glass with the ice. Top with milk, leaving room for the maple vodka. Cascade the maple vodka into the glass and enjoy.

(Steinhart Distillery)

TASTING NOTES: BLUEBERRY GIN (47.5% ABV)
Steinhart proves there is no flavour shortage in Nova Scotia. This bountiful gin balances juniper, blueberry jam, cloves, lavender, and rose, then unwinds on the palate with lemon, ginger, and sprouting pine.

STILL FIRED DISTILLERIES
ANNAPOLIS ROYAL, NS

What led two commercial divers to take the plunge into distilling? For Owen Ritchie and Andrew Cameron, it was a calling. Owen grew up selling bologna, bullets, and fishing rods at his family's Lequille Country Store, and then entertained himself between long days under water with a home distilling kit. Things changed, though, when he and Andrew attended Seattle's Artisan Craft Distillers Institute. The two friends returned determined to convert a 420-square-metre warehouse across the street from the store into a distillery.

They wanted to manage all aspects of the distilling life cycle, beginning at square one. They recruited spirits enthusiast and renowned metal artist Daniel McSparron to help them build the first legal still ever to be designed and constructed entirely in Nova Scotia. It so resembled a giant's shiny steel diving helmet that they named it Kirby, in honour of the Kirby Morgan Company, which manufactures professional diving gear. The 600-litre column still quickly converts into a pot still by snapping on a head.

Demand soon surpassed Kirby's capacity, and in response the team hand-built a second still, also compatible with Kirby's pot still head, and they fitted it with a water jacket to efficiently control temperature. They named this one Morgan—again, after the diving gear company. At the same time, they upgraded their reflux column to a five-metre 14-plate tower.

Products now include their bestselling Granny's Apple Pie Moonshine, a combination of Ritchie's granny's apple pie recipe with Still Fired moonshine. For Fundy Gin, they macerate several botanicals, including local juniper and Bay of Fundy dulse, in triple-distilled spirit. Dulse is a handpicked seaweed that has been sun-dried. Fundy Gin provides a taste of the sea without having to go for a dip in the bay. More recently they have added rum and whisky to their line-up.

(continued)

9548 Route 8
Annapolis Royal, NS B0S 1A0
(902) 471-7083
www.stillfireddistilleries.com

FOUNDED 2015

OWNERS Owen Ritchie and Andrew Cameron

STILLS Own design, named Kirby and Morgan

PRODUCTS Gin, moonshine, rum, vodka

AVAILABLE Onsite, Lequille Country Store, Halifax airport, farmers' markets

NEAREST NEIGHBOURS Barrelling Tide Distillery (page 270) – 1 hr, 10 min; Ironworks Distillery (page 278) – 1 hr, 45 min

TASTING NOTES:
GRANNY'S APPLE PIE MOONSHINE
(20% ABV)

Granny's apple pie—if Granny has a neck tattoo. A mulled cider–like fusion of fresh-pressed apple cider and Still Fired moonshine. A cinnamon-forward spice blend accents the moonshine and apple's sweet buttery texture. Serve warm during the cooler months and on ice during the summer. Easily smuggled into prison if your granny is doing time.

COCKTAIL:
STILL FIRED ARUGULA GIMLET
MAKES 1 COCKTAIL

1 cup fresh baby arugula, plus extra
    to garnish
2 oz Fundy Gin
1 oz simple syrup
¾ oz fresh-squeezed lime juice
Handful of ice cubes

In a shaker, combine all of the ingredients. Shake until the arugula is mostly crushed. Pour in a Martini glass and garnish with arugula leaves.

(Still Fired Distilleries)

THE NEWFOUNDLAND DISTILLERY COMPANY
CLARKE'S BEACH, NL

Peter Wilkins's commute gives new meaning to long walks on the beach. Threading your way among jellyfish and the occasional killer iceberg (watch the blockbuster movie *Titanic*) is a way of life in his hometown of Clarke's Beach. Until late 2019, when it moved 10 minutes down the street, the distillery overlooked Conception Bay from what was once a general store called Garfield Ralph's. Wilkins remembers the old shop fondly, and he still wears a cap that he bought there. Garfield Ralph's sold everything from hardware, oilskin coats, and wedding dresses to coffins, but closed when the owner took up permanent residence in one of the latter.

Wilkins and his business partner, William Carter, planned from day one to produce craft spirits that showcase the island's ingredients. Their aquavit, for example, is the first legally distilled spirit in Newfoundland with every component grown in the province. However, it's gin that keeps the stills working overtime. Their first gin incorporates three local botanicals—juniper, savory farmed atop Mount Scio, and Newfoundland's esteemed cloudberry.

For their Seaweed Gin, the team replaces cloudberry with Grand Banks seaweed. The barley base spirit they distil onsite is passed through their copper pot stills with the addition of seaweed, juniper, and savory. Once diluted to 40% abv, the gin is macerated again with the botanicals. Although this is their bestseller, their Gunpowder & Rose is close at its heels.

Why gunpowder and rose? In the 1600s, when the British navy gave its sailors a daily ration of rum, they would mix a sample with gunpowder before lighting it to prove its quality. Good rum flared, whereas grog merely fizzled. This maritime tradition inspired Wilkins and Carter to add edible gunpowder to aged Jamaican-style amber rum. They make this edible gunpowder by using local charred birch and sea salt from the Newfoundland Salt Company. They also add wild Newfoundland roses to the rum for aromatic contrast, capping off a flavour tour of Newfoundland from the comforts of Clarke's Beach.

14 Conception Bay Highway
Clarke's Beach, NL A0A 1W0
(709) 786-0234
www.thenewfoundlanddistillery.com

🐦 @NLDistilleryCo

📷 @thenewfoundlanddistilleryco

FOUNDED 2017

OWNERS Peter Wilkins and William Carter

STILLS 1,000-litre Specific Mechanical pot

PRODUCTS Aquavit, gin, rum, vodka

AVAILABLE Onsite, Newfoundland Liquor Commission and Liquor Express stores

NEAREST NEIGHBOURS Wooden Walls Distilling (page 288) — 1 hr; Glenora Inn and Distillery (page 275) — 19 hr (including ferry)

TASTING NOTES:
GUNPOWDER AND ROSE RUM (40% ABV)

Don't expect this spiced rum to deliver a cannonball to the face. It's a precise sniper's bullet of refined flavours. A cleverly floral and sophisticated salt-and-peppery brine supports vanilla and sweet brown sugar. If the navy gave this rum to sailors headed into battle, they'd think they were aboard the *HMS Pinafore*.

WHISKY ON THE ROCK

t was a dentist who converted the old Whitbourne, Newfoundland, community hospital into a modest winery. Dr. Hilary Rodrigues made fruit wine, powdered fruit supplements, and now and again he fired up a still that looked like used tank parts. The story goes that the Sofac les Alambics pot still was manufactured in Condom, France, in 1993 and saw action on the French archipelago of Saint-Pierre and Miquelon, about 25 kilometres off the coast of Newfoundland. After Rodrigues acquired the still in 2012, it spent more time developing a tarnished black patina than producing spirits. The still that marked distilling's official return to Newfoundland has been silent for years now, without ever having distilled Newfoundland-grown grains, but Newfoundland's legal distilling story does not end there.

In 2017, when the first drops of alcohol came off The Newfoundland Distillery Company's still (page 285), Peter Wilkins saw them as drops of joy. Wilkins is a one-time professional drinker. A decade before opening the distillery, he and British comedian Dom Joly travelled the globe filming the television series *Dom Joly's Happy Hour*. The six-episode series caricatured travel television while exploring national traditions via drink.

Drinking his way around the world gave Wilkins a broad perspective on international spirits. Unknowingly, he was cross-training to give distilling a go. Wilkins met his Newfoundlander wife in a Czech bar. While in Canada to meet her family, he also met Cordon Bleu–trained master chef William Carter.

Carter insists on simple recipes that use the freshest ingredients available. His celebrated career has seen prime ministers, royalty, and celebrities dine on his cuisine. When they met, Carter confided to Wilkins that he dreamed of making whisky. Wilkins did too, but the three-year wait for it to mature put him off. Why not try gin? They applied Carter's tried-and-true cooking techniques to distillation—the best-quality Newfoundland ingredients, processed pure and in a straightforward manner. When they tasted their first creation, the partners worried that the romance of making it had completely skewed their objectivity. Nevertheless, they packed up a few bottles and travelled to the UK, where they hosted blind tastings. The reviews were positive. Had distilling arrived again in Newfoundland? Yes, but only for a short time.

In November 2018 a harrowing explosion at the distillery sent two employees to hospital. Fortunately, they recovered, but it was a month before they were back on their feet. Just to be safe, the distillery's three original copper pot stills were retired. Once again, Newfoundland was without an operating still.

Wilkins and Carter do not easily give up, though, and they have now installed a brand new, Canadian-made 1,000-litre Specific Mechanical copper pot still with a spirit head and columns. Finally, Newfoundland is ready to make whisky. Carter's ultimate aim is to produce a definitive Newfoundland whisky made from bere, a barley-like grain the Vikings brought here over 1,000 years ago. But bere is expensive and difficult to find. So, while that plan is on hold, they are using malted barley from a local farm. Has distilling finally landed on The Rock? The answer is an emphatic "Yes, b'y." ■

WOODEN WALLS DISTILLING
ST. JOHN'S, NL

140 Harbour Dr.
St. John's, NL A1C 5N8
www.woodenwalls.ca

🐦 @WoodenWallsDist

📷 @woodenwallsdistilling

NEAREST NEIGHBOUR The Newfoundland
Distiller Company (page 285) — 1 hr

The first distillery in St. John's is named for the wooden-walled steamships that modernized the fishing industry and contributed to the city's culture. An important landmark also helped build the city. For 150 years, Templeton Trading Inc. operated as a hardware store at 140 Harbour Drive in downtown St. John's before finally closing in 2016. Now a distillery has taken up residence within the Templeton space, hoping to write the building's next chapter. Sip gin and vodka cocktails in the sit-down tasting room and listen while Peter Madden and Chris Dowden recount tales of the neighbourhood stories about the location's exciting history, and their plans to make whisky and rum there.

OTHER DISTILLERIES

While writing and researching this book, distilleries just kept springing up. This shows just how vibrant the industry has become. Here are some distilleries not covered in the book that are also part of Canada's microdistilling movement. For even more updates, please visit www.canadiandistilleries.com.

BRITISH COLUMBIA

BESPOKE SPIRITS HOUSE DISTILLERY
Parksville, BC
www.bespokespiritshouse.com

ENDLESS SUMMER DISTILLERY
Kelowna, BC
www.endlesssummerdistillery.com

ESTATE THURN DISTILLERY
Summerland, BC
www.bodega117.com

KOOTENAY COUNTRY CRAFT DISTILLERY
Slocan, BC
www.kootenaycountry.ca

MONTIS DISTILLING
Whistler, BC
www.montisdistilling.com

MOUNT 7 SPIRITS CRAFT DISTILLERY
Golden, BC
www.facebook.com/mount7spirits

URBAN DISTILLERIES AND WINERY
West Kelowna, BC
www.urbandistilleries.ca

VERNON CRAFT DISTILLERS
Vernon, BC
www.vernoncraftdistilleries.com

WYNNDEL CRAFT DISTILLERIES
Wynndel, BC
www.wynndelcraftdistilleries.ca

THE PRAIRIES

BACK 40 DISTILLERY
Camrose, AB
www.back40distillery.com

BRIDGELAND DISTILLERY
Calgary, AB
https://bridgelanddistillery.com

BROKEN OAK DISTILLING CO.
Grand Prairie, AB
https://brokenoak.ca

COLD LAKE BREWING & DISTILLING
Cold Lake, AB
https://coldlakebrewingdistilling.com

ELK ISLAND SPIRITS CO.
Sherwood Park, AB
www.elkislandspirits.com

GREENWOOD DISTILLERS
Sundre, AB
www.greenwooddistillers.ca

GRIT CITY DISTILLERY
Medicine Hat, AB
https://gritcity.ca

KRANG SPIRITS, INC.
Cochrane, AB
www.krang.com

LATITUDE 55
Grand Prairie, AB
www.latitude55.ca

WEST OF FIFTH DISTILLERY
Barrhead, AB
http://shady-lane-estate.mybigcommerce.com

ERRINGTON LAKE DISTILLERY
Kindersley, SK
www.erringtonlakedistillery.com

HUDSON BAY DISTILLERS
Landis, SK
www.hudsonbaydistillers.ca

MINHAS SASK DISTILLERY, WINERY AND BREWERY
Regina, SK
www.minhassask.ca

ROCKY MOUNTAIN BIG HORN DISTILLERY
Yellowhead County, AB
http://rockymountainbighorn.ca

SMOOTH 42 CRAFT DISTILLERY
Brownlee, SK
https://smooth42.ca

STUMBLETOWN DISTILLERY
Saskatoon, SK
www.stumbletown.ca

TIPPA INC.
Okotoks, AB
http://tippa.ca

TROUBLED MONK
Red Deer, AB
https://troubledmonk.com

ONTARIO
BARNSTORMER BREWING & DISTILLING CO.
Barrie, ON
www.barnstormerbrewing.com

DURHAM DISTILLERY
Whitby, ON
https://durhamdistillery.ca

ELORA DISTILLING COMPANY
Elora, ON
https://eloradistillingcompany.com

MAVERICK CRAFT DISTILLERY
Oakville, ON
https://maverickdistillery.com

MUSKOKA BREWERY AND DISTILLERY
Bracebridge, ON
https://muskokabrewery.com/the-distillery

NIAGARA DISTILLERY
Niagara Falls, ON
https://niagaradistillery.com

PERSIAN EMPIRE DISTILLERY
Peterborough, ON
www.persianempire1.com

SILVER FOX DISTILLERY
Arthur, ON
www.facebook.com/silverfoxdistillery

SPRING MILL DISTILLERY
Guelph, ON
www.springmilldistillery.com

QUEBEC
BEAUREGARD BRASSERIE DISTILLERIE
Montreal, QC
www.beauregardbrasseriedistillerie.com

BLUEPEARL DISTILLERY
Montreal, QC
https://bluepearldistillery.com

DISTILLERIE BOILEAU
Boileau, QC
www.distillerieboileau.com

BRASSERIE DISTILLERIE CHAMP LIBRE
Mercer, QC
https://champlibre.co

DISTILLERIE DE LA CHAUFFERIE
Granby, QC
https://lachaufferie.ca/fr

DISTILLERIE CÔTE DES SAINTS
Mirabel, QC
www.facebook.com/Distilleriecotedessaints

CIDRERIE ENTRE PIERRE & TERRE
Franklin, QC
www.entrepierreetterre.com

DISTILLERIE GRAND DÉRANGEMENT
Saint-Jacques, QC
www.grandderangement.ca

DISTILLERIE L&M
Trois-Rivières, QC
https://distillerielm.com

DISTILLERIE MITIS
Candiac, QC
www.distilleriemitis.com

DISTILLERY DU QUAI
Bécancour, QC
www.facebook.com/distillerieduquai

DISTILLERIE OUSHKABE
LaSalle, QC
www.oushkabe.ca

DISTILLERIE TROIS-LACS
Salaberry-de-Valleyfield, QC
www.distillerietroislacs.ca

LES SPIRITUEUX UNGAVA
Cowansville, QC
www.ungavaco.com

DISTILLERIE WILSY
St-Placide, QC
www.wilsy.ca

TROIS LACS DISTILLERY
Salaberry-de-Valleyfield, QC
www.distillerietroislacs.ca

ATLANTIC CANADA
DEVIL'S KEEP DISTILLERY
Fredericton, NB
https://devilskeepdistillery.ca

DISTILLERY CHECKLIST

LEGEND: VW = VISITORS WELCOME; V = VODKA; G = GIN; W= WHISKY; O = OTHER; * = SPIRIT AGING

☑ DISTILLERY	VW	V	G	W	O
ALBERTA					
Alberta Distillers Limited		✓		✓	
Black Diamond Distillery	✓	✓	✓	✓	✓
Black Velvet Distillery	✓			✓	
Burwood Distillery	✓	✓	✓		✓
Confluence Distilling	✓	✓	✓		
Eau Claire Distillery	✓	✓	✓	✓	✓
The Fort Distillery	✓	✓	✓		
Hansen Distillery	✓	✓	✓	✓	✓
Highwood Distillers	✓	✓		✓	✓
Last Best Brewing & Distilling	✓		✓	✓	✓
Lone Pine Distilling	✓		✓		
Old Prairie Sentinel Distillery	✓	✓	✓	✓	✓
Park Distillery	✓	✓	✓	✓	✓
RAW Distillery	✓	✓	✓	✓	✓
Red Cup Distillery	✓				✓
Rig Hand Distillery	✓	✓	✓	✓	✓
Stone Heart Distillery	✓	✓			
Strathcona Spirits Distillery	✓	✓	✓	*	
Wild Life Distillery	✓	✓	✓	*	
BRITISH COLUMBIA					
The 101 Brewhouse + Distillery	✓	✓	✓		
After Dark Distillery	✓	✓	✓	*	✓

☑ DISTILLERY	VW	V	G	W	O
Alchemist Distiller	✓		✓		✓
Ampersand Distilling Company	✓	✓	✓		✓
Anderson Distilleries	✓	✓	✓		✓
Arbutus Distillery	✓	✓	✓	✓	✓
Bohemian Spirits	✓	✓	✓	*	✓
Bruinwood Estate Distillery	✓	✓	✓		✓
Central City Brewers & Distillers	✓		✓	✓	✓
Copper Spirits Distillery	✓	✓	✓		✓
Crow's Nest Distillery	✓	✓		✓	
Deep Cove Brewers and Distillers	✓	✓	✓		✓
de Vine Wines & Spirits	✓	✓	✓	✓	✓
Dragon Mist Distillery	✓	✓	✓		
The Dubh Glas Distillery	✓		✓	✓	✓
Elder Bros. Farms Distillery	✓				✓
Fernie Distillers	✓	✓	✓	*	✓
Forbidden Spirits Distilling Co.	✓	✓	✓		✓
Gillespie's Fine Spirits Ltd.	✓	✓	✓		✓
Goodridge & Williams Craft Distillers	✓	✓	✓	✓	✓
Island Spirits Distillery	✓	✓	✓		✓
Jones Distilling	✓	✓	✓	*	✓
Legend Distilling	✓	✓	✓	✓	✓
The Liberty Distillery	✓	✓	✓	✓	
Long Table Distillery Ltd.	✓	✓	✓		✓

DISTILLERY	VW	V	G	W	O
Lost Boys Distilling	✓	✓	✓		✓
Lucid Spirits Distilling Co.	✓	✓	✓	*	✓
Mad Laboratory Distilling	✓	✓	✓		✓
Maple Leaf Spirits	✓				✓
Merridale Cidery & Distillery	✓	✓	✓	✓	✓
Monashee Spirits Craft Distillery	✓	✓	✓	*	✓
The Moon Distilling Co.	✓	✓	✓	*	✓
New Wave Distilling	✓	✓	✓		✓
North West Distilling Co.	✓	✓	✓	✓	
Odd Society Spirits	✓	✓	✓	✓	✓
Okanagan Craft Spirits Distillery	✓	✓	✓	✓	✓
Okanagan Crush Pad	✓		✓		✓
Old Order Distilling Co.	✓	✓	✓	*	✓
One Foot Crow Craft Distillery	✓	✓			
Pacific Rim Distilling	✓	✓	✓		
Pemberton Distillery	✓	✓	✓	✓	✓
Phillips Fermentorium Distilling Co.	✓		✓	*	✓
Resurrection Spirits Inc.	✓	✓	✓	✓	✓
Roots and Wings Distillery	✓	✓	✓	*	
Salt Spring Shine Craft Distillery Ltd.	✓	✓	✓		✓
Shelter Point Distillery	✓	✓	✓	✓	✓
Sheringham Distillery	✓	✓	✓	✓	✓
Sons of Vancouver Distillery	✓	✓			✓
Spinnakers Brewpub	✓	✓	✓	*	✓
SR Winery & Distillery	✓				✓
Stealth Distillery	✓	✓			

DISTILLERY	VW	V	G	W	O
Stillhead Distilling Inc.	✓	✓	✓	✓	✓
Tailored Spirits	✓	✓	✓		
Taynton Bay Spirits	✓	✓	✓		✓
Tofino Craft Distillery	✓	✓	✓		✓
Trench Brewing & Distilling Inc.	✓	✓	✓		
True North Distilleries	✓		✓	✓	✓
Tumbleweed Spirits	✓	✓	✓	✓	✓
Victoria Caledonian Distillery	✓			✓	
Victoria Distillers	✓	✓	✓	✓	✓
Wayward Distillation House	✓	✓	✓		✓
The Woods Spirits Co.	✓		✓	*	✓
Yaletown Distilling Company	✓	✓	✓	✓	

MANITOBA

DISTILLERY	VW	V	G	W	O
Capital K Distillery	✓	✓	✓	*	✓
Gimli Distillery				✓	
Patent 5 Distillery	✓	✓	✓	*	

NEW BRUNSWICK

DISTILLERY	VW	V	G	W	O
Blue Roof Distillers	✓	✓	✓		
Distillerie Fils du Roy	✓	✓	✓	✓	✓
Gagetown Distillery & Cidery	✓	✓	✓	✓	✓
Moonshine Creek Distillery	✓				✓
Sussex Craft Distilling	✓				✓
Winegarden Estate Ltd.	✓				✓

NEWFOUNDLAND

DISTILLERY	VW	V	G	W	O
The Newfoundland Distillery Company	✓	✓	✓	*	✓
Wooden Walls Distilling	✓			*	✓

DISTILLERY	VW	V	G	W	O
NOVA SCOTIA					
Authentic Seacoast Distillery & Brewery	✓	✓		✓	
Barrelling Tide Distillery	✓	✓	✓		✓
Caldera Distilling	✓			✓	
Coldstream Clear Distillery	✓	✓	✓		✓
Compass Distillers	✓	✓	✓	*	✓
Glenora Inn and Distillery	✓			✓	
Halifax Distilling Company	✓				✓
Ironworks Distillery	✓	✓	✓		✓
Nova Scotia Spirit Co.	✓	✓	✓		✓
Raging Crow Distillery Inc.	✓	✓	✓		✓
Steinhart Distillery	✓	✓	✓		✓
Still Fired Distilleries	✓	✓	✓	✓	✓
ONTARIO					
All or Nothing Brewhouse & Distillery	✓		✓	*	✓
Beattie's Distillers Inc.	✓	✓	✓	*	✓
Black's Distillery	✓	✓	✓	*	✓
Canadian Mist Distillers			✓		
Copperhead Distillery & Spirits Ltd.	✓	✓	✓	*	✓
Crosscut Distillery	✓	✓	✓	*	
Dairy Distillery	✓	✓			✓
Dillon's Small Batch Distillers	✓	✓	✓	✓	✓
Dixon's Distilled Spirits	✓	✓	✓	✓	✓
Forty Creek Distillery	✓	✓		✓	✓
Frape & Sons	✓			*	
Grand Spirits Distillery	✓	✓	✓	✓	✓

DISTILLERY	VW	V	G	W	O
Hiram Walker & Sons Distillery	✓	✓	✓	✓	✓
Junction 56 Distillery	✓	✓	✓	✓	✓
King's Lock Craft Distillery	✓	✓	✓	✓	✓
Kinsip House of Fine Spirits	✓	✓	✓	✓	✓
Last Straw Distillery	✓	✓	✓	✓	✓
Limited Distillery	✓			*	✓
Magnotta Distillery	✓	✓	✓		✓
Mill Street Distillery	✓		✓	✓	✓
Murphy's Law Distillery	✓				✓
Niagara College Distillery	✓				
Niagara Falls Craft Distillers	✓	✓	✓	✓	✓
Nickel 9 Distillery	✓	✓	✓	*	✓
North of 7 Distillery	✓	✓	✓	✓	✓
Pepprell Distilling Co.	✓		✓		
Polonée Distillery Inc.	✓	✓			✓
Reid's Distillery	✓		✓		
Rheault Distillery	✓	✓		✓	✓
Spirit of York Distillery Co.	✓	✓	✓	✓	✓
Still Waters Distillery	✓			✓	
Tawse Winery and Distillery	✓	✓	✓	*	✓
Top Shelf Distillers	✓	✓	✓	✓	✓
Vieni Estates Inc.	✓				✓
Wayne Gretzky Estate Winery & Distillery	✓			✓	✓
The White Distillery	✓	✓	✓		✓
Willibald Farm Distillery	✓		✓	✓	✓
Wolfhead Distillery	✓	✓		✓	✓

☑ DISTILLERY	VW	V	G	W	O
☐ Yongehurst Distillery Co.	✓	✓	✓	✓	✓

PRINCE EDWARD ISLAND

	VW	V	G	W	O
☐ Deep Roots Distillery	✓			*	✓
☐ Matos Winery & Distillery	✓				✓
☐ Myriad View Artisan Distillery Inc.	✓			✓	✓
☐ Prince Edward Distillery	✓	✓			

QUEBEC

	VW	V	G	W	O
☐ 1769 Distillery Inc.		✓	✓	✓	✓
☐ Absintherie des Cantons	✓		✓		✓
☐ Artist in Residence Distillerie	✓	✓	✓	*	✓
☐ Distillerie Beemer	✓	✓			✓
☐ Cirka Distilleries	✓	✓	✓	*	
☐ Distillerie du Fjord	✓		✓		✓
☐ Intermiel	✓				✓
☐ Les Vergers Lafrance	✓	✓	✓		✓
☐ Distillerie Mariana	✓	✓	✓		✓
☐ Menaud Distillerie et Brasserie	✓	✓	✓		
☐ Cidrerie Michel Jodoin	✓	✓			✓
☐ Distillerie de Montréal	✓		✓		✓
☐ Distillerie Noroi	✓		✓		
☐ O'Dwyer Distillerie Gaspésienne	✓		✓	*	✓
☐ Old Montreal Distillery	✓		✓		
☐ Brasserie & Distillerie Oshlag	✓	✓	✓	*	✓
☐ Distillerie le Pirate du Nord			✓	*	✓
☐ Distillerie Puyjalon Inc.	✓	✓	✓	*	✓

☑ DISTILLERY	VW	V	G	W	O
☐ Distillerie de Quebec	✓	✓	✓		
☐ Distillerie du St. Laurent	✓		✓	✓	✓
☐ Distillerie Shefford	✓			*	✓
☐ Maison Sivo	✓			✓	✓
☐ La Société Secrète	✓	✓	✓		✓
☐ Les Distillateurs Subversifs	✓	✓	✓		✓
☐ Thompson Distillery	✓	✓	✓		✓
☐ Tower Hill Road Distillery					
☐ Valleyfield Distillery				✓	✓
☐ Vice & Vertu Disilleries	✓		✓	*	
☐ Wabasso Distillerie			✓	*	✓

SASKATCHEWAN

	VW	V	G	W	O
☐ Bandits Distilling Inc.	✓	✓	✓	*	✓
☐ Black Fox Farm & Distillery	✓	✓	✓	✓	✓
☐ Last Mountain Distillery	✓	✓	✓	✓	✓
☐ Lost River Distillery	✓	✓			
☐ Lucky Bastard Distillers	✓	✓	✓	✓	✓
☐ Outlaw Trail Spirits Company	✓	✓			✓
☐ Radouga Distilleries	✓	✓			✓
☐ Sperling Silver Distillery	✓	✓	✓	✓	✓

YUKON

	VW	V	G	W	O
☐ Klondike River Distillery		✓			
☐ Yukon Brewing	✓		✓	✓	✓
☐ Yukon Shine Distillery		✓	✓		

GLOSSARY

ABSINTHE: An aniseed-flavoured spirit made with the wormwood shrub and other botanicals.

ABV: Alcohol by volume—indicates the percentage of alcohol in a given amount of liquid.

ACERUM: A spirit distilled from fermented Quebec maple sap ingredients, following rules defined by Acerum's protected designation of origin.

AGED GIN: Gin that has been matured in oak barrels, which impart colour and flavour (*see also* **gin**).

ANGELICA ROOT: A common gin botanical that helps integrate other botanical flavours and adds an earthy, dry note to gin's flavour profile.

AQUAVIT: A Scandinavian-derived spirit traditionally distilled with caraway and dill as the core flavours.

ARAK: A West Asian distilled spirit, usually made by fermenting and distilling crushed grapes, with aniseed added for the second of three distillations.

BÁIJǓI: A Chinese distilled spirit (translates to "white spirit") made by fermenting grain with a fermentation agent called *qu* before distillation.

BASE SPIRIT: A neutral alcohol distilled from grain, fruit, root vegetables, cane sugar, or honey to a high abv; may be redistilled or macerated with botanicals to create gin.

BIERSCHNAPPS: A schnapps made by distillilling beer (also known as **bierschnaps**). (*see also* **schnapps**).

BITTERS: A spirit flavoured by the infusion of botanicals to a high concentration and used as an ingredient in cocktails.

BOTANICALS: Plant materials, roots, leaves, stems, flowers, seeds, that give spirits such as gin, absinthe, bitters, and aquavit their distinctive flavours.

BOTTLING STRENGTH: The abv level to which spirits are usually reduced, using pure water; often 40% abv, for bottling.

BRANDY: A spirit distilled from grape pomace, fruit, or wine and sometimes aged in wooden casks.

CHILL FILTERING: The process by which spirits are cooled, then filtered to remove components that would settle out over time and create cloudiness in the bottle (also known as **cold filtering**).

COCKTAIL RIMMER: A salt- or sugar-based mixture that adheres to the wet rim of a cocktail glass.

COLUMN STILL: A tall metal cylinder filled with horizontal perforated plates, over which fermented mash passes back and forth as it descends the column. Alcohol and congeners are stripped out as steam rises from the bottom of the column, until they pass from the top of the column to a condenser.

CONDENSER: A series of tubes that are cooled from the outside to condense vapours from distillation into liquid state.

CONGENER: Any of a broad range of compounds that give spirits their flavours.

CONTINUOUS STILL: A column still to which fermented mash can be added and distillate removed in uninterrupted streams over long periods of time.

CORIANDER SEED: A common gin botanical that adds a spicy citrus profile as well as floral tones.

DISTILLATION: The separation of individual components of a solution by heating it to a temperature where some components will vapourize but others will not, and then collecting the vapours.

DOUBLE-STRAINING: The process of straining the liquid from a cocktail through a standard strainer and a fine mesh strainer simultaneously into a glass.

DRY SHAKE: The process of shaking ingredients using a cocktail shaker without ice.

EAU-DE-VIE: A clear brandy distilled from fermented fruit such as raspberries, pears, or apples.

ENZYME: A naturally occurring protein that causes specific chemical reactions to occur. Prior to fermentation, enzymes convert starch to sugar by breaking certain chemical bonds in the starch.

EXPRESSING: The aromatic process of squeezing a citrus rind over a cocktail to release its essential oils over the drink.

FERMENT: As a verb: to convert sugar to alcohol and carbon dioxide though metabolic activity in yeast. As a noun: the process of fermenting or the time during the process when fermentation occurs.

FERMENTABLES: Sugars and other carbohydrates that may be fermented by yeast.

FERMENTER: The vessel in which fermentation occurs.

FINISH: The flavour and feel that is left behind by a spirit after it has been swallowed. Also used to describe how long said flavour and feeling last.

FLAVOURED VODKA: Vodka that has been flavoured with either natural or artificial flavours and generally sweetened with sugar (see also **vodka**).

FRUIT BRANDY: A brandy distilled from fermented fruits. Applicable to a broad spectrum of spirits, including eau-de-vie, Calvados, Pálinka, and Poire Williams.

GARNISH: An ingredient added to a cocktail as a decorative element to enhance presentation.

GENEVER: A spirit category originating in the Netherlands, made from a base spirit of malted grain wines with the addition of botanicals such as juniper.

GIN: A popular spirit made by infusing neutral or near-neutral spirits with plant flavours (see **botanicals**).

GIN BASKET: A wire basket or other permeable container that holds gin botanicals above the boiling liquid in a still so that the vapours will pass through and pick up flavours as they rise to the condenser.

GRAIN NEUTRAL SPIRIT (GNS): Flavourless alcohol produced by distilling and redistilling fermented grain-derived sugars until all detectable congeners are removed. Some newer distillers have inverted the acronym to NGS. Neutral spirits are also distilled commonly from fruit, roots, and cane sugar.

INFUSED VODKA: Vodka that is flavoured, generally by infusing it with natural ingredients without the addition of sugar.

I-STILL: A unique Dutch-made still that can be monitored by Wi-Fi and operated remotely using a smartphone.

JUNIPER: An essential ingredient in gin that gives the spirit its iconic pine and cedar flavours.

LICORICE ROOT: A common gin botanical that adds sweetness and a smooth mouthfeel to gin.

LIGNIN: A complex molecule found in wood and the outer coating of grain. Lignin is the primary source of wood- and grain-derived flavours.

LIQUEUR: A low-alcohol, sweetened spirit of at least 23% abv, flavoured by plant materials such as extracts, juices, herbs, fruit, and/or spices. Liqueurs may contain cream and natural or artificial flavours and colours.

MACERATION: The process of steeping botanicals or ingredients in alcohol to extract their flavours.

MALT: Grain, usually barley, that has been partially sprouted to activate enzymes, then dried.

MALTINGS: A facility where grain is malted.

MARRYING: The practice of putting spirits that have been blended into barrels or vats for a period of time to let the mixture equilibrate.

MASH: As a verb: to mix ground grain, fruit, potatoes, etc., with water in preparation for fermentation. As a noun: a slurry of fermentable materials and water.

MASH BILL: The mix of grains used to make whisky.

MOUTHFEEL: The way a spirit feels in the mouth. Usually characterized as creamy, mouth-coating, thin, or watery.

MUDDLE: The process of gently crushing an ingredient in a shaker or glass with a wooden muddling tool.

NOSE: As a verb: to smell spirits for the purpose of identifying aromas. As a noun: the aromas found by methodically smelling spirits.

ORRIS ROOT: A common gin botanical that aids in binding other botanical flavours together. It can also add a floral sweetness to a gin's aroma.

PALATE: The flavour and feel of a spirit in the mouth. Also, the ability to differentiate subtle differences in flavour and mouthfeel.

PALETTE: The particular range of spirits and botanicals that a blender uses—just as artists use a specific range of colours, each blender has a flavour palette.

PALLET: The wooden base on which barrels are placed to facilitate storage and transportation by forklift.

POITIN: A traditional Irish spirit distilled from grain, sugar beets, molasses, or potatoes in a small pot still. Can also be used as a term for an aged Irish-style moonshine or illicitly distilled whisky.

POMACE: The skins, seeds, stems, and pulp that remain after pressing fruit for juice.

POT STILL: A large vessel, usually made of copper, in which fermented mash is heated to cause the alcohol and congeners to evaporate so that they can be separated from water and undesirable congeners.

RECTIFIER: Traditionally, someone who purchased raw alcohol and made palatable whisky by filtering it and adding flavouring compounds. Today, the term describes the final column still used to produce, or rectify, new distillate.

RECTIFYING: A process of making raw whisky more drinkable by adding or removing certain flavours. Traditionally, whisky was rectified by filtering through charcoal and/or adding flavourings and colour.

RUM: A spirit made from fermented molasses or other cane sugar. In Canada, rum must be aged for at least one year.

SCHNAPPS: A dry high-proof spirit of German origin, generally made by distilling fermented fruit juices.

SHAKE: The process of shaking ingredients in a cocktail shaker with the addition of ice.

SHŌCHŪ: A Japanese traditional spirit made from grains or vegetables such as sweet potato, barley, or rice. Shōchū's alcohol content averages between 25% and 37%.

SINGLE MALT: A whisky made in a single distillery, using only grain that has been malted (*see also* **malt**).

SINGLE SHOT DISTILLATION: The process of making gin by combining base spirit and botanicals in a pot still and distilling them together.

SPENT MASH: The remains of the mash after filtration or distilling. Usually quite rich in yeast and protein and used to feed animals and as a fertilizer.

SPIRYTUS: A highly rectified spirit originating in Poland and bottled at 95% abv. It is used as a base for liqueurs and other infusions.

STILL: A mechanical device used to separate alcohol and congeners from water by heating them and taking advantage of differences in boiling temperatures.

STIR: The process of mixing ingredients with the use of a barspoon.

STRAIN: The process of straining the contents of a shaker while pouring them into a glass.

TERROIR: Adapted from the common winemaking term. In spirits, terroir is the result of how a distiller captures the character of the area surrounding the distillery—for example, by using local grains or botanicals associated with the surrounding area.

TWIST: A citrus-peel garnish that is twisted over a cocktail to release its essential oils.

VACUUM DISTILLATION: Distillation at low temperature, in a vacuum, to preserve the delicate flavours of heat-sensitive congeners. Sometimes called cold distillation.

VAPOUR INFUSION: Adding flavours by placing botanicals in the vapour stream of the still rather than directly in the liquid mash or spirit that is being distilled.

VERMOUTH: Red or white wine that has been fortified with spirits, then flavoured with aromatic herbs and spices. Sometimes sweetened. Often used as an ingredient in cocktails.

VODKA: A clear, theoretically flavourless spirit obtained by distilling spirits several times and often filtering them through charcoal to remove any residual flavours.

WHISKY: A spirit of at least 40% abv derived from fermented grain. In Canada, this spirit must be matured in oak barrels for at least three years.

YEAST: A single-celled organism that consumes sugar, turning it into ethanol and carbon dioxide. Yeasts also produce many of the desirable congeners in spirits.

BIBLIOGRAPHY

Bart-Riedstra, Carolyn. *Images of Canada: Stratford*. Charleston, SC: Arcadia Publishing, 2002.

Broom, Dave. *Gin: The Manual*. London: Mitchell Beazley, 2015.

Brymner, Douglas. *Report on Canadian Archives*. Ottawa: Maclean, Roger & Company, 1895.

Campbell, Jonah. *Eaten Back to Life*. Picton, ON: Invisible Publishing, 2017.

Carr, Deborah. *In Vino Veritas: How an Old German Tradition Becomes New Brunswick's Windfall*. Baie Verte, NB: Winegarden Estate Ltd., 2009.

De Kergommeaux, Davin. *Canadian Whisky: The New Portable Expert*. Vancouver: Appetite by Random House, 2017.

Faith, Nicholas. *The Bronfmans: The Rise and Fall of the House of Seagram*. New York: St. Martin's Press, 2006.

Greene, Philip, and Dale DeGroff. *The Manhattan: The Story of the First Modern Cocktail, with Recipes*. New York: Sterling Epicure, 2016.

Heron, Craig. *Booze: A Distilled History*. Toronto: Between the Lines, 2003.

James, Rick. *Don't Never Tell Nobody Nothin' No How: The Real Story of West Coast Rum Running*. Madeira Park, BC: Harbour, 2019.

Livermore, Don. *Quantification of Oak Wood Extractives via Gas Chromatography—Mass Spectrometry and Subsequent Calibration of Near Infrared Reflectance to Predict the Canadian Whisky Ageing Process*. PhD thesis, Heriot-Watt University, 2010.

MacKinnon, Tanya Lynn. *The Historical Geography of the Distilling Industry in Ontario: 1850– 1900*. Master's thesis, Wilfrid Laurier University, 2000.

Newman, Kara, and John Lee. *Shake. Stir. Sip: More than 50 Effortless Cocktails Made in Equal Parts*. San Francisco: Chronicle Books, 2016.

Poirier, Bernard. *Whisky with Dinner*. Burnstown, ON: General Store Publishing House, 1989.

Price, Ruth. *The Politics of Liquor in British Columbia, 1920–1928*. Vancouver: Simon Fraser University, 1979.

Schobert, Walter. *The Whiskey Treasury*. Castle Douglas, Scotland: Neil Wilson Publishing, 2002.

Simonson, Robert. *3-Ingredient Cocktails: An Opinionated Guide to the Most Enduring Drinks in the Cocktail Canon*. Berkeley, CA: Ten Speed Press, 2017.

Simonson, Robert, and Daniel Krieger. *The Old-Fashioned: The Story of the World's First Classic Cocktail, with Recipes and Lore*. Berkeley, CA: Ten Speed Press, 2014.

Smith, David T. *The Gin Dictionary*. London: Mitchell Beazley, 2018.

Teacher, Matt. *The Spirit of Gin*. Kennebunkport, ME: Cider Mill Press, 2014.

Thompson, Scott, and Gary Genosko. *Punched Drunk: Alcohol, Surveillance and the LCBO, 1927–1975*. Black Point, NS: Fernwood Publishing, 2009.

Walsh, Victoria, and Scott McCallum. *A Field Guide to Canadian Cocktails*. Vancouver: Appetite by Random House, 2015.

CREDITS

ACKNOWLEDGMENTS

Thank you to all the distillers, large and small, who welcomed us so graciously into their distilleries and shared with us their plans, dreams, and accomplishments.

Before the book arrives with our names on the cover and we develop instant amnesia about all the people it really took to conceive, write, and publish it, our sincere gratitude to Denise Bukowski, and her staff at the Bukowski Agency for support, advocacy, and reality checks. Thank you and deep appreciation to Appetite publisher Robert McCullough and to Penguin Random House editor Katherine Stopa for their patience and encouragement in turning an idea into a book. It is now 2020; our discussions began in 2017. And thank you, Andrew Roberts. You designed the book we hoped you would.

Author Dave Broom is a positive influence and a kind man. Thank you, Dave. Kevin Burns read every word and made numerous helpful suggestions, which is author's code for thanking him without letting on he did so in tracking mode and came up with many a neat turn of phrase. Our editor at Appetite, Katherine Stopa, did so too. Thank you both. Nevertheless, there will be errors and stumbling locutions because we didn't always pay attention.

We are most grateful to Janet de Kergommeaux, who did much of the preliminary web research, and Anthony Tremmaglia for his cartography vision. Jan Westcott and CJ Helie, of Spirits Canada, provided details of sales, production, and economic impacts, as did Tyler Dyck of the British Columbia Distillers Guild. Rachel Dorion of Bacardi-Martini helped dig up Canadian facts about Jose Bacardi.

Among the many who helped us in many ways, we especially thank Lawrence Graham, Frank Hudson, and Heather Leary of the Victoria Whisky Festival and Frank Scott of the New Brunswick Spirits Festival. Thanks also to Clay Risen for drawing global attention to Canadian whisky. Alex Hamer was enormously helpful in BC and beyond, as was Charlene Rooke. Thomas Chen supported our work in many ways. Kara Newman included us in her tour of Montreal. Johanne McInnis hosted us in New Brunswick, as did Graham MacKenny. Andrew Ferguson, Evan Eckersley, and Jay Wheelock were key supporters in Calgary. Crystal Coverdale and Grant Stevely were our hosts in the Okanagan, as were Bob Baxter, Alan Hansen, and Jasmine Sangria in Yukon. Emmett Hossack was an enthusiastic supporter and welcome travel companion.

FROM DAVIN:

My greatest thanks is reserved for my family: Chris, Tori, Danielle, Amanda, Matt, Seneca, Ronan, Laurie, Al, Kristen, Heather, Drew, Sarah, Olivia, Jordan, Jonathan, Marco, Karyn, Donna, Dad, and the memory of my mother. My family in Victoria understood when I ignored them to finish writing this book. Thanks to Aunts Vi and Hope, cousins John, Thor, Laurie, and Judy, and to Aunt Heather and Uncle Denis.

And most of all, my deep love, gratitude, and affection for my wife and best friend, Janet. Oh, and Chewie!

FROM BLAIR:

In addition to all the people above, thanks to family and friends, especially Mom, Dad, Jeff , Kevin, and Andrew. Derele and Les Scharfe for sharing their appreciation for wine and spirits, and Jim Hamilton for unknowingly setting me on the path. Steve Veale for teaching writing through experience, and Zane Lamprey, Karen, and Casey at Drinking Made Easy for opening the doors.

Above all, to Lina for her love, support, laughs, and endless inspiration. And to Wesley and Isla, this book will be perfect for show-and-tell. ■

INDEX

NOTE: (TN) AFTER A PAGE NUMBER DENOTES TASTING NOTES

RECIPE INDEX